THE HEALTH CRISIS

Opposing Viewpoints®

Other Books of Related Interest in the Opposing Viewpoints Series:

AIDS
Biomedical Ethics
Chemical Dependency
Death and Dying
Drug Abuse
Poverty
Social Justice

Additional Books in the Opposing Viewpoints Series:

Abortion
American Foreign Policy
American Government
The American Military
American Values
America's Elections
America's Prisons
The Arms Race
Censorship
Central America
China
Civil Liberties
Constructing a Life Philosophy
Crime & Criminals
Criminal Justice
The Death Penalty
Economics in America
The Environmental Crisis
Israel
Latin America and U.S. Foreign Policy
Male/Female Roles
The Mass Media
The Middle East
Nuclear War
The Political Spectrum
Problems of Africa
Religion in America
Science & Religion
Sexual Values
The Soviet Union
Teenage Sexuality
Terrorism
The Vietnam War
War and Human Nature

THE HEALTH CRISIS

Opposing Viewpoints®

David L. Bender & Bruno Leone, *Series Editors*

Bonnie Szumski, *Editor*

OPPOSING VIEWPOINTS SERIES ®

Greenhaven Press   San Diego, CA

No part of this book may be reproduced or used in any form or by any means, electrical, mechanical, or otherwise, including, but not limited to, photocopy, recording, or any information storage and retrieval system, without prior written permission from the publisher.

Library of Congress Cataloging-in-Publication Data

The Health crisis.

  (Opposing viewpoints series)
  Bibliography: p.
  Includes index.
  1. Public health—United States. 2. Medical care—United States. 3. Social medicine—United States.
I. Szumski, Bonnie, 1958-   . II. Series.
RA445.H3373 1989   362.1'0973   88-24317
ISBN 0-89908-438-9
ISBN 0-89908-413-3 (pbk.)

"Congress shall make no law . . .
abridging the freedom of speech,
or of the press."

First Amendment to the US Constitution

The basic foundation of our democracy is the first amendment guarantee of freedom of expression. The *Opposing Viewpoints Series* is dedicated to the concept of this basic freedom and the idea that it is more important to practice it than to enshrine it.

Contents

Chapter 3: Should Government Provide More Health Care Benefits for the Elderly?

Chapter 4: Are Health Care Costs Too High?

Chapter 5: Is a Holistic Lifestyle Healthier?

Chapter 6: How Can Health Be Improved?

Why Consider Opposing Viewpoints?

"It is better to debate a question without settling it than to settle a question without debating it."

Joseph Joubert (1754-1824)

The Importance of Examining Opposing Viewpoints

The purpose of the Opposing Viewpoints books, and this book in particular, is to present balanced, and often difficult to find, opposing points of view on complex and sensitive issues.

Probably the best way to become informed is to analyze the positions of those who are regarded as experts and well studied on issues. It is important to consider every variety of opinion in an attempt to determine the truth. Opinions from the mainstream of society should be examined. But also important are opinions that are considered radical, reactionary, or minority as well as those stigmatized by some other uncomplimentary label. An important lesson of history is the eventual acceptance of many unpopular and even despised opinions. The ideas of Socrates, Jesus, and Galileo are good examples of this.

Readers will approach this book with their own opinions on the issues debated within it. However, to have a good grasp of one's own viewpoint, it is necessary to understand the arguments of those with whom one disagrees. It can be said that those who do not completely understand their adversary's point of view do not fully understand their own.

A persuasive case for considering opposing viewpoints has been presented by John Stuart Mill in his work *On Liberty*. When examining controversial issues it may be helpful to reflect on this suggestion:

> The only way in which a human being can make some approach to knowing the whole of a subject, is by hearing what can be said about it by persons of every variety of opinion, and studying all modes in which it can be looked at by every character of mind. No wise man ever acquired his wisdom in any mode but this.

Analyzing Sources of Information

The Opposing Viewpoints books include diverse materials taken from magazines, journals, books, and newspapers, as well as statements and position papers from a wide range of individuals, organizations and governments. This broad spectrum of sources helps to develop patterns of thinking which are open to the consideration of a variety of opinions.

Pitfalls To Avoid

A pitfall to avoid in considering opposing points of view is that of regarding one's own opinion as being common sense and the most rational stance and the point of view of others as being only opinion and naturally wrong. It may be that another's opinion is correct and one's own is in error.

Another pitfall to avoid is that of closing one's mind to the opinions of those with whom one disagrees. The best way to approach a dialogue is to make one's primary purpose that of understanding the mind and arguments of the other person and not that of enlightening him or her with one's own solutions. More can be learned by listening than speaking.

It is my hope that after reading this book the reader will have a deeper understanding of the issues debated and will appreciate the complexity of even seemingly simple issues on which good and honest people disagree. This awareness is particularly important in a democratic society such as ours where people enter into public debate to determine the common good. Those with whom one disagrees should not necessarily be regarded as enemies, but perhaps simply as people who suggest different paths to a common goal.

Developing Basic Reading and Thinking Skills

In this book carefully edited opposing viewpoints are purposely placed back to back to create a running debate; each viewpoint is preceded by a short quotation that best expresses the author's main argument. This format instantly plunges the reader into the midst of a controversial issue and greatly aids that reader in mastering the basic skill of recognizing an author's point of view.

A number of basic skills for critical thinking are practiced in the activities that appear throughout the books in the series. Some of the skills are:

Evaluating Sources of Information The ability to choose from among alternative sources the most reliable and accurate source in relation to a given subject.

Separating Fact from Opinion The ability to make the basic distinction between factual statements (those that can be demonstrated or verified empirically) and statements of opinion (those that are beliefs or attitudes that cannot be proved).

Identifying Stereotypes The ability to identify oversimplified, exaggerated descriptions (favorable or unfavorable) about people and insulting statements about racial, religious or national groups, based upon misinformation or lack of information.

Recognizing Ethnocentrism The ability to recognize attitudes or opinions that express the view that one's own race, culture, or group is inherently superior, or those attitudes that judge another culture or group in terms of one's own.

It is important to consider opposing viewpoints and equally important to be able to critically analyze those viewpoints. The activities in this book are designed to help the reader master these thinking skills. Statements are taken from the book's viewpoints and the reader is asked to analyze them. This technique aids the reader in developing skills that not only can be applied to the viewpoints in this book, but also to situations where opinionated spokespersons comment on controversial issues. Although the activities are helpful to the solitary reader, they are most useful when the reader can benefit from the interaction of group discussion.

Using this book and others in the series should help readers develop basic reading and thinking skills. These skills should improve the readers' ability to understand what they read. Readers should be better able to separate fact from opinion, substance from rhetoric and become better consumers of information in our media-centered culture.

This volume of the Opposing Viewpoints books does not advocate a particular point of view. Quite the contrary! The very nature of the book leaves it to the reader to formulate the opinions he or she finds most suitable. My purpose as publisher is to see that this is made possible by offering a wide range of viewpoints which are fairly presented.

David L. Bender
Publisher

Introduction

"The only way to keep your health is to eat what you don't want, drink what you don't like, and do what you'd rather not."

Mark Twain

Some say that Americans' concern for their own health borders on the neurotic. Exercise, food, and mental health fads abound, and an ever-conscious fear of disease causes many people to question how they can improve their health. This leads to an essential question: Is it possible to control all aspects of our health, or is illness an inevitable consequence of our humanity?

The idea that Americans can and should take control of their own health is pervasive. Medical reports published in the popular press admonish Americans for their high fat, high protein diets that are suspected of causing heart disease and cancer. Health experts also chastise the large numbers of Americans who lead sedentary lifestyles that promote obesity and other health complications. Statistics show the alarming number of deaths that theoretically could be prevented by eliminating smoking and improving dietary and exercise habits: 500,000 Americans die every year from lung cancer associated with cigarette smoking, and close to one million die from heart-related ailments that are thought to be aggravated by high blood pressure and cholesterol levels. In addition, medical evidence suggests that cancer of the colon, breast, and liver are diet-related. These findings, while by no means conclusive, have led more and more people to choose different foods and take up some form of exercise. And many of those who do not change their lifestyles are left perpetually worrying about whether they should.

On the other side are people, including scientists and doctors, who claim that this constant vigilance over health has become so exaggerated as to harm the mental and physical health of many Americans. Elizabeth Whelan, executive director of the American Council on Science and Health, argues, "The cancer death rate has not increased substantially during the past few decades, but the notion that cancer is more prevalent and a by-product of industrial society seems to feed on itself." Critics like Whelan claim that the news media sensationalize medical reports. Self-help

13

books and seminars repeat this exaggerated information until it is widely accepted as fact. Whelan and others believe that many of the resulting fads may actually increase physical injury and cause nutritional deficiencies. These critics assert that people will always be plagued by disease and that constant emphasis on prevention and control is misplaced. No one chooses to get cancer, and insistence that changing one's diet or exercise habits could have prevented it is simply a new form of blaming the victim. As Marcia Angell, a medical doctor, contends, "A view that attaches credit to patients for controlling their disease also implies blame for the progression of the disease."

Six chapters are included in *The Health Crisis: Opposing Viewpoints*. They are Is There a Health Crisis? Does Private Industry Make Health Care More Efficient? Should Government Provide More Health Care Benefits for the Elderly? Are Health Care Costs Too High? Is a Holistic Lifestyle Healthier? and How Can Health Care Be Improved? As the reader delves into these basic issues one thing is certain: Americans will continue to worry about and look for ways to improve their health. The viewpoints in this book debate whether their efforts will be successful.

Is There a Health Crisis?

Chapter Preface

Humanity is facing many frightening health problems over which it has little control. Disasters such as the Chernobyl nuclear meltdown and the Love Canal chemical dumpings have caused widespread health dangers. And modern-day plagues such as AIDS continue to prove that people are not immune to disease. These facts seem to suggest that world health is not improving.

But are these concerns justified? Medical technology and an increased awareness of the causes and prevention of disease have freed people throughout the industrialized world from many diseases that were once rampant.

Whether or not world health has improved is the subject debated in this chapter.

*"The very technology we have created
to . . . rid ourselves of disease is now attacking
us through toxic chemicals."*

World Health Has Worsened

Joseph D. Weissman

Joseph D. Weissman is a medical doctor who began examining
the link between disease and environmental toxins after his son-
in-law died of a heart attack. In the following viewpoint, Weissman
argues that chemicals and wastes entering the air, food, and water
are the cause of many of the serious diseases that plague people
in the twentieth century.

As you read, consider the following questions:

1. What "toxins" does the author argue people must avoid to
   stay healthy?
2. What is the most harmful myth related to health,
   according to Weissman?
3. How does the author believe chemicals in the environment
   pollute our food?

Most people are unaware that they can choose a life of excellent health, remaining active, trim, and alert. They assume instead that ailments arise from causes beyond their control—from fate or genetics or the bad luck of encountering a virus. Or they do not really believe that serious illnesses will touch them, rationalizing that they are somehow protected by a merciful God, that they have always had good luck, that because their parents and grandparents lived long and healthy lives, they too will be untouched. They believe they can live the high-risk modern lifestyle—eating whatever they want, doing whatever they choose—and still feel healthy indefinitely.

However, there are strong indications that in addition to genetics, choices of diet and lifestyle in our industrial societies play a very large part—perhaps the largest—in whether we will remain vibrant past our prime or fall prey to various ailments. My research reveals that many diseases have developed within the last two hundred years as probable by-products of the Industrial Revolution. The very technology we have created to make our lives easier and to rid ourselves of disease is now attacking us through toxic chemicals that have been introduced into our environment and food supply both intentionally and accidentally, without our realizing their full cumulative effects.

There is virtually no soil or water supply in the developed world that remains unpolluted by these toxins, and consequently they are also in almost all of the food we eat, the water we drink, and the air we breathe.

Avoiding the Poison

How, then, can we choose to avoid these poisons and live active, vibrant, longer, and healthier lives? It is impractical to consider moving millions of people to a tropical island or to the jungles of Africa or the outback of Australia, places still relatively untouched by progress. Nor is the solution to rid ourselves of our technology and industry; we are now dependent upon the marvels we have created.

In the long run, for the sake of our children and grandchildren, we must find ways to have our technology without the toxins, but that will surely take longer than our own lifetimes to accomplish. Since it took more than two hundred years to accumulate the current extensive pollution, it may take as long, if not longer, to get rid of it.

Our own choice—if we choose to live—is a more personal one, and one that must be made with full responsibility for our own bodily health. If we make this choice, we face numerous other choices, some of which may be exceedingly difficult for us. We must become involved in decisions about what we eat and drink and about the safety of our environment.

Most people have been aware for some time that obesity, use of tobacco and alcohol, and lack of proper exercise can be harmful to health. Much less familiar are the dangers related to animal food sources, drinking water, beverages, and processed foods, all of which contain toxic chemicals associated with technological society. These toxins and their actions within our bodies are what we must avoid to remain healthy. I believe that they cause many of the diseases that are so prevalent in the twentieth century. . . .

Health Myths

During our era, a number of myths have grown up around the subjects of disease, health, and longevity. Though many of those myths are only popular misconceptions, some are also an accepted part of medical belief. True, we have made great strides in medicine and science in the twentieth century; there is no denying that. But to make further meaningful progress we shall have to get rid of some of the mistaken ideas that stand in the way of full understanding of what has been and remains to be achieved.

The most serious myth, one accepted by medical science and the public alike, is that most of the major noninfectious diseases of the twentieth century have always been with us, simply a part

WARNING: LIVING IS DANGEROUS TO YOUR HEALTH!

19

of the human condition from the very beginning, and have only been brought to light in recent times because of improved diagnosis and greater life expectancy.

Closely linked to that myth is another, that many of these diseases are "degenerative." Fatalistically, we have come to accept that cancer, coronary heart disease, Alzheimer's disease, arthritis, diverticulosis, diabetes, and other ailments are to be expected with advancing years.

But both assumptions are patently untrue and inadvertently self-serving, like the related myth that we are living longer and healthier lives today as a result of scientific advancements. That one clearly ignores or overlooks facts of history and encourages the general public's confidence in medical science.

Better Health in the Past

Consider these facts. One hundred years ago
• *coronary artery disease* (also called coronary heart disease) was virtually unknown in Europe and America. The first description of coronary occlusion (blockage associated with coronary artery disease) appeared in the medical literature in 1910. Today coronary artery disease is the leading cause of death.
• *cancer* caused approximately 3.4 percent of all deaths in Europe and America. A century earlier it was responsible for less than 1 percent. Now cancer is the second leading contributor to death, claiming 1 out or every 4 men and 1 out of every 5 women.
• *diabetes* was extremely rare; 2 out of every 100,000 Americans had the disease, compared with 1 in every 20 (more than 12 million Americans) today. Diabetes and its complications are the third most common cause of death.
• *Alzheimer's disease* did not exist. The condition was first recognized in 1907 by the German physician Alois Alzheimer. Presumably because of its rarity until recently, it has not yet been included in the U.S. vital statistics tables. Over 3 million Americans have this condition, which is considered the fourth leading cause of death.

If these facts are a surprise to you, consider that I am a physician and should have long been aware of them—but I wasn't. The information was shocking; I discovered that the billions spent on research, newer diagnostic techniques, organ transplants, coronary bypass procedures, chemotherapy, radiation, and various drugs have not appreciably altered the advance of killer diseases.

Aging Population Is Not To Blame

We have been led to believe that the incidence of many of these killer diseases is a function of an aging population and is nothing more than a result of bodies growing older, wearing out, and falling apart. However, this does not account for the number of younger people who suffer from Crohn's disease, arthritis, cancer, heart attacks, multiple sclerosis, and other ailments that have been on the rise in the twentieth century.

Where have all these conditions come from? Certainly not from the aging process alone. Young people today acquire them, and older people in previous centuries didn't. Today even newborns and very young children can be victims of cancer and leukemia. This was unheard of at the turn of the century. Moreover, there is reason to believe that seemingly unrelated conditions affecting children and young adults—congenital birth defects, sterility, endometriosis, premenstrual syndrome, Down's syndrome, and behavior and learning disorders, to name a few—may have a common bond with the killer diseases. In short, all the evidence suggests that in relatively recent times a great number of diseases have been on the rise, undeterred by the advances of modern medicine.

High Rates of Cancer

The bottom line is that 400 million pounds of toxic chemical still pour into our nation's waters each year. An NRDC [Natural Resources Defense Council] review of New York State Department of Environmental Conservation files shows what this means for the quality of our rivers and lakes in just a single state. More than 2,500 pounds of heavy metals are disgorged into the Hudson and Mohawk rivers each day. According to a 1984 New York State Assembly report, 23 companies discharge up to 3,000 pounds of toxic chemicals a day into the Niagara River, which provides drinking water to 380,000 people; scientific analyses of the river and its sediments have detected more than 100 toxic substances, including solvents, plasticizing chemicals, and heavy metals. In recent years, biologists have also found extremely high rates of cancer among fish in a number of rivers and lakes badly contaminated with industrial chemicals.

Jonathan King, *Troubled Water,* 1985.

It is difficult to understand how people, physicians in particular, can believe the myth that the so-called degenerative diseases have been around forever but have only recently been discovered because of improved diagnostic skills. This belief does not conform with the facts. Many physicians in earlier centuries were expert diagnosticians who used simple but effective techniques that are now a lost art.

Their ability to diagnose and describe both rare and common infections solely through the senses of smell, taste, touch, sight, and hearing is well known. And they were able to do this for centuries prior to the birth of the germ theory in the 1880s, without benefit of knowing the cause of the conditions.

21

It hardly seems likely that these excellent observers would have been incapable of recognizing and describing the modern-day killers, particularly in the final stages, when diagnosis is relatively easy. We must assume, for lack of descriptive evidence, that the killer diseases were absent.

Longer Life Span?

It will be necessary to dispel another myth—that our ancestors did not suffer from the "degenerative" diseases because they died young of infections and therefore did not live long enough to acquire them. In virtually every grade-school health class, we are told that because of the miracles of modern medicine we can expect a life span considerably longer than our ancestors enjoyed.

The real explanation for the apparently longer modern life span lies in statistical averages. Mortality rates among infants and children in earlier centuries were high because of infectious diseases. Those who died young, particularly those who died in infancy, brought the *average* life span down considerably. However, many people lived to a ripe old age once they survived their youth. If, for example, you had reached the age of 45 back in 1849, the year of the Gold Rush in California, your life expectancy would hardly have been different from that of a 45-year-old today; now you might have an advantage of 3 to 5 years, and that is all.

It is life expectancy from *birth* that has changed most dramatically, and that is because of our improved chances of surviving infancy. Babies born today can expect to live 25 years longer than infants did 100 years ago. In 1850 the average life expectancy from birth was 40 years; it rose to 50 by 1900; it is approximately 76 today. But that is only a *statistical average*. It is not the maximum possible life span.

Maximum life span is the greatest age obtainable by a member of a species. In humans, this maximum has been 110 to 120 years and has not changed appreciably in recent times. In Europe 15,000 years ago, average life expectancy was about 28 years, but maximum life span was not much different among the people of the Roman Empire from what it is today in the United States.

The Industrial Revolution

During the last two hundred years the world has undergone a unique period of rapid industrialization. The Industrial Revolution brought with it new manmade chemicals: chlorine and its compounds, coal-tar derivatives, pharmaceuticals, petrochemicals, and so forth. Steam and electrical power, the internal-combustion engine, and the mass production of consumer and industrial goods made their debut.

All industry, past and present, creates by-products and wastes that require disposal. The only means of eliminating them are

22

burning (with the subsequent development of toxic smoke), disposal in nearby waterways, or burial. The emergence of industrialization, with its production of masses of waste, coincided with the discovery—and presumably the first appearance—of many new diseases.

Underground waste disposal ultimately intrudes upon water aquifers, and burning wastes pollutes the air; thus toxic materials are deposited in farming areas and finally make their way into water and food supplies. All foods are affected: fruits, vegetables, grain, fish, poultry, meat, eggs, dairy products. Some foods store more toxins than others, for some are bioconcentrators and biomagnifiers.

The Dangers of Chemicals

In light of what we have learned in recent years, we can no longer plead ignorance. The predictable—and predicted—results of our massive and indiscriminate use of these poisons are now showing up as epidemics of cancer, miscarriages, birth defects and other health disorders.

For many of us, it is already too late, for the damage that has been done is irreversible. But for all of us, the truly tragic thing is that we are continuing down a road that we should know full well is leading us to a disaster of unprecedented proportions. And every day that passes, the problem becomes greater, as does the price we will inevitably have to pay when the day of reckoning arrives.

Lewis Regenstein, *America the Poisoned*, 1982.

Generally, *all* animals are bioconcentrators—from fish, mollusks, and birds to cattle, sheep, and humans. The absorption and retention of poisons in animals is far greater than in plants. The greatest concentrations of toxins occur in animal fat and cholesterol, for many chemical toxins are fat-soluble; however, muscle tissue, eggs, and milk are not exempt.

The X Factor

The various toxic substances in the environment constitute the X factor. This term derives from the Greek *xenobiotics*, a word research scientists use to describe substances foreign and harmful to living creatures, including man. Though some X factors occur naturally in the environment (for example, certain chemicals found in plants or created by volcanic activity), by far the greater number owe their existence to human intervention; these include manmade poisons, pollutants, reactive chemicals, free radicals, radioactive substances, heavy metals, and most pharmaceuticals and chemical food additives. It is the intrusion of the X factor that

23

has been the major cause of the appearance of new, manmade diseases.

Most medical theories that attempt to explain the causes of various diseases do not adequately account for the absence of these diseases historically and in existing primitive societies. Our ancestors, like present-day primitive peoples, were virtually free of "degenerative" diseases.

Even meat-consuming peoples such as the Eskimo, Pygmy, Masai, Samburu, and Navajo have had no multiple sclerosis or lupus, little coronary artery disease, and very little cancer. Heredity does not explain it, since their relatives who migrate to industrialized areas of the world begin to develop "diseases of civilization."

In addition to exercise, one crucial factor appears to explain the lack of "degenerative" diseases in these groups: They have, or did have, relatively pure sources of food and water. They drank water that was not altered by chlorine or other disinfectants. Their food sources—cattle, camels, birds or fish—had access to pure water and food untainted by industrial smoke and pesticide residues. In other words, they were not exposed to the X factor.

Water in primitive lands—as was the case with water in developed countries before the late nineteenth century—is not disinfected. There are no industries and factories pouring waste pollutants into the immediate environment, and so plants, marine life, and land animals are not tainted by dangerous chemicals. Finally, primitive peoples have not incorporated food additives, excessive salt, bleached sugar, and bleached flour into their diet.

It has been well documented that undeveloped societies undergo a change in health patterns once they adopt the diet and lifestyle of developed societies. When the early Spaniards came to the American Southwest, they brought sheepherding to the Navajo Indians. But the change to a high-fat diet of lamb and mutton did not introduce the "degenerative" diseases to the Navajo. They continued their sheepherding for centuries after the Spaniards left, with no ill effects. In the twentieth century they acquired automobiles and other amenities of civilization. They were able to leave their Arizona and New Mexico reservations to buy food, alcohol, and tobacco products, and at that point their health patterns began to change. They now suffer from the same "degenerative" ailments as other Americans.

Contaminants Easily Spread

But how is it possible that chemical pollutants in our environment can contaminate our food sources so easily?

As mentioned previously, all animals, including humans, are bioconcentrators and biomagnifiers. Pesticides and other poisonous chemicals do enter the food chain from the soil to fruits and vegetables, but in most cases the toxins absorbed by plants remain at the same level of concentration as in the original soil. However, animals concentrate and store the poisons they eat. Many of these toxins are fat-soluble and make their home in the fatty tissue and cholesterol areas of the host animal. Biomagnification causes the amount of these poisons to increase dramatically over time, since the animal continues to ingest and store more poisons. Older and larger cattle, fish, and poultry have greater amounts of toxins than younger ones.

While the greatest concentration of toxins is in the cholesterol and fatty tissue, other tissue is also affected.

The X factor appears in liver and muscle tissue as well as in milk and eggs. Eating lean beef or restricting the animal food intake to fish, egg whites, nonfat milk, or skinless white meat of poultry solves little and is a compromise of dubious value.

Nearly Total Contamination

If our meat, fish, and poultry were as free of toxins as the animal products consumed by primitive peoples in the undeveloped world, we might be able to continue to be omnivorous. However, the contamination of our soil and water now seems to be nearly total; there is little unpolluted grazing land left to us. This problem is, of course, complicated by the development of agribusiness, in which cattle and poultry are raised en masse and fattened by the use of hormones, waste tallow supplements, antibiotics, and chemically sprayed grain and feed.

Fat, cholesterol, and animal protein are not inherently bad for us; our ancestors were well able to handle them. It is the toxins we have added to them that cause the harm.

But if humans are bioconcentrators, don't we still accumulate toxic substances from fruits and vegetables? Yes, we do. But by emphasizing plant foods in our diet and eliminating animal foods, we are minimizing the dangers as much as possible. The toxin levels in animals are many times—in some studies, as many as sixteen times—those in plants.

And those in plants are high enough. For example, a study by the Natural Resources Defense Council found that 44 percent of fruit and vegetable produce contained residues of nineteen different pesticides; 42 percent of the sample contained more than one pesticide, some as many as four. The consumption of foods containing two or more pesticides is especially risky, for synergistic action can take place, with the toxic effects of one pesticide being enhanced by exposure to other toxins.

Toxins Accumulate

It is true that most food contains only infinitesimal amounts of synthetic colors, preservatives, fertilizers, pesticides, hormones, and antibiotics, but most of these substances do not leave our

25

bodies. They remain stored within us to combine with toxins from our next meal and our next, until there are enough to affect our health adversely.

Pesticide monitoring is carried out daily by the U.S. Food and Drug Administration and the Department of Agriculture. But this monitoring is simply that—monitoring. It does not prevent pesticides from being used.

There are currently more than three hundred pesticides registered for use on food crops. When we consider that these are used on plant food for animals and are then concentrated and magnified within the cow, pig, or chicken, interacting with the hormones and antibiotics they are given, we can begin to comprehend the magnitude of our own toxin consumption. Combine the lower level of toxins from our plant foods with the concentrated and magnified toxins from animal foods, and we are literally poisoning ourselves each time we eat.

While we wait for society as a whole to behave responsibly and repair the ecological damage we have done, it is important for individuals to take responsibility for themselves and to avoid drinking, eating, or breathing the chemical poisons that threaten them. Because it is impossible to avoid all xenobiotics, other steps, such as taking vitamin and mineral supplements and giving the body proper exercise, are also necessary to fight or counteract the dangers.

"At a time when we should be rejoicing about
our unprecedented state of good health . . . we
are living in a fog of despair and nosophobia,
literally defined as the morbid fear of illness."

World Health Has Improved

Elizabeth M. Whelan

Elizabeth M. Whelan is the executive director of The American
Council on Science and Health (ACSH), a national consumer
education association. ACSH is committed to providing consumers
with scientifically balanced evaluations of issues relating to food,
chemicals, the environment, and health. In the following viewpoint, Whelan argues that the health risks posed by environmental pollution are grossly exaggerated. The real threats to
Americans' health, she believes, are smoking and alcohol and drug
abuse.

As you read, consider the following questions:

1. What is the mortality rate from environmental toxins,
   according to Whelan?
2. Why does the author argue that worrying about the
   environment is purely nostalgia?
3. Does the author believe nature is always good? Why or
   why not?

Elizabeth M. Whelan, speech delivered before the New York Academy of Sciences in
New York, September 22, 1987.

27

I saw a bumper sticker this weekend that said life causes cancer. And I sympathize with people's resignation and bewilderment. I wish to share my thoughts on how our public health priorities in the United States are inverted and confused, how we as a nation in pursuit of good health are squishing ants while the elephants run wild, and why this may be one of the most critical domestic issues facing the U.S. today, with both our high standard of living and our unprecedented state of good health in imminent jeopardy.

Gaul may have been divided into three parts but my brief comments are divided into four parts:

1. A profile of the problem
2. Possible explanations for why the problem exists
3. How we as scientists might contribute to the solution, and
4. What the consequences may be if we don't

1. *The Problem*

In defining my concern about inverted health priorities, I start with some assumptions, among them that those of us who work in public health accept that those people who daily protect their health and those who regularly assume risks have exactly the same mortality rate: 100 percent. The difference is in the timing. Our goal in public health is to provide individuals with the type of information which will allow them to die young at a very old age. In other words, we want to offer folks a shot at avoiding premature mortality.

We obviously have limited resources with which to reach this goal, so we want to put our efforts in preventive medicine on efforts that pay off. We must never lose sight of the reality that the legitimate purpose of any public health regulation—whether it restricts lifestyle factors, bans a chemical, evacuates a population or anything else—is to prevent premature disease and death, and only that. It is not the role of public health personnel to harass industry, to remove from the market useful products and terrify people about hypothetical risks. Nor is it their role to take action in the name of public health when there is no scientific evidence that such activity will promote the public's health. . . .

The Main Causes of Death

Note that in total some 2 million Americans die each year from all causes. We estimate that fully half of these two million deaths are premature. What are the main causes of premature death?

Cigarette Smoking

The latest peer-reviewed literature indicates that nearly 500,000 premature deaths can be linked with tobacco use, almost exclusively cigarette smoking. That works out to one in four U.S. deaths each year linked to smoking, smokers being at extraordinarily increased risk of heart and lung disease, cancers of many sites, in-

News item: Americans are suffering from an over-consumption of food that contributes to heart disease, high blood pressure, diabetes, etc.

News item: Heavy smokers & drinkers run a 15-times greater risk of developing cancer of the mouth & throat.

ROTHCO

cluding lung, bladder, pancreas, esophogeal and cervical—and other maladies as well. A thoracic surgeon on my Board refers to his operating room as "Marlboro Country."

For purposes of perspective, it is important to keep in mind how *new* are cigarettes—and their health devastation. Just to pick one widely known individual: the day that the President of the U.S. was born, cigarettes were not commercially available. Obviously tobacco has been in use since before Columbus's time, but before cigarettes were introduced tobacco was used in a relatively harmless way.

Alcohol Abuse

About 100,000 annual deaths [are] due to alcohol abuse, including alcohol's role in auto fatalities, suicide, homicide, liver disease, cancer and other conditions. A distinction, of course, can be drawn between alcohol and cigarettes, in that a) cigarettes are hazardous when used as intended, while alcohol can be consumed by most people without assumption of health risks; and b) while there is no known health benefit associated with tobacco inhalation, there is a growing literature on the protective effect of alcohol (when consumed in moderation) on cardiovascular health and extended longevity.

Use of Other Addictive Substances

Our rough estimate is that there are some 35,000 premature annual deaths from other forms of drug abuse, including AIDS as acquired through shared needles.

Neglect of Preventive Care/Poor Treatment

29

Some 275,000 deaths are attributable here, including a hefty portion due to individuals not taking advantage of screening techniques to detect diseases that can be treated.

Hazardous Life Styles

We include here reckless driving, promiscuous sexual practices, lack of working smoke detectors, and other causes, totalling about 45,000 annual premature deaths. The number of AIDS deaths will increase dramatically in the next few years, accounting for perhaps as many as 65,000 deaths in the year 1991 alone.

These, then, are the real public health risks we face today.

American Consumers' Fear Exaggerated

But what are American consumers focusing on? Well, if you take as your measure of concern the areas reported in the nation's media, and the activities of our local, state and federal regulatory agencies, the concerns, among others, are those listed in Table I. We could add to that list, urea formaldehyde foam, asbestos in hairdryers, hair dyes, irradiated foods, sugar, and more.

TABLE I

SELECTED MUCH PUBLICIZED
HYPOTHETICAL CAUSES OF DEATH

Trace Levels of:	Estimated Number of Deaths*
Dioxin	0
PCBs	0
EDB	0
Chloradane, heptachlor, DDT (and all other pesticides)	0
Ionizing radiation from U.S. nuclear power plants	0
Lead in air and water	0
Food additives (saccharin, BHA, nitrites, etc.)	0

*Best estimate is close to zero.

The best estimate we have on premature mortality due to these alleged causes is approximately zero. With specific regard to cancer mortality, Richard Doll and Richard Peto in their classic publication "The Causes of Cancer" suggest an upper limit of 2 percent of cancers due to outdoor environmental pollution. Regarding food additives, specifically antioxidants, they suggested a negative effect on cancer, in the sense that those compounds may protect against, rather than contribute to the disease.

And we could note, under hypothetical risks, some much-publicized events as well as specific chemicals: The so-called

30

disasters at Three Mile Island and Love Canal. TMI killed or injured no one. The radiation exposure to those near the plant was risk equivalent to inhaling four puffs of a cigarette in a life-time or crossing the street five times. As for the "tragedy" at Love Canal, a blue ribbon panel appointed by Governor Mario Cuomo found no evidence of acute health effects linked to chemical exposure. Yet, you may recall that President Jimmy Carter ordered 700 Love Canal families evacuated at a cost to taxpayers of millions of dollars after an EPA [Environmental Protection Agency] report alleged the residents were victims of chromosomal damage.

Americans Are Healthier

Fortune magazine did an in-depth statistical analysis of American life separated by three decades, 1956-1986. . . .

If Ralph Waldo Emerson was right in his belief that the first wealth is health, *Fortune* continued, Americans are getting even richer. We can expect to live five years longer than in 1960, fewer adults die of heart attacks, and even racial differentials in life expectancies are narrowing. The average white life expectancy today is six years longer than that of blacks, but the gap was eight years in 1960. *Fortune* concluded that, in health care, Americans "are richer now than ever before."

S. Lon Connor, *American Medical News,* February 5, 1988.

And this is the result of misdirected priorities: an enormous amount of media attention, and subsequent regulatory activity being directed at remote, perhaps even hypothetical risks. In reviewing these misplaced priorities, I am reminded of the incident in *Alice In Wonderland* where Alice attends a tea party and the Mad Hatter proclaims that it is time to bring the meeting to order and direct undivided attention to the non-issues. . . .

Irresponsibly Blaming Technology

2. Item 2 on my list of 4. Why is the most educated, health-conscious society in the world inverting health priorities? Why do we seem so willing to dismantle our technological society in what we believe to be the pursuit of good health? Why is this insistence on a "zero risk at any cost" approach applied to regulations about PCBs and dioxin, but not to cigarettes?

I do not have time to go into depth here. But I think the problem can be traced to some widespread but inaccurate premises.

First, there is the prevailing idea that Model T health is better than today's turbo-charged machines. It is just our bad luck to be living in an age of pesticides, lawn care chemicals, radiation from nuclear power plants and a legion of "unnatural" substances.

If we could motor back to a more simple, pristine time, we're told, life and health would be so much better. This, of course, is nostalgic nonsense. Early in this century the life expectancy at birth was about 46 years, 35 if you were non-white. Infectious diseases such as typhoid, TB, diphtheria, pneumonia and whooping cough were all common. A spectrum of life-saving pharmaceuticals and medical technology, control of communicable/infectious disease, and improved understanding of nutrition have contributed to good health, not detracted from it, and created a society where the life expectancy is in the mid 70's and still rising.

No Cancer Epidemic

Though the popular wisdom is otherwise, the cancer death rate has not increased substantially during the past few decades, but the notion that cancer is more prevalent and a by-product of industrial society seems to feed on itself. Recall W.C. Field's famous remark, "always carry a flagon of whiskey in case of a snakebite . . . and furthermore, always carry a small snake." But conventional wisdom here is not fact. There is no cancer epidemic in the United States. Except for the dramatic rise in lung cancer, rates of other sites have stabilized or declined in recent decades.

Second, despite our advanced educational system, science and technology pose somewhat of a mystery to many Americans. And it is always easier to fear the unknown and the unfamiliar. Cigarettes are known and familiar: dioxin and nuclear power plants are not. Consider a comparison between a nuclear power plant and a swimming pool. Can you imagine a TV camera zooming in on a pool with a grim voiceover telling us "there is enough water in this pool to drown 10,000 people?" Related to this is the peculiar human tendency to avoid, at all costs, being introspective. How much more comforting it is to blame the corporation and big government for our ills than it is to examine critically our own personal lifestyles and the primary role our actions may play in determining our fate. How willing we seem to tolerate enormous risks which lie within our control, while protesting the hypothetical risks perceived as outside our control.

Third, Americans are likely to focus on "chemicals" as a cause of disease because there *have* been some legitimate horror stories. Occupational exposures—asbestos, vinyl chloride, beta naphthalmine immediately come to mind—have caused preventable deaths. There have been cases of loss of life involving manmade chemicals—from carelessness, accidents and downright greed. We know that. We must recognize that prudent and constant vigilance is necessary to prevent health-threatening exposure to potentially hazardous substances. There is no debate about this. But many Americans, however, are unable to distinguish between proper chemical regulation and monitoring versus banning or purging of useful, non-health-threatening chemicals and compounds. And the most critical of toxicological adages seems lost on them: "Only the dose makes the poison."

Fourth, we must acknowledge the prevailing view that natural is good and safe and synthetic is evil—a view strongly reinforced by today's food products that boast of "no artificial anything." Associated with this view is a) that only synthetic chemicals cause cancer in man or animals and b) animal testing is an infallible means of extrapolation to man, thus the media's frequent use of the word carcinogen—or cancer causing agent—as if synonymous for animal and man.

Nature Abounds in Toxins

The reality here, of course, is that nature abounds in toxins and carcinogens; and that animal tests, particularly at high doses, have not been validated as accurate predictors for human cancer and other diseases.

Fifth, in attempting to understand the willingness to eliminate any chemical that causes cancer in animals, many consumers— and regulators—have accepted uncritically the assumption that there are no risks to banning—or not approving—a technology. This is clearly naive. Consider, for example, the risks of not using pesticides: we compete with insects for food.

The Best System in the World

Most public discussion of the U.S. medical system lacks full perspective on this enormous complex. Over the entire USA, we have 7,000 hospitals, 600,000 doctors, millions of other employees, and a capital investment that exceeds $100 billion. To finance that huge system, we spend almost 11 percent of our national income.

Those vast resources give us what is usually the best medical care in the world. In no other country are the latest advances in medical science—new operations, new drugs, or new machines—available so rapidly to so high a percentage of the people. The Food and Drug Administration does delay the approval of some safe and effective new drugs far longer than other countries do, but even this agency now recognizes the need to do better.

Harry Schwartz, *USA Today*, July 8, 1987.

The ultimate health threat, then, at least in less developed countries, is starvation. But then there is the intermediary risk of eating food infested by insects penetrating the grain kernels and introducing microbial and fungal contamination. But we did not hear of the risks of not taking risks when, for example, EDB was banned. And are there no risks to not approving drugs? Ask the relatives of heart attack victims denied the clot-dissolver TPA, a currently unapproved drug.

Sixth, many corporations are now reinforcing public fears of synthetic chemicals and food processing. Sure "natural organic" is scientific nonsense and there is contradictory evidence about fiber and colon cancer, let's claim it anyway. A major baby food company is advertising that it does not use the agricultural chemical Alar. As mentioned, large supermarket chains are boasting that their produce is grown without benefit of pesticides . . . and the message is reinforced that the way to good health is to avoid "chemicals."

Cigarettes a Real Threat

Seventh and finally, the fear of chemicals, in food, air, water. The media focuses on these and other hypothetical risks, and consumer goods must be understood in the context of the reality that the manufacturer of the leading cause of death—cigarettes—has substantial clout in editorial policy, particularly in U.S. magazines and newspapers. With nearly a three billion dollar annual advertising and promotional budget, it is no wonder that cigarette companies have been rewarded with editorial silence in American publications. You have seen the cover of *Newsweek* or *Time* featuring sugar as a hazard to health, or highlighting illicit drugs as a cause of disease, or front page features on the poisoning of America, but you have never seen an in-depth story on the hazards of smoking. A few courageous editors print the truth about cigarettes even though their publications run cigarette ads, but by and large we at the American Council have been unable to find any significant articles on the hazards of smoking in magazines which take cigarette ads, which is almost all of them. When you cannot write about the number one cause of environmentally related death, you have lots of pages to fill with hypothetical causes.

3. And to point #3 on my list of 4: what can we as scientists do about this? I think you can gather from what I have said so far that we have an exciting opportunity to make significant advances against premature death and disease in this country. But the primary killers in our society aren't hidden away in some toxic dump. They are not lingering in the atmosphere outside a nuclear power plant. They are not lurking in your muffin mix. We know them. They are assailable. And for most of them, miracle drugs are not needed.

We can—today—prevent the major causes of disease and death in this country by altering our lifestyles. But more progress requires focus and direction. Unfortunately, we are like the airline pilot that radios "I have some good news and bad news. The good news is that I am making excellent time. The bad news is that I am lost." At a time when we should be rejoicing about our unprecedented state of good health—and the exciting opportunity to become even healthier—we are living in a fog of despair and nosophobia, literally defined as the morbid fear of illness. And we are blaming our sophisticated society for problems that simply do not exist. As I mentioned, part of the problem can be laid at the doorstep of corporate America which seems all too willing to abandon science in favor of short-term sales.

On the other hand, our representatives—the ones which allocate taxpayer money for disease prevention—carry much of the responsibility for our mixed-up priorities. The Environmental Protection Agency receives *twice* as much money to mitigate hypothetical dangers than does the National Cancer Institute to fight the leading cause of death, cigarette smoking. Congress is allocating 14 billion dollars for Superfund when, as noted in a recent study by the Cato Institute, there is no evidence of any significant health risks associated with chemicals within that law's regulatory domain.

Scientists Need To Come Out of the Closet

The question I pose is:

How can we expect the use of sound science in regulation— whether that applies to a long used product like saccharin, or some new application of biotechnology—when the vast majority of the scientific community has remained largely mute when scientific principles and information are publicly distorted? Ten years ago I asked myself that question. The answer was that my fellow professionals were in classrooms and laboratories, and terrified at the prospect of appearing on the *Today* program or answering the questions from a *New York Times* reporter. They shunned the spotlight because they didn't speak the language of consumers, and had no interest in presenting their ideas to the mass media. Further, they were so highly specialized that they hesitated to venture outside their fields to give the media a glimpse of the "big picture" on the public health scene. . . .

The public needs to understand not just the risks and hazards of modern living, but also the extraordinary benefits and opportunities associated with advances in technology. Poll after poll reveals the high degree of credibility among the public and media that scientists enjoy. One poll conducted among journalists [in 1985] gave scientists a 94 percent credibility rating. They gave their own colleagues 53 percent and government officials 15 percent. . . .

4. Which brings me to my final point. . . . It is senseless to pretend that the national purse has no bottom. It's therefore essential that we choose, out of the infinite number of things we could do, the small set that contributes the most public health protection.

It is wasteful and unprincipled to chase after residues in our food when cigarettes, AIDS, alcohol and drug abuse are costing hundreds of thousands of lives, billions upon billions in medical costs and untold human suffering. Yet there's also another consequence of failing to reorder our environmental and health priorities:

We will suffer as a nation—as a people—when precious human and monetary resources are wasted, and it is often those who need help the most that get hurt the most. If we fail to develop our domestic energy resources out of fear of technology, we face higher energy prices, dependence on foreign nations and the same type of economic disruptions that were common in the 1970s.

If we needlessly pull effective products from the agricultural fields, there is a great danger of insect infestation, less food, higher consumer costs. If we continue to fail to approve in a timely fashion potentially life saving or pain relieving drugs because those preparations may carry intrinsic but small risks, we will all suffer. If we reject the extraordinary applications of biotechnology—a field related by some as having a level of importance similar to the discovery of fire—because we fear it, the loss will be incalculable.

Hazards That Do Not Exist

If we continue to generate a maze of legislation to protect us from hazards that do not exist, all of us will pay more for everything from products as related as automobiles and gasoline to those as unrelated as pharmaceuticals and drycleaning.

The end results of hyperbole about risk is higher taxes, less food, fewer jobs, fewer consumer goods, stagnant economic growth. In other words, a diminished standard of living, all ostensibly in the interest of promoting public health, but with no perceived or measurable health benefit whatever. I believe that the growing fear of technology and the associated regulatory efforts to purge our land of hypothetical risks at any cost, is nothing short of economic suicide. In the long term, we will pay for the failure to use our resources wisely—namely diminished quality of life in the United States is a legacy unfit for the next generation.

More than 40 years ago, Sir Winston Churchill said, "Science has given to this generation the means of unlimited disaster or progress. There will remain the greater tasks of directing knowledge lastingly toward the purpose of peace and human good." That is a thought none of us should forget.

"By the year 2000, unless astonishing progress is made . . . , there will be a cumulative total of 5 million cases of AIDS in America alone."

The AIDS Crisis Will Worsen

William H. Masters, Virginia E. Johnson, and Robert C. Kolodny

The AIDS epidemic is the most severe and widespread health crisis facing the world today. But will AIDS continue to spread, infecting more of the heterosexual population and becoming much worse? In the following viewpoint, William H. Masters, Virginia E. Johnson, and Robert C. Kolodny argue that it will worsen. They predict five million AIDS cases in the United States alone by the year 2000. Masters and Johnson are co-authors of several landmark studies in the field of human sexuality. They are also the founders of the Masters and Johnson Institute in St. Louis, Missouri. Kolodny is medical director of the Behavior Medicine Institute and a member of the Board of Directors of the Masters and Johnson Institute.

As you read, consider the following questions:

1. According to the authors, what is wrong with the AIDS information the public receives now?
2. Why do the authors believe the number of AIDS cases is underreported?
3. What is the consequence of this underreporting, according to the authors?

AIDS is a frightening disease. The fears engendered by the AIDS epidemic tap into the very roots of our human condition: fear of the unknown, fear of blood, fear of sex, fear of disease, fear of helplessness, fear of desertion and loneliness, fear of death. Such fears are not, of course, entirely irrational. AIDS is a killer, and our uncertainty about the exact magnitude of the AIDS epidemic only magnifies our anxieties. . . .

We as individuals and as a society must turn from a sense of relative complacency in dealing with the realities of the currently exploding epidemic and make a personal and public commitment to prevention as a primary issue. . . .

One thing is absolutely clear: until a cure is found, the best weapon we have in the fight against AIDS is information. But information that suggests scientific certainty where no such certainty exists, or information that presents an optimistic outlook primarily to prevent panic and hysteria, is a violation of the responsibility that scientists should vigorously protect and that the public should vociferously demand. . . .

The Numbers of a Global Epidemic

In 1986 a spokesman for the World Health Organization estimated that on a global basis there were 100,000 cases of AIDS, 300,000 to 500,000 people with other symptoms of infection with the AIDS virus, and somewhere between 5 million and 10 million symptom-free carriers of the virus, many of whom will ultimately develop full-blown cases of AIDS. By late 1987 45,000 cases of AIDS had been reported in the United States alone. In Western Europe about 7,000 cases had been reported. In Africa about 50,000 cases had probably occurred. Indeed, cases had been identified in more than 110 countries, including Russia, Japan, Australia, India, and the People's Republic of China.

AIDS Underreported

These numbers are, we believe, serious underestimates of the actual number of cases that have occurred. There are several explanations for such underreporting. In some countries, for instance, there were clearly political overtones to the issue, especially in the early days of the epidemic. To report an alarmingly large number of cases of AIDS was to run the risk of decreased tourism, with its economic consequences, and to admit to a major public health problem, which might be taken by some to imply unhygienic conditions, inadequate public education, and so forth. Furthermore, many countries were unwilling, because of their religious or cultural heritage, to acknowledge a problem that initially seemed to be concentrated among homosexuals, bisexuals, and IV drug abusers.

In the United States and Europe there were several different problems that together resulted in substantial underreporting, which to a large degree has continued up until the present. First, physicians in many locales could not diagnose AIDS because they were not personally familiar with the syndrome. (Most physicians who graduated from medical school before 1979 probably never encountered a case in school or in their postgraduate training.) Second, until the blood test for antibody to the AIDS virus became available in mid-1985, the diagnosis was chiefly made on the basis of clinical recognition, with little direct laboratory evidence to support a physician's impression. Third, some physicians have used other diagnoses, euphemistic or misleading, in order to protect patients and their families from the ignominy of a diagnosis of AIDS. (Recall, for example, the situation with regard to Liberace and Roy Cohn.) We estimate that for this reason alone, 20% of all AIDS cases in the United States and Europe have not been reported.

In a variation on this theme, many physicians do not report cases of AIDS until after the patient has died. This may sometimes be because the physician fears that becoming known as an "AIDS doctor" will adversely affect his or her practice. It may also reflect other considerations. For instance, a physician may be motivated by a strongly humanitarian urge in such situations. Sometimes

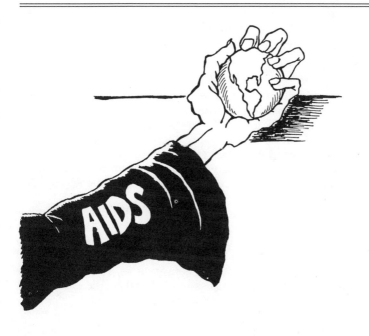

© Borleau/Rothco

the motivation is more questionable, though, as in the case of Stewart McKinney, a congressman from Connecticut, whose illness with AIDS appears to have been concealed from the electorate despite rumors of his condition; while his death from AIDS was finally acknowledged, such instances of delayed reporting, if common, would badly skew the government's efforts to monitor the rate of increase of the disease and its geographic distribution.

The other major reason for a significant underestimate of the actual number of AIDS cases was a technical one: between 1982 and late 1987 the CDC [Centers for Disease Control] insisted on unduly restrictive criteria for diagnosing cases of AIDS, as many workers in the field pointed out. Although there was certainly some scientific rationale for maintaining a relatively unchanging set of diagnostic criteria (as the CDC itself noted, such a case definition "has provided useful data on disease trends because it is precise, consistently interpreted, and highly specific"), there were marked disadvantages too. Once it became clear in 1985 that emaciation and dementia were common features of the AIDS syndrome, and that thousands of infected people who were showing these symptoms were in fact severely ill (with many going on to die), it was a curious form of scientific denial not to permit these cases to be diagnosed as AIDS. The result of this insistence on unrealistically narrow criteria for case reporting was not just to underestimate the number of cases but to make it seem that the rate of increase in the overall number of AIDS cases in the U.S. was declining, when in fact just the opposite was happening.

Reports Are Too Conservative

The bottom line of all of these considerations is that there has been such serious underreporting of the actual incidence of AIDS that the statistics as of late 1987 were off by some 50%. This means that in the U.S. there has probably been a cumulative total of at least 67,000 cases of AIDS from the time the epidemic began until the end of 1987. In Africa, where underreporting is even more serious, it is likely that the cumulative total as of the end of 1987 was 100,000 or more.

This problem is not just an academic one. If the baseline number of cases used by epidemiologists and public health officials to estimate future trends of this epidemic has been off by so much to begin with, then "official" estimates of the toll the world will see in the future are also far too conservative. For example, the U.S. Public Health Service has estimated that by the end of 1991 there will be a cumulative total of 270,000 cases of AIDS in this country alone, with 179,000 deaths. But this estimate was based on the "official" reported statistics available as of mid-1986. Today, taking into account the strong probability of a larger baseline number of cases even at that time, as well as more realistic estimates of the rate of conversion from the symptomless stage of infection with the AIDS virus to the full-blown AIDS syndrome, we believe that by the end of 1991 the actual number of AIDS cases in America will exceed 500,000, with more than 300,000 deaths. Worldwide there will be at least 2 million cases of AIDS, with well over 1 million deaths. By the year 2000, unless astonishing progress is made in the development of a vaccine to prevent this infection, there will be a cumulative total of 5 million cases of AIDS in America alone. Worldwide there will be 25 million cases. The enormity of this threat—and the world's failure to respond swiftly enough with both funding for research and planning for this frightening future—should not be taken lightly.

"In my judgment, the future [of AIDS] looks bright if we are willing to solve the pressing problems facing us."

The AIDS Crisis Will Become Less Severe

Edward N. Brandt Jr.

Edward N. Brandt Jr. is a medical doctor and chancellor of the University of Maryland at Baltimore. In the following viewpoint, Brandt contends that an AIDS vaccine will be produced in the early 1990s and that this vaccine will lower and eventually contain the spread of AIDS. He concludes that the world is dealing effectively with the AIDS crisis.

As you read, consider the following questions:

1. Why is the author confident that an AIDS vaccine will be produced?
2. Does Brandt believe educational programs have been successful?
3. What three steps does the author view as necessary to controlling the AIDS epidemic?

Edward N. Brandt Jr., "What Lies Ahead?" *The World & I*. This article appeared in the November 1987 issue and is reprinted with permission from *The World & I*, a publication of *The Washington Times Corporation*, copyright © 1988.

The first cases of an illness later named Acquired Immunodeficiency Syndrome (AIDS) were detected in early 1981, and the first description, based on five cases, was reported in the June 6, 1981, issue of *Morbidity and Mortality Weekly Report* (MMWR), a publication of the U.S. Centers for Disease Control (CDC). The original cases were in homosexual men, but in 1982, cases also appeared in people with hemophilia and in others receiving transfusions of blood and blood products. Cases also began to be reported in intravenous (IV) drug abusers who shared needles. Hence, by 1983, the possible causes had been narrowed to an infectious agent that could by transmitted by sexual intercourse (anal or vaginal) and by infected blood and blood products.

As of August 31, 1987, 40,795 cases in adults and 571 in children had been reported to CDC. In adults, 26,968 cases or 66 percent were in homosexual or bisexual men, and 9,786 or 24 percent in IV drug abusers. All other categories—transfusions, heterosexual transmission, and undetermined—accounted for 5 percent or less each. In children, 78 percent of cases involve an infected mother, since AIDS is transmitted by the mother's blood before or during birth, with an additional 17 percent due to transfusions of blood or blood products. . . .

From these data, it is clear that the number of cases were at least doubling each year until 1984, but since then, the rate of increase has decreased to about 50 percent per year. The exact meaning of this is not clear. . . .

Scientific Advances

An important scientific issue is that of vaccines. There are a number of possible approaches and all of them are under study. The first human trials of a candidate vaccine will begin shortly, and other vaccines are in development. A successful vaccine must be capable of generating neutralizing antibodies that will prevent the virus from entering the cell and probably also stimulate cellular immunity as well. Furthermore, it must do so without risk of causing the disease. The next one or two years will give us some data about the timing of a successful vaccine.

The epidemiology of HIV infection is now clear. It is transmitted by semen, vaginal secretions, and blood or blood products. It is *not* transmitted by casual contact, insects—including mosquitoes—or inanimate objects such as towels, dishes, toilet seats, and the like. Furthermore, the HIV is easily killed by a 1:10 dilution of sodium hypochlorite (household bleach), and it survives outside the human body for only very short periods of time.

This epidemic has been characterized by the greatest scientific advances in the shortest period of time in history. The causative agent was discovered, characterized, and cultured in less than three years. At the same time, it was possible to develop a test to detect the presence of antibodies in blood. In less than five years, a drug that benefits infected people appeared for clinical use. The epidemiology has been clearly delineated, and guidelines to prevent the spread defined and circulated. It is a remarkable record.

The HIV is spread primarily by sexual intercourse and by infected needles used by intravenous drug abusers. Since sexual activity is a highly emotional topic in American society, the HIV epidemic is controversial. Furthermore, the mortality rate is quite high, with over 90 percent of persons developing AIDS in 1981 now dead.

Irrational Fear

The mortality rate had led to fear, even hysteria, in the American public. Fear leads to irrational behavior as witnessed by the threats to and burning of the house of the Ray family in Arcadia, Florida; the denial of the right to attend school to infected children; and the denial of medical and dental care to infected people of all ages. There are also anecdotal reports of denial of employment, denial of insurance coverage, and even denial of embalming of dead AIDS victims. There are calls for a quarantine of infected persons, as well as mandatory testing of many groups such as applicants for marriage licenses, pregnant women, persons with sexually transmitted diseases, and even the entire American population.

AIDS Not a Middle-Class Disease

The news media have tried to mainstream AIDS by convincing heterosexuals that it was going to sweep through the nation's singles bars the way it swept through the gay community in the early 1980s. Now, that is utterly dishonest. This is never going to be a middle-class, heterosexual disease.

Randy Shilts, *The Village Voice*, February 23, 1988.

In my view, all of these have resulted from the fear penetrating our society. It is important to emphasize that no responsible public health official or organization has endorsed mandatory testing except for blood, tissue, or organ donors.

This societal response has brought new attention to privacy and confidentiality issues in matters of health. Legal protections including not only court cases but also legislation to protect the rights to privacy have been introduced and, in some cases, passed. Educational programs have been developed throughout the country, and nearly 300 community organizations largely staffed with volunteers have come into being.

The U.S. Public Health Service has estimated that at least 270,000 cases will be reported by 1991 and more than 179,000 deaths. These projections are based upon the estimate of infected people and the likely numbers to develop AIDS. That means more than 230,000 new cases in the next four years. Furthermore, based on current experiences, at least as many cases of ARC [AIDS-Related Complex] will be reported. Hence, there could be as many as 200,000 to 250,000 people requiring medical care by 1991.

Someone once said that in predicting the future of science, five-year projections will be too optimistic and ten-year projections too pessimistic. However, AIDS has been characterized by rapid scientific advances primarily because of the rich store of basic knowledge that has been accumulated in the past 20 years. If we learn anything from the epidemic of HIV infection, it should be the necessity of a strong, vital basic research enterprise in the United States. Without that, we would probably still be trying to characterize and define this new disease.

Examination of the future of HIV infection must take into account several different scenarios. For example, will there be a vaccine? Will there be an effective treatment, at least to control the disease? What will be society's attitude toward those infected? I predict that we will have at least a satisfactory vaccine and drugs capable of controlling the disease process in the early 1990s. Furthermore, I believe the educational programs now in development will lead to great public understanding and a resurgence of the compassion that our society extends to those afflicted with other illnesses. Yet, one cannot ignore the possibility that none of these will be true, and we could see a "worst case" situation.

In any scenario, there are 1 million to 1.5 million infected people now, and many of them will develop symptoms and require health care irrespective of the implementation of effective preventive measures. That translates into more than 200,000 people requiring care by 1991, with the resultant strain on the health care system. At present, there is clearly an inadequate number of physicians, nurses, and other staffers capable of caring for that large number. Educational programs are now under way to correct this deficiency.

Problems Will Be Solved

Assuming that the problem is solved, and I am convinced it will be, based on current figures the annual cost to the nation will exceed $4 billion. This projection is minimal, and others project 1991 costs to be $8.5 billion. Furthermore, over half of those costs will come from public funds, such as Medicaid and Medicare, and that will severely tax both state and federal funding sources. Indeed, without much question, at least 10 states will have to increase their funding of Medicaid dramatically. . . .

In summary, three steps must be taken to preserve the quality and availability of health care for all people, given the epidemic of HIV infection. The first is education and preparation of additional physicians, nurses, and hospital staffs to provide care for the increased number of cases of ARC and AIDS. Expansion of treatment of ARC and AIDS in nonhospital settings is the second. The third step must be resolution of the payments for care of indigent patients. All of these are being addressed, and I believe enough will be accomplished to prepare us for the next five to ten years. However, the public must support these steps. . . .

AIDS Could Fall in Place

With so many scientists focused on AIDS, at any moment one of them could stumble across an idea that makes everything fall into place.

Stuart Gannes, *Fortune*, December 21, 1987.

The United States will see several dramatic changes over the next five to ten years. There will be marked changes in sexual behavior, characterized by a reduction in sexual partners, especially "casual" partners, and increased use of condoms. Intravenous drug abuse will lessen, and there will be expansion of treatment sites and effectiveness for current abusers. Indigent care will receive increased attention with improved public funding for it, and the increasing number of people with ARC or AIDS will receive treatment at home or out of hospitals. Finally, the fear in our society will be addressed successfully by education.

In my judgment, the future looks bright if we are willing to solve the pressing problems facing us. It will require understanding and political courage and will. I have no doubt that it can and will be done, but every American must assume some responsibility. Without that, the future will be one of loss of fundamental human rights by some people, and thereby by all.

Distinguishing Bias from Reason

When dealing with controversial issues, many people allow their feelings to dominate their powers of reason. Thus, one of the most important critical thinking skills is the ability to distinguish between statements based upon emotion or bias and conclusions based upon a rational consideration of the facts.

The following statements are taken from the viewpoints in this chapter. Consider each statement carefully. *Mark R for any statement you believe is based on reason or a rational consideration of the facts. Mark B for any statement you believe is based on bias, prejudice, or emotion. Mark I for any statement you think is impossible to judge.*

If you are doing this activity as a member of a class or group, compare your answers with those of other class or group members. Be able to defend your answers. You may discover that others come to different conclusions than you do. Listening to the rationale others present for their answers may give you valuable insights in distinguishing between bias and reason.

> R = *a statement based upon reason*
> B = *a statement based upon bias*
> I = *a statement impossible to judge*

47

1. There is virtually no soil or water supply in the developed world that remains untouched by toxins.

2. In the long run, we must find ways to have our technology without the toxins. Since it took more than two hundred years to accumulate the current extensive pollution, eliminating the toxins will surely take longer than our own lifetimes to accomplish.

3. Public health priorities in the US are inverted and confused; we as a nation in pursuit of good health are squishing ants while the elephants run wild.

4. Combine the hundreds of pesticides magnified in animal fat with the hormones these animals are given, and we are literally poisoning ourselves each time we eat.

5. Eating lean beef or restricting the animal food intake to fish, egg whites and non-fat milk solves little. Manmade toxins appear in liver and muscle tissue as well as in milk and eggs.

6. Despite claims to the contrary, the primary killers in our society are not lurking in your muffin mix.

7. AIDS is underestimated in less developed countries because announcing a large number of AIDS cases risks a decrease in tourism, fosters an impression of the country as unhygienic, and, by admitting to the presence of homosexuals, clashes with cultural taboos.

8. The prevailing idea that Model T health is better than today's turbo-charged machines is, of course, nostalgic nonsense.

9. The causative agent of AIDS was discovered, characterized and cultured in less than three years. Thus I predict we will have at least a satisfactory vaccine by the early 1990s.

10. How much more comforting it is to blame the big corporations for our ills than to examine critically our own lifestyles.

11. Life expectancy from birth has changed dramatically and caused an upward surge in the *average* life expectancy without changing the 120 year maximum life span among humans.

12. Many corporations are now reinforcing public fears of synthetic chemicals and food processing.

Periodical Bibliography

The following articles have been selected to supplement the diverse views presented in this chapter.

Carol Adelman, Jeremiah Norris, and Susan Raymond	"A New Rx Is Needed for World Health Care," The Heritage Foundation *Backgrounder*, July 9, 1987. Available from The Heritage Foundation, 214 Massachusetts Ave. NE, Washington, DC 20002.
Geraldine Dallek	"A Health Crisis That Need Not Be," *Los Angeles Times*, May 31, 1988.
Ann Giudici Fettner	"The Facts About Straight Sex and AIDS," *The Village Voice*, February 23, 1988.
Gary Hancock	"Why AIDS Matters," *New Internationalist*, March 1987.
Jeffrey E. Harris	"The AIDS Epidemic: Looking into the 1990s," *Technology Review*, July 1987.
David C. Jones	"Perspective on AIDS," *Vital Speeches of the Day*, January 1, 1988.
Sandra Panem	"Planning For the Next Health Emergency," *Issues in Science and Technology*, Spring 1988.
John Pekkanen	"AIDS: The Plague That Knows No Boundaries," *Reader's Digest*, June 1987.
David Pence	"The AIDS Epidemic," *Vital Speeches of the Day*, February 1, 1988.
Allen Salzberg, interviewed by Kathleen Klenetsky	"AIDS Study Shows 13 Million Dead or Sick by 2005," *21st Century Science & Technology*, May/June 1988.
Jon Tinker	"Responding to AIDS as a Global Emergency," *The Christian Science Monitor*, November 19, 1987.
Michael Woods	"The War on AIDS," *The World & I*, November 1987.

Does Private Industry
Make Health Care
More Efficient?

Chapter Preface

Health care in the United States has traditionally been handled through a patchwork of private insurance and health care providers and government-supported medicare and medicaid. The relative efficiency and merits of this system are debated in this chapter.

Many people argue that private industry is the most equitable and efficient way to deliver health care. They believe it is everyone's right to choose their own form of medical care. Free market principles, these advocates believe, allow consumers to choose the best doctors and the most reliable insurance.

Opponents argue that millions of people who cannot afford health insurance and are not covered by medicare and medicaid simply go without medical care. This leaves society with the burden of a high infant mortality rate and a higher disability and unemployment rate. These ills, they contend, are the products of private industry's greed and can only be eradicated with more government involvement in providing health insurance. While it seems unlikely that the US will ever adopt a national health insurance program similar to those in socialist countries, those people who continue to go without health insurance assure that the current private system will still generate debate.

"By introducing market incentives into private and public health policies, it is possible to deliver services more efficiently."

For-Profit Strategies Improve Health Care

Committee for Economic Development

The Committee for Economic Development (CED) is an independent research and educational organization of business executives and educators. CED proposes policies to promote steady economic improvement and helps "business to earn and maintain the national and community respect essential to the successful functioning of the free enterprise capitalist system." In the following viewpoint, CED argues that private industry's involvement in health care has increased efficiency and kept costs down. The authors believe that the government's role should be limited to helping the poor receive care.

As you read, consider the following questions:

1. Why does CED believe the large share of the gross national product devoted to health care is not necessarily a problem?
2. What improvements has private industry made in the health care system, according to the authors?
3. What role do the authors believe government should play in health care?

Committee for Economic Development, *Reforming Health Care: A Market Prescription* (New York, 1987). Used with permission.

Since the mid-1970s, U.S. health care policy has confronted three major interrelated problems: cost, access, and quality. The first and most visible problem is how to reduce the rapid escalation of health care costs. The primary theme of this policy statement is that such a reduction can be achieved most efficiently through market incentives in the financing and delivery of health care services. The second problem is that the greater reliance on market principles is likely to make it more difficult to assure access to health care for all Americans. Success in solving the problem of escalating costs will eliminate many indirect subsidies, thereby reducing access to affordable health care for a higher proportion of the population. The third problem is that as health care reforms respond to the problems of cost and access, research and development (R & D) and the diffusion of new technologies may be slowed, thus harming the quality of care.

The major purchasers of care, business and government, are becoming much more cost-conscious and are introducing new systems of paying doctors, hospitals, and other providers of services. In response to buyer pressure, these providers are beginning to develop more integrated and cost-effective delivery systems. These changes have helped to control health care costs, but prices are still rising significantly. Indeed, the rate of inflation for medical care was 7.7 percent in 1986, a rate about seven times greater than the rise in the Consumer Price Index. Moreover, the aging of the U.S. population and costs associated with technological innovation may cause health care to claim a larger share of the nation's gross national product (GNP) in the future.

Health Care's Cost Increases

Twenty years ago, health care was a $42-billion-a-year industry, with the government financing 26 percent of expenditures; but by 1985, the industry had grown to $425 billion, with the government financing 41 percent. From 1966, when Medicare and Medicaid were implemented, until 1980, the cost of the combined programs doubled every four years. Although annual increases have slowed considerably in the 1980s, public expenditures on these two programs, financed by payroll taxes and general revenues, continue to grow at a faster rate than overall government spending (of which they represent a significant share).

In the private sector, the cost of employer-based health insurance escalated rapidly during the 1970s. Despite a slowdown in the rate of growth in the average annual health insurance premium, employer contributions amounted to $1,549 per person in 1984, or 7.4 percent of payroll. The cost of providing health care insurance for employees and, in many larger corporations, for retirees, along with the cost of payroll taxes for financing government health programs, has significantly increased fixed labor costs.

In some industries, this has probably discouraged employment growth. . . .

The rising share of GNP devoted to health care is not a problem per se. Higher outlays have contributed to a healthier, more productive work force, and the resulting productivity gains have led to a higher rate of economic growth. Thus, focusing only on the *share* of GNP going to health can be misleading.

We should think of health care outlays in much the same way we think of expenditures for education: as an *investment* in human capital. Spent wisely, such outlays stretch the productive potential of the populace and pay dividends in the long run. Moreover, only a small increment to GNP growth arising from additional health expenditures is needed to make such extra outlays cost-effective.

Health Care Needs Free-Market Strategies

The chief virtue of the free market is that it translates consumer demand into powerful incentives for providers to offer adequate supplies of goods and services at reasonable prices and to increase their efficiency through constant innovations in design, production, and distribution. But the history of the U.S. health care system has ignored this virtue. It has attempted to regulate demand by manipulating costs and supply. The predictable effects have been economic distortion and inefficiency. The challenge is to free America's health care system from the escalating costs of over-regulation, which increasingly denies access to large segments of the population and threatens the quality of health care for all Americans.

Edmund F. Haislmaier, Heritage Foundation *Backgrounder*, October 23, 1987.

But two conditions must be met for this investment rationale to be justified: First, it is important to direct existing and additional health care expenditures to those services and population groups likely to produce the highest return on the investment. This poses difficult allocation decisions for society. Additional expenditures on prevention of illness and accidents are likely to result in a larger payoff than greater emphasis on acute or long-term care. Should some acute care services be denied if there is a low probability that the patient will recover and be a productive member of the work force? Similarly, GNP will rise more rapidly if most of the increased expenditures are invested in youths and prime-aged workers whose improved health will contribute most to productivity growth. Second, the money must be spent in an efficient way, which requires a system of market signals and incentives that make both the consumers of health services and those who provide them cost-conscious in their use of resources.

Of course, health expenditures are more than economic investments in human capital. They also reflect society's desire to minimize the pain and suffering associated with illness. But in the long run, the ability to achieve the goal of reducing pain and suffering depends heavily on the extent to which investments in health care are economically efficient and produce the return necessary for financing that social goal.

Balancing Benefits and Costs

The rapidly escalating cost of financing private and public health care programs is clearly the dominant policy problem facing the U.S. health care system. We believe that by introducing market incentives into private and public health policies, it is possible to deliver services more efficiently. Such a strategy involves a redirection of policy away from the traditional regulatory approach.

Over the years, the growing amount of resources devoted to the health industry has produced substantial benefits. Industries supplying services responded to increased demand by rapidly developing new medical procedures to produce more successful patient outcomes. The higher level of demand encouraged manufacturers of medical devices and pharmaceuticals to develop new products that have provided benefits in excess of the cost to the patients receiving them.

Perhaps the greatest benefit has been that by the 1980s, the vast majority of Americans had access to high quality services. In 1950, only about half of the civilian population was protected by one or more forms of private health insurance; but by 1984, the proportion had risen to 80 percent. The huge Medicare and Medicaid programs guaranteed all the elderly and a substantial proportion of the poor access to basic health care.

The system of providing health care services through a wide range of government and privately financed providers has created considerable diversity in the actual provision of care. This diversity has encouraged different approaches to treating illness in a variety of institutional settings. Compared with more monolithic health care systems, it has given many patients some degree of choice of provider and has probably also contributed to improvements in the quality of services. . . .

Health care markets have special dimensions. For example, people buying health insurance rely heavily on agents—the government, employers, and insurance carriers—for information on the types and availability of health plans. Patients depend on other agents—usually physicians—in making decisions about the need for specific services. Health care consumers are not often sensitive to price, especially when they require treament for potentially life-threatening or terminal illnesses and accidents. Nevertheless, market principles can operate successfully when health insurance is originally purchased and when individuals require routine medical care. When consumers make these types of decisions, we can expect them to accept a greater share of the financial consequences of their choices.

Government Safeguards Necessary

In the case of most products and services, if individuals are unable to make the purchase, or if they fail to protect themselves against unforeseen risk, they are expected to accept the consequences. But inability to purchase needed medical services can have serious personal consequences that our society is reluctant to impose on individuals. We believe safeguards are needed to assure that those who lack the resources to insure themselves receive assistance. But if an efficient system of safeguards and subsidies is in place, the purchase of health care services can follow the basic principles of a market economy.

Government Cannot Improve Health Care

The prospects are grim for a free market for medical care. Congress is inundated with proposals to establish a system of national health insurance with federal regulators controlling health-care spending.

But government cannot promise a more efficient health-care system. In fact, the evidence suggests the opposite is true—comprehensive regulation raises costs and lowers the quality of medical care.

Fern Schumer Chapman, *USA Today,* July 8, 1987.

As a nation's economy grows, the share of resources devoted to health care will probably increase. Two decades ago, there was an urgent need for the nation to increase expenditures on health care. But the reimbursement system in both the public and the private sectors provided no market signals that would have enabled those paying for the increased expenditures to determine whether the escalating costs were producing any significant improvements in health. As more resources were invested, the additional benefits began to diminish. . . .

A commitment to two important goals—making health care available to all and ensuring a high rate of medical innovation—will mean that health care expenditures will continue to rise. But the rate of increase will depend on how efficiently the services are delivered. Market incentives can improve the trade-off between cost constraint and greater availability of services and can also reduce, or indeed obviate, the need for the nation to devote a higher proportion of its resources to health care. As economic growth continues, society may, of course, decide to continue to devote more of its total resources to health care, but it must also be prepared to give up the potential benefits of investing these resources in other ways.

Helping the Indigent

Even with greater reliance on market incentives government will still have a crucial role in improving the performance of health care markets and intervening when market outcomes leave some people with inadequate access to care. Government policies can provide incentives to constrain cost escalation while stimulating innovations and efficiently insuring care for the indigent. Direct subsidies can alleviate the adverse side effects of a more market-oriented approach to cost management. But these effects are not always immediately visible, and the political will to address them could be lacking. Extensive government regulation, however, is not justified.

Greater use of incentives in private-sector health care policies can hold down costs if they make the consumer of health care a more efficient buyer of insurance and if they encourage the use of lower-cost providers. Traditionally, employees have had little choice of benefit plans, and reimbursement followed a cost-plus model that encouraged consumers to select high-cost providers. The introduction of cost sharing makes consumers more aware of the differences among the premium costs of benefit packages, so that they are more likely to consider selecting lower-cost plans. Consumer choice can still be preserved for those who want plans with more extensive services and little or no cost sharing, but the consumer will have to give up some income to pay for the additional premium.

Incentives can also be applied to the use of routine care. By supplying improved information on the cost of services and requiring a variety of checks on whether a service is medically necessary, the employer is in a position to control rising costs through limiting the use of unnecessary services or high-cost providers.

Finally, by adopting market incentives in their health care plans, employers can redirect insurance priorities toward those of greatest benefit to individuals: protection against the high cost of unpredictable accidents or illness. Until recently, many private plans provided first-dollar coverage for routine care but little protection for some forms of catastrophic illness. This meant, for example, that the *entire* cost of a 20-day hospital stay was paid for by the insurance company but no costs were covered after the 20th day. A similar approach was adopted by Medicare when it was implemented in 1966. Insurance for all types of illness should be available, but market incentives will gradually produce a higher priority for protection against catastrophic illness and begin to emphasize coverage for cost-effective preventive services. Greater application of market principles can also constrain cost escalation associated with the traditional reimbursement system, which pays for any services prescribed by the physician.

The private sector has begun to adopt market incentives through the redesign of health care plans. We support these changes and favor the strengthening of this trend. Public policies, too, have been reformed to slow down the escalation of government health expenditures. These public and private health care policy changes have reduced the rate of increase in costs, but more extensive use of market incentives will be necessary if health care costs are to continue on a more moderate trend. . . .

Market Incentives Will Improve Care

The challenge for health care policy is to meet the goal of cost constraint and at the same time stimulate health care innovations and improve access to quality care. Greater use of market incentives will eventually provide health care services more equitably and in a cost-sensitive way. Part of these cost savings can be used to finance indigent care. As market incentives are introduced, health care resources will be allocated more efficiently among types of services covered and among groups in society. From society's point of view, if this type of reallocation occurs, the return on the nation's investment in health care will increase. But although health care policies can be designed to increase the overall rate of access to services, a market-driven health care policy will mean that some groups which previously had access to relatively generous health care benefits at little personal cost will eventually have to pay more of the cost themselves or reduce their consumption of services. . . .

The Role of the Market System

In markets for most products and services, economic efficiency is enhanced if government intervention is minimal and competition thrives. Efficiency is achieved through the strong incentive for suppliers to minimize costs and respond to demand by allocating resources to their most productive uses. The market also enhances the goal of innovation by providing powerful incentives for management to surpass both its own past performance and that of its competitors. But private-sector markets do not always achieve the desired results; outcomes may be socially unacceptable. In health care, this is especially important because some reasonable minimum level of access for everyone is as important as the goals of good cost management and a high rate of innovation. . . .

Competitive conditions vary among health care markets. For example, the market for hospital services is dominated by nonprofit institutions that often have fewer incentives to minimize cost through efficiency and innovation than for-profit institutions do.

Available evidence suggests, however, that the profit motive does not appear to result in any significant difference between the care provided to patients and the cost efficiency for either type of institution. At the other extreme, the production of new drugs and medical equipment is provided almost entirely by for-profit businesses. These private-sector organizations continuously search for profitable opportunities through the expansion of market share and the development of new products in response to consumer demand for more effective treatment. . . .

Employers Can Make a Difference

The fact that the U.S. health care system is dominated by employment-based health plans provides employers with a unique opportunity to overcome the lack of information individuals have about the services offered. The specialized experience of health plan benefit managers and those designing plans in the insurance industry can significantly increase consumer and employer information about the range of prices and quality of services available. We believe employers can both give employees protection against illness and at the same time provide incentives for providers to compete for a share of the demand for services.

While there are obvious limitations on the extent to which market principles can be expected to achieve the goals of health care policies, government intervention also has serious limitations. Indeed, in some cases the growth of the government role is actually the primary cause of the failure of private markets.

Extensive government intervention in the market for hospital services through Medicare illustrates how public policy can contribute to market failure. . . .

Government's Role

A combination of more reliance on market incentives and more explicit recognition of government's role in health care markets is the type of strategy most likely to achieve the health care policy goals of cost restraint and increased innovation and, at the same time, improve government policies to ensure access to a reasonable level of medical care for all. Government should continue to intervene in health care markets whenever private markets cannot do the job. Market-type incentives have a central role in the reform of all health care policies in the public as well as the private sector.

"The free-market system has never delivered good health care to everyone at a reasonable cost."

For-Profit Strategies Damage Health Care

Robert L. Dickman, Amasa B. Ford, Jerome Liebman, Sharon Milligan, and Alvin L. Shorr

Robert L. Dickman, Amasa B. Ford, and Jerome Liebman are medical doctors who teach at Case Western Reserve University School of Medicine in Cleveland, Ohio. Sharon Milligan and Alvin L. Shorr have degrees in social work and also teach at Case Western Reserve University in the School of Applied Social Science. In the following viewpoint, the authors describe the United States' current health care policy as a patchwork quilt. They admonish the US government for the lack of a consistent national health policy that would provide care to all. The current system, which is a mixture of private industry and federal control, encourages inefficiency, unequal care, and exploitation, they conclude.

As you read, consider the following questions:

1. Why do the authors believe the US must have a national health policy?
2. What do the authors blame for the high cost of health care? Why?
3. What benefits do the authors see in a government-imposed national health care system?

Robert L. Dickman, Amasa B. Ford, Jerome Liebman, Sharon Milligan, Alvin L. Shorr, "An End to Patchwork Reform of Health Care," *The New England Journal of Medicine*, vol. 317, pages 1086-1088, 1987. Copyright © 1987 by the Massachusetts Medical Society. Reprinted with permission.

Our system of health care may be said to be one of the longest-lived, most expensive demonstration projects in history—a test of the efficacy of "free-market" health care. The time has come to step back and evaluate the project. We conclude that although superb care has been delivered to some persons in some places, the free-market system has never delivered good health care to everyone at a reasonable cost. Although the Hill-Burton Act, Medicare, Medicaid, health maintenance organizations (HMOs), and other partial measures have improved access to health care, the system during the past few years has shown signs of destabilization. We think a unitary system—that is, a national health insurance program or a national health service—ought now to be seriously considered.

The Need for a Unitary System

From the perspective of practicing physicians and social scientists, we offer three general reasons that the country ought now to move to some sort of unitary system.

First, if one reviews the long development of health services in this country, it is impossible to avoid the conclusion that a central error has been the absence of a vision of a whole health care system supported by a public determination to achieve it. No interested party—not organized medicine, providers, the government, or consumer groups—sought the system of health care that we now have. Instead, it consists of a patchwork of separate responses to various problems, with each reform creating a new distortion.

The early struggle for a free-market system, between 1920 and 1950, was won by organized medicine, the insurance industry, and employers. In time, however, unions bargained aggressively for improved health plans which led to higher costs and provided the impetus for prepaid group practice. Commercial insurance companies, taking heart from the success of the Blues [Blue Cross and Blue Shield], skimmed off low-risk, low-cost enrollees. As a result of the ensuing price competition, the Blues became increasingly incapable of providing protection to such high-risk groups as the aged. Major population groups were failing to benefit equitably from the improved capacities of health service providers. Early political and economic successes of organized medicine and its allies had set the stage for a major entry by government into health care.

In the wake of World War II, that entry took the shape of government-financed expansion in four major health care areas: hospital construction, costing $13 billion in 15 years; medical research, particularly within teaching hospitals; . . . the Veterans Administration system; and mental health programs. Although these developments met readily apparent needs, their combined

© Pat Fink/Rothco

effect on health care delivery as a system was mainly accidental. The Hill-Burton Construction Act tended to correct an inequitable distribution of hospitals among states but favored middle-income communities within states. In time, it contributed to the excess of hospital beds within large cities, which in turn contributed to uncontrolled health care costs. Devotion to medical research on the part of teaching hospitals, although valuable in its own right, tended to produce a withdrawal from primary care to the community—an effect not sharply evident until later, when medical schools were subjected to the financial pressures of the 1980s. Meanwhile, reform in terms of equity of care and access for the disadvantaged was long delayed.

Health Care Reforms

Thus, the ground was prepared for the demands for health care reform in the 1960s. L.E. Lewis et al. assessed 11 reform efforts initiated during that period, ranging from the attempt to renew and encourage family practice as a specialty to the multibillion-dollar Medicare and Medicaid programs. These reforms represented efforts to overcome existing barriers to access, such as maldistribution of physicians and lack of economic resources. There is little doubt that the aged and the poor gained from these reforms. The overall assessment of the effect on the system, however, was that "most of the programs focused on one barrier [to access] have either failed to demonstrate the desired impact or else have created secondary, almost intolerable side effects. The multi-barrier approaches have demonstrated impact but have proved politically and economically unfeasible." The reason is that we have long had a market economy in health care; lately, the government has become a powerful player, but it is only one player. Practitioners, hospitals, insurance companies, the pharmaceutical industry, and corporate medicine (the newest entrant) are other players. Patchwork reforms have been undertaken, only to be allowed to wither away. . . . Or, as in the encouragement of family medicine, reforms may be allowed limited growth without improving health services in general. Substantial innovations, such as HMOs, have been transformed· and caught up in market processes—that is, they have themselves become bargaining chips in the free market rather than correctives of the system, as was originally intended. Moreover, the innovations that the market absorbs, such as Medicaid, tend to become essential to it, so that attempts to alter them, when their problems are identified, encounter political obstacles equivalent to those faced in attempting to alter sectors of the defense industry. . . .

Reforms Add New Problems

In short, our experience with a free-market health care system in which improvement or reform is approached piecemeal is that correcting one serious problem leads to another, sometimes more serious; addressing one health care objective (quality, access, equity, or reasonable cost) leads to slighting others.

Now the nation is preoccupied with the issue of cost in health care. We spend at least three times as much per person on health care as other Western countries, without producing demonstrably better health. Furthermore, when mortality is used as an indicator, the United States consistently exhibits one of the highest degrees of inequality in health among 32 industrialized nations. According to E. Ginzberg, "The answer to why costs continue to rise lies in our open system of health care payments in the United States, which depends on the decisions of federal and state legislatures, large and medium-sized corporations, and consumers." That is, the reason lies in our free-market system. Evidently, a cost-effective health care system cannot be pasted together like a collage.

Our second general reason for considering a unitary, national health care system has to do with the continuing erosion of physicians' autonomy and patients' choices. A health care system largely driven by the market has led to problems that encroach on the intimacy of the doctor-patient relationship. It is clear that physicians in the United States are much more besieged with paperwork and have more people looking over their shoulders than do their Canadian or British counterparts. It is not fitting that in caring for our patients we should be engaged in constant negotiation with them about what their insurance will or will not cover, or that we should have to make medical decisions for them that are based on positive or negative incentives, depending on their particular insurance programs. No one wants to think that physicians make choices for these reasons, but evidence abounds and common sense suggests that the free-market system has a strong influence on the decisions that physicians make. . . .

Public Dissatisfaction

Our third general argument is that, although it has for a long time been conventional wisdom that structural reform of health care delivery is not politically feasible, the politics of the matter are shifting. Although the American public consistently reports general satisfaction with its personal health care arrangements, almost one quarter agree with the statement, "Our health care system has so much wrong with it today that we need completely to rebuild it." Three quarters subscribe to an evidently more moderate statement, that the health care system "requires fundamental change." The views of practicing physicians are very influential, perhaps more so than the views of any other leadership group, yet they are becoming less influential year by year. Two thirds of the public say they are "beginning to lose faith in doctors." These opinions indicate a sense of crisis about health care and suggest that organized medicine's influence on policy development may be declining.

Privatization Diminishes Care

By treating heath care as a commodity, privatization has diminished the quality of services and made them less available to those less able to pay. The for-profit chains may provide quality care for some patients, but the poor, whose complex medical problems often require more expensive care, typically lose out. That is because for-profit hospitals gravitate to suburban communities and prosperous regions, where the expanding population tends to be well off, young and healthy, and where unions are generally weak. . . . They prefer to treat insured patients with uncomplicated diagnoses, requiring frequently used but expensive diagnostic tests, services and drugs over those with costly chronic illnesses requiring long-term, labor-intensive care or rarely used, highly specialized equipment. For-profit hospitals often are built without the emergency rooms on which the poor rely for routine care, due to shortages of doctors and clinics in their neighborhoods.

Mimi Abramovitz, *The Nation,* October 17, 1987.

These are merely attitudes; material changes are taking place as well. As we have indicated, American medicine is finding the very principles that it thought a free market would ensure—professional autonomy and free choice by patients—to be increasingly compromised. Physicians have been well prepared to resist government pressures, but they are less prepared to resist corporate and bureaucratic pressures. As A.S. Relman observed, in corporate arrangements "economic imperatives may weaken what should be a strong fiduciary relationship between doctor and patient." Physicians are increasingly becoming members of bureaucracies, anyway; the reasons that they opposed structural reorganization for so long no longer apply—certainly not with the same force.

As for the patients and the public, it is well understood that increasing numbers of the poor and nearly poor cannot afford health care. More to the point of political power, of the 29 million Americans under 65 years of age in 1979 who lacked private health insurance, three fourths were not below the official poverty line. The next four years added 6 million people to the preretirement group without coverage, partly because employers had started to restrict health insurance. These 35 million or so who are not poor, most of whom are employed persons and their dependents, are more likely than the poor to be voters and members of influential interest groups. Moreover, those who are covered find their ties to their personal physicians weaker for the same reasons that physicians find themselves increasingly interfered with—that is, because medical corporations and the insurance industry have joined the government in imposing controls. Many patients feel harassed by, among other things, an indecipherable paper flow related to insurance coverage and payments. They are sent to unfamiliar physicians and inconvenient hospitals. They face a barrage of advertising for supplementary insurance that, in turn, consumer groups warn against.

A Novel Opportunity

Thus, the free-market system in its current form is alienating a substantial part of the tacit alliance—middle-class patients and voters, physicians themselves, and the advocates of the disadvantaged who believed they could make progress incrementally—that for so long prevented the adoption of a national health insurance program. We think that those who look objectively at the political possibilities now will see a novel opportunity to create a national health care system.

The only reasonable solution to current problems (never mind the problems of the future, such as the projected spending of 11.6 percent of the gross national product—a new high—for health care by 1990) is a unitary, national system. Judging by Canadian and British experience, it would permit us to bring the cost of medical care under control. If nothing else (and there is much else), saved administrative costs alone might amount to 8 to 10 percent of current total costs. A national system could help us deal with such neglected issues as the maldistribution of medical resources, the declining quality of care to the urban poor, and the cost of medical education. As hospitals take steps to regulate their costs, one of the first casualties will certainly be medical education, whose previously hidden cost has in the past largely been added to the bill for patient care. Explicit funding of clinical education will then become necessary. Other obvious advantages to a unitary, national system would be improved access for those now uninsured or only partially insured. The elderly, Medicare notwithstanding, are included among the underinsured, as recent controversy about extended coverage for them has made clear.

It is important to make wisely informed choices about the exact nature of the national health care system. Impatience runs high, and proposals are being called novel that merely have the merit of being old enough to have been forgotten.

Profit Before People

The unmitigated quest for profit is the driving force of capitalism. In the United States today health care has become yet another commodity to be bought and sold in the marketplace like automobiles or table cloths. Those with the cash can purchase a longer life or a better life, and those without cannot. The system that controls the distribution of the commodity of health care, in order to maximize profit, is immune to ethical considerations implied by the system. The principle of the universal right to comprehensive health care is vastly overshadowed by the principle of the universal right to property ownership and profit. This is, in the crudest sense, profit before people.

David Lawrence, *Political Affairs,* December 1987.

We cannot continue this patchwork approach to health policy. If we have learned anything at all from history, it is that tinkering—especially multibillion-dollar tinkering—inevitably creates new problems. Current talk about reform often involves ambiguous terms such as "national system" and "national plan." It is time to address the major unitary alternatives—national health insurance and a national health service—and to debate their relative merits.

We believe that those of us who cherish our relationship with patients should look honestly at what has happened to our profession over the past decade. Are we prepared in the name of the market system to work for corporate masters, to face ever-increasing costs and medical indigency, and to be deluged with regulations and complex reimbursement programs? If we are not, then we should at least examine the possibility of starting over and making medicine the humanitarian profession it once was.

"On the whole, HMOs provide quality health care at a reasonable price."

HMOs Improve Health Care

Thomas R. Mayer and Gloria Gilbert Mayer

The rise of for-profit alternatives in health care has become a source of consternation for many health care professionals and consumers. One of these alternatives is health maintenance organizations or HMOs, in which members pay a low monthly fee and receive unlimited health care. This innovation has been both deplored and praised. In the following viewpoint, Thomas R. Mayer and Gloria Gilbert Mayer praise HMOs because they save money while providing quality care. Thomas R. Mayer is assistant clinical professor at the University of Minnesota in Minneapolis and has a full-time family practice at the Park Nicollet Medical Centers and MedCenters Health Plan. Gloria Gilbert Mayer is a registered nurse with a doctorate in education from Columbia University in New York.

As you read, consider the following questions:

1. How do HMOs save money, according to the Mayers?
2. What do the authors criticize about the traditional fee-for-service health care system?
3. How do HMOs differ from socialized medicine, according to the authors?

Reprinted by permission of the Putnam Publishing Group from THE HEALTH INSURANCE ALTERNATIVE by Thomas R. Mayer and Gloria Gilbert Mayer. Copyright © 1984 by Thomas R. Mayer and Gloria Gilbert Mayer.

The HMO system alleviates some of the problems of providing high-quality and consistent health care. In fact, HMOs began for the very purpose of providing excellent care at an affordable price.

Your regular HMO membership fee pays for most of your health care in advance, no matter how much care you may need. There is no deductible and few additional charges.

All of this sounds very rosy—but are HMO fees reasonable? Do they really compete with the cost of medical insurance?

The answer to this is a very definite *yes*. In fact, HMO costs have to be reasonable and competitive, or no one would join them. The tremendous growth of HMO membership (from approximately four million members nationwide in 1970 to 10.8 million in 1982) and of the number of HMOs in the U.S. (from 33 in 1970 to 265 in 1982) provides ample evidence that HMOs' rates are competitive with those of insurance. Since HMO membership and the number of HMOs in this country both continue to grow at a rapid rate (about 10 percent per year), we feel safe in saying that HMOs are the health care wave of the future.

Health maintenance organizations are owned and operated by a wide variety of different organizations—hospitals, clinics, employers, universities, industries, groups of physicians, medical societies, state and city governments, and even by insurance companies. And if insurance companies (HMOs' major competitor) are operating health maintenance organizations, we can be sure that HMOs are here to stay. . . .

Founders Are Doctors

The most common founders of HMOs are groups of physicians who specialize in a wide variety of medical areas. Working together, they can provide most of the health care services the HMO's members will need; the rest is provided by an HMO-affiliated hospital.

Although virtually every HMO in the country offers a comprehensive range of personnel and facilities—hospitals, physicians, clinics, support staff, and so on—the administrative structure behind these varies widely. Some HMOs own their own facilities, which provide care only to HMO members. The facilities might be in one or several locations.

Other HMOs consist of a clinic, a number of staff physicians, other medical and support personnel, and an affiliated hospital and affiliated specialists. The HMO member goes to the HMO clinic for most of his health care; for anything beyond the scope of what the clinic can handle, he is sent to either the affiliated hospital or an affiliated physician practicing the appropriate specialty. The hospital and physicians usually spend most of their time providing pay-as-you-go health care for non-HMO members, but they are also under contract with the HMO to provide their services to HMO members. The services of these physicians and the hospital are covered by your regular HMO membership fee.

Some HMOs call this fee just that: a *fee.* Some call it a *premium* (like an insurance premium). Some give it the generic name: a *payment.* Whatever it is called, its function is the same. We shall refer to this as a *membership fee,* since this is the least confusing and ambiguous term. Membership fees are normally paid monthly or quarterly. . . .

The Benefits of HMOs

Although HMO premiums may be more than standard health insurance plans, the total costs of health care to the individual are lower because of substantially lower out-of-pocket expenditures. Furthermore, HMOs provide the additional benefit of preventive care, which is frequently excluded from standard plans. Finally, HMOs provide a total system of health care, helping the patient understand a frequently confusing system of numerous medical specialties, types of delivery settings and treatment plans.

National Committee for Quality Health Care, *Critical Condition,* 1988.

Some HMOs are nonprofit, some profit-making, and some actually a combination of the two. We have found that the costs and quality of care have no relationship to whether or not the HMO is operated for profit. . . .

Most medical care in this country is offered on what is called a *fee-for-service* basis. That is, a specific service (or set of services) is provided, and the consumer is billed for only those services. He is expected, of course, to pay that bill promptly. Health insurance makes no change in this system: the services continue to be provided on an item-by-item basis, and the bill for those services is paid shortly thereafter, either by the consumer himself or by the insurance company. The only difference is in who pays the bill.

Expensive Health Care

If we look carefully at this system, we can see how it has contributed to expensive health care costs, and to unnecessary hospitalization—even to unnecessary surgery in extreme cases.

Most medical insurance pays for your medical care only when you become ill. This means doctors and other health professionals are paid by insurance companies primarily for healing the sick, and virtually not at all for helping healthy people stay healthy. Rather than having a system that supports people who are sick and then curing them, wouldn't it make more sense to have a system that enables people to stay healthy?

69

The fee-for-service system presents a second and bigger problem. Most health insurance provides more thorough coverage for a person's health bills when he is in the hospital than when he simply makes a visit to a doctor or clinic. Also, the physician is paid through insurance on daily hospital visits when he treats a patient in the hospital. So it winds up often being cheaper for the patient and more lucrative for the doctor to put the patient in the hospital! Hospitals have gone along with this somewhat bizarre trend by basing their admission criteria not only on the actual need of the patient but on his insurance coverage as well.

There are further effects of all this. Because people are sometimes hospitalized needlessly, insurance companies pay out more money for hospitalization than they should. And because curing the sick almost always costs more (in the long run) than keeping healthy people as healthy as possible, insurance companies wind up spending more on this end of things too. Ultimately, the result of this increased spending is higher insurance premiums for the consumer.

We are not apportioning blame here. In fact, neither doctors nor hospitals nor insurance companies are particularly to blame for what has happened. There is no conspiracy going on, nor do the motives of any of these groups seem to be underhanded. Nevertheless, the problems of the fee-for-service health care system remain. And clearly something better can be devised. A national health insurance creates its own set of problems—and it is exceedingly unlikely that we will see it come to pass, at least in the next decade or two.

The clear and present solution to the health care dilemma, we feel, is the HMO. *In fact, the development and growth of HMOs in this country represent a reversal of the traditional economics of health care. . . .*

Do HMOs Skimp on Quality?

When some consumers reach this point, they wonder: "But I want to be assured of quality care. Since HMOs want to keep costs down, won't they have a tendency to skimp on the services they offer?"

The answer to this is a resounding *no.* Studies have shown over and over that trying to skimp or cut corners in health care invariably results in *increased* costs. The cheapest and most practical health care consists of careful preventive medicine, a strong patient education program, and thorough and responsive treatment of all illnesses as soon as they become apparent. It also means having and using modern, up-to-date medical equipment and excellent personnel—and it means using the right staff members at the right times.

There is another reason why the quality of health care in HMOs is generally high. The organizations are monitored under both formal and informal programs to ensure that the quality of health care remains high. This monitoring, called *peer review*, is required for federally qualified HMOs by law under the HMO Act of 1973. This is done by physicians and other health care professionals outside of the HMO. Private physicians outside of an HMO are not required to receive such a review.

In many, many studies of HMOs reported in the professional medical literature, the quality of health care offered by them has been found to be as high as or higher than the health care of traditional fee-for-service medicine.

HMOs Reduce Costs

National HMOs have introduced a corporate structure to the health care industry, which it has never had before. For the HMO member, this means potentially lower costs and the availability of quality health care nationwide. For the individual HMOs, it means all the advantages of large-scale operation and development: increased capital for expansion and development, increased efficiency through administrative streamlining, greater political and legislative clout, and greater standardization of systems and procedures. . . .

As with any change, the consumer will have a mixed bag of advantages and disadvantages from this system. Increased competition should put a brake on escalating health care costs, to at least keep them in line with inflation. (The likelihood of any actual decrease in the cost of health care is very slight, since a portion of cost increases always comes from technological improvements and advances.) The competition in the marketplace will undoubtedly improve the availability of health care.

Thomas R. Mayer and Gloria Gilbert Mayer, *The Health Insurance Alternative,* 1984.

We feel obligated to add here that we are speaking in generalities. Private doctors, hospitals, and HMOs all make some mistakes; none is perfect. It is of course possible that you may receive poor or improper care at *any* health care facility or from any medical worker. And some HMOs are better than others—just like hospitals and private physicians. But on the whole, HMOs provide quality health care at a reasonable price.

Services vs. Costs

One of the major benefits of HMO membership is that services are generally not tied to costs. This means you never have to worry about whether you can afford a trip to the doctor. Suppose you find a small lump on the back of your neck. You do not have to worry about whether a trip to the doctor is worth the expense, because after all "it's probably nothing." Instead, you can (and should) go to see a doctor at your HMO as soon as possible.

Another major benefit of HMO membership is location. Many HMOs have everything—doctors (including physicians in most specialties), a lab, a clinic, and a hospital—all in one complex. This means that no matter what kind of care you or your family needs—an ear examination, a broken bone set, a proctological inspection, or major surgery—it can all be taken care of at the same site. Even if several members of your family have different health problems, they can be dealt with in the same complex, sometimes even at the same time. This can result in savings of time and trouble.

Some large HMOs in major cities have "satellite" offices in the suburbs. These satellites are to HMOs what branches are to banks. This brings the HMO closer to you.

Both HMOs and conventional health insurance are *prepaid* medical plans. That is, in both cases you pay a regular fee to cover your future health care costs.

HMOs have several distinct benefits over conventional health insurance, however. . . .

1. HMOs never have a deductible; virtually every medical insurance policy does.

2. HMOs generally cover a wider range of care and services than most insurance policies.

3. Insurance policies often pay only 80-90 percent of certain charges. Most HMOs provide many or all of these same services without requiring *any* co-insurance payment from the consumer. . . .

Misconceptions About HMOs

If I join an HMO and need to see a doctor, won't I just be given whatever doctor is available at the time?

No. When you join an HMO, you will usually be asked to choose a *primary physician*. This will be the person responsible for most of your medical care, and the doctor you will see for checkups and for most health problems. The primary physician will act very much like a private family physician, and usually you have the option of having the same primary physician for each family member. Ideally, you and your primary physician will establish a strong and compassionate rapport, just as you would with any good doctor. However, if you are unhappy with your primary physician for some reason, you can have a different one assigned to you.

Some HMOs do not assign primary physicians. Instead, they will give you a list of affiliated private physicians to choose from. You can then choose your own doctor, just as you would under the fee-for-service system.

Doctors in an HMO are on salary, so they don't make as much as most private physicians. Doesn't this mean that they're generally young, less experienced, and less competent than private doctors?

There are several misconceptions in this statement. First, "private" or "higher paid" does not necessarily mean "better."

Second, just because a physician has chosen to work in an HMO, this does not mean he is incapable of establishing a private practice. For one thing, many HMO doctors *are* in private practice, and they provide care to HMO members and private patients alike. For another, some physicians prefer working for an HMO despite the lower income, because they are spared the effort, anxiety, and expense of maintaining an office and handling billings, and because they have a more bearable workload than most physicians in private practice.

Third, it is indeed true that the *average* HMO doctor is slightly younger than the average private physician. But age alone does not make someone competent. And if you do feel that age is important, ask for an older doctor to be appointed as your HMO primary physician. . . .

Socialized Medicine?

Aren't HMOs nothing more than socialized medicine?

No. HMOs are "socialized" only in the sense that they do not provide health care on the usual fee-for-service basis (and some even do this, for those who want it). But HMOs compete directly with other health care organizations and providers—private physicians, hospitals, clinics, insurance companies, and other HMOs—for your business. Many of them are in business to make a profit, and certainly even the nonprofit ones try to stay in the black. We could hardly call this socialist. "Socialized medicine" normally refers to some form of national health care, in which the federal government runs most or all of the health care services in the country with no charge to the taxpayer other than increased taxes. HMOs are nothing of the sort. They are private and individual organizations that make their own rules and policies, for the most part. HMOs exist as an alternative to traditional medical insurance—not as an attempt to become nationalized or to become the only option.

"The HMO . . . demands the continued recruitment of ever more passive and compliant providers in order to obscure the reduced quantity and quality of service delivered."

HMOs Do Not Improve Health Care

William H. Anderson

William H. Anderson believes the current HMO system erodes the quality of health care. In the following viewpoint, Anderson argues that to remain profitable, HMOs must encourage the sick and disabled to drop out and find new, healthy members to replace them. Anderson argues that this is an unacceptable way to cut the costs of health care. He believes that health care *is* expensive, and a more equitable way of distributing care must be found. Anderson is an academic physician teaching at Harvard and Tufts Universities. His special interests are connections among biology, psychology, and politics.

As you read, consider the following questions:

1. What two assumptions do HMOs make that are unrealistic, according to Anderson?
2. How do HMOs construct barriers to service, according to the author?
3. Why does Anderson believe that managers are so important to the way an HMO is run?

William H. Anderson, "HMOs' Incentives: A Prescription for Failure," *The Wall Street Journal*, January 2, 1987. Reprinted with permission of The Wall Street Journal © 1988 Dow Jones & Company, Inc. All rights reserved.

Health maintenance organizations are new systems for the delivery of health care in a service-rationed and cost-controlled manner. They enjoy increasing public acceptance and a corresponding market share of insurance programs. They now claim to provide care for more than 25 million people. Current enthusiasm obscures certain internal contradictions that may make HMOs unstable in the long run. Both managers and "providers" (hospitals and physicians) have their behaviors shaped by incentive systems that are antagonistic to actual health-care delivery. Unless these incentives are modified, the HMO structure will not endure.

Health-care planners have embraced the HMO concept for more than 15 years. Unfortunately, they started with two erroneous assumptions. First, they thought that HMOs would be aggressive proponents of preventive medicine. But the most important preventive measures are under the control of the patients and not the physicians. The best preventives are avoidance of smoking, drinking, obesity and indolence. The HMO doctor has little power to alter these.

Second, the planners assumed that managers are altruists. The initial design did not require the HMO to be stable in the long run. Managers by training and inclination do not consider long-term stability as a high priority. The planners failed to design incentives for managers that would encourage such stability.

Generous Compensation

Managers decide the policies and strategy of each competing HMO. A manager's most important incentive is generous compensation, which requires a large positive cash flow for the organization. This situation is satisfied only by increasing the number of healthy subscribers and by minimizing the expenditures for delivery of service.

The manager's strategy is to attract subscribers who will not use services, to avoid enlisting those who might, and to extrude those who have become sick. Managers are not encumbered by a need to develop a stable long-term delivery system, since their skills (unlike those of the providers) are easily transferred to other industries.

What management strategies would seem most attractive? Three rules immediately become apparent:

1) *Increase the advertising budget.* This ensures an adequate flow of applicants from which the desired healthy people and low resource users may be recruited. Modern marketing methods will be highly effective in attracting demographic subgroups that can be expected to yield the least demand for services. Kevin Higgins reported in Marketing News that a major Midwestern HMO increased its subscribers from 41,000 to 500,000 in an 18-month period in 1984-85 by use of a $12 million advertising budget.

2) *Construct barriers to services so as to create dissatisfied subscribers more frequently among those who utilize services the most.* It is beneficial if resource users are sufficiently annoyed by the lack of available care that they drop out of the plan, thereby taking their demands for service to a competitor. Waiting time, geographical inconvenience and reduced service may be some of the means employed. A well-established and prestigious New England HMO with 200,000 members gained 100,000 new ones but lost 81,000 of the original members in a recent 12-month period. This is an annual turnover rate of 40%.

3) *Create disincentives to the providers.* Of course, it is necessary to have physicians and hospitals identified as care providers for the HMO plan. But once having enrolled them, their compensation should be marginally lower than that awarded by other insurance carriers. This will tend to make the providers marginally less interested in serving your subscribers and so will create another barrier to care delivery. Two major Boston area HMOs have reduced physician compensation by failing to redistribute a contingency reserve.

In an environment of physician and hospital surplus there are always new providers available, and those who are most "manageable" may be selected. In the past 20 years the physician-to-patient ratio in the U.S. has increased 48%.

Ed Gamble. Reprinted with permission.

Thus, the incentives for the managers, however well-intentioned they might be, are skewed toward the *pretense* of care delivery. There is a clear disincentive actually to provide care. Managers trained to seek short-run solutions cannot be blamed for pursuing their own self-interest. It is up to us to design incentives for them that provide for long-term stability.

We usually choose a particular medical insurance when we are healthy. Thus the potential subscriber need only be shown a "Potemkin village" of physicians and hospitals. Those who later become sick and hope to use resources may be disappointed by a lack of convenient or quality service. They may then take their business to a competitor.

How does this incentive system impinge on physicians and hospitals? In an HMO that pays them marginally less than they receive from competitors, these providers may suggest that sick subscribers change to other HMOs. In those with a capitation-fee model, providers are encouraged to keep users satisfied, somehow, by any means except provision of expensive care. In this case hospitals and physicians are rewarded for satisfying subscribers' wants, but not necessarily their needs. Those who remain scrupulous in their duty to the patient will advise the sickest to go to the HMO with the best record of care delivery. This will further unbalance the system in favor of the HMO with the least real service.

Thus the HMO as now structured, and in an oligopolistic environment, essentially depends on the continued infusion of new healthy subscribers at a rate that equals or exceeds the number of sick dropouts. It identifies the sickest members and encourages them to leave the plan. It demands the continued recruitment of ever more passive and compliant providers in order to obscure the reduced quantity and quality of service delivered.

HMOs Are Unstable

The scheme, in whatever guise, is unstable. Eventually it exhausts its pool of potential new subscribers. This time may come soon or late depending on demographic factors.

Some will argue that this pessimistic view is not supported by current observation, and that HMOs provide needed and wanted care at competitive prices. But the future behavior of individuals and organizations is best predicted by the structure of their incentives. Good intentions are eventually eroded by a relentless gradient of self-interest. The advertising budgets, dropout rates and provider surpluses are real. And the incentive structure of HMOs is now clearly visible. The end-stage HMO environment will consist of a predominant organization in each geographical area having a membership consisting of the young and the healthy. Advertising will be ubiquitous and creative. For those subscribers who insist on care, service will be provided at a necessary minimum. The system will benefit no one but the managers, and then only for a limited time. But it may be a bit less expensive than its former competitors.

At this point the managers of the HMO will look for more challenging positions in other industries. Their replacements will be less experienced and probably less skilled. Eventually the lack of service will be visible to all and the structure will collapse, leaving a void in the health-care system and large numbers of demoralized physicians and disillusioned patients awaiting the construction of another delivery mechanism.

HMOs Recruit the Healthy

HMO and Medicare competition are both much hotter. A lot of companies look at different insurance plans and change employees' benefits every year. For the employee that means all new coverage and finding a new doctor. That's fine if you're 20 years old and healthy but not if you're 55 with heart problems. There's just no continuity of care. I think continuity of care is a thing of the past.

Toni Martin, *American Medical News*, January 1, 1988.

What is to be done? We must build a new structure using valid assumptions: that the patients are responsible for preventive measures and that managers and providers primarily pursue self-interest. Then it may be possible to develop incentives for physicians, hospitals and managers that are congruent with promotion of health in an enduring system of quality, equity and tolerable cost.

This prescription requires that we face a plain but unpleasant fact: that health-care resources are finite, and limited by our desires to spend money for other things. We have become accustomed to use of our resources for wants rather than dreary needs. Yet we cannot expect perfection in medicine, sue to enforce this expectation, and then ask that it be cheap, or that others pay for it. Quality, equity and cost are related variables. We cannot determine each arbitrarily by law.

"The reasons for supporting a national health program are fairly straightforward: (1) it is the moral and principled thing to do . . . ; (2) it makes sense; and (3) people want it."

A Government-Run Health Care System Is Best

Vincente Navarro

Among the major Western industrialized nations, the United States is one of the few that does not have some form of national health insurance. American society's traditional inclination toward minimal government involvement has always prevented its adoption. In the following viewpoint, Vincente Navarro criticizes this attitude. He believes health care should be viewed as a human right and must be provided by the government in a national health insurance program. Navarro teaches social policy at the Johns Hopkins University. His most recent book is *Crises, Health and Medicine: A Social Critique.*

As you read, consider the following questions:

1. What is the root problem of US health care, according to the author?
2. What facts does the author cite to argue that US health care has declined?
3. Why does Navarro believe health care should be federally financed?

Vincente Navarro, "The Unhealth of Our Medical Sector," reprinted with permission from the Spring 1987 issue of *Dissent*, a quarterly publication of the Foundation for the Study of Independent Social Ideas, Inc., 521 5th Ave., New York, NY 10017.

The U.S. health care non-system is inhuman and inefficient. Among major Western industrialized nations only the U.S. and South Africa do not uphold the principle that health is a human right. The major political and medical establishments say we have neither the resources nor the popular will to make the commitment to health a human right. Both arguments are wrong.

The problem is clearly not lack of resources. What this argument ignores is that we already spend more on health care than any other nation on earth. Nearly 11 percent of our GNP [Gross National Product] is spent on health services, making the health sector the third largest economic activity in the nation.

In spite of these enormous expenditures, we still have problems with our health care system, problems unmatched by any other country in the West: wrong priorities, high costs, and poor health care. Some examples:

• From 1980 to 1985, more U.S. children died because of poverty, hunger, and malnutrition than the total number of American battle deaths in the Vietnam War.

• Today one child dies of poverty, hunger, and malnutrition on average every fifty minutes.

• A child from a black or white low-income family has only half the chance of surviving the first year of life as a child from a higher income family.

• A migrant farm worker is likely to live slightly more than one-half the number of years that a corporate executive lives.

• On average, a worker is killed or dies because of work-related conditions every five minutes.

• Three million families were refused medical care in 1985 because they could not pay for it.

• Thirty-eight million people do not have any form of health insurance coverage, public or private; 36 percent of them are children.

• Fifty-nine percent of poor and near-poor blacks and 63 percent of Hispanics were uninsured for all or part of the year in 1984.

• Twenty years after the establishment of Medicare (the insurance program for the elderly) senior citizens still have to pay on average 22 percent of their health care bills out of their own pockets.

The Need for Universal Care

These are but a few examples of an unacceptable reality. The political and medical establishments ignore this reality or put it aside as a problem of certain small sectors of the population. But the problems of high cost of health care and limited health coverage of the poor are the exacerbated forms of problems faced by the majority of the U.S. population. Health costs are the major cause of personal bankruptcy. These are not only minority problems—they are majority problems.

Most of these problems are preventable. Other countries offer more comprehensive and universal health care coverage and have better health indicators and more popular health services than ours, and cost much less than ours do. Great Britain, for example, with 5.6 percent of its GNP spent on health services, offers comprehensive and universal health coverage, with 85 percent of the British people pleased with their National Health Service. A somewhat similar situation exists in Canada. In the U.S., we spend almost double (10.8 percent of the GNP) what Great Britain does, but still 16 percent of our population doesn't have any form of health coverage and the majority of our citizens still pay directly for large amounts of their health bills. Not surprisingly, 72 percent of our population feel that the U.S. health care system needs profound changes. And 62 percent favor a national health program, even if the establishment of this program would call for higher taxes (which it would not).

Why This Situation?

The root of the problem is the profit orientation of our health care system, the economic rationale that sustains it, the entrenched interest groups that it reproduces, and the enormous waste that it generates. In 1983, the profit in some areas of the health sector was as follows: for the drug industry, $5.6 billion; for medical and

K. Lemieux/*Medical Self-Care*. Reprinted with permission.

equipment suppliers, $1.8 billion; for insurance and other financial institutions, $2.1 billion; and for health institutions (including hospitals), $2.8 billion.

But the problem is not only profits. It also includes the enormous apparatus needed to sustain those profits and the interest groups they benefit. In 1983, for example, $15.6 billion was spent on insurance overhead, $26.9 billion on hospital administration, $4.1 billion on nursing home administration, $31.1 billion on physicians' overhead, $2 billion on marketing, and $38.2 billion on excessive physicians' income.

A lot of profit and obscenely high salaries are being made from sick people. The greedy are indeed exploiting the needy. Much of these profits and expenditures is both unnecessary and harmful.

The interest groups that benefit from such greed and waste will oppose changes. And their political influence is enormous. . . .

Under the Current Administration

The health situation has worsened during the Reagan administration. For instance:

• Infant mortality is no longer declining at the rate it had for the last twenty years. And the mortality rate of infants between 28 days and one year of age has increased.

• The gaps between black and white infant mortality rates and between low-income and high-income families are the largest since 1940.

• The number of people who do not have health coverage has increased from 1982 to 1984 by five million.

• The number of families who have been refused health care because they could not pay has increased from 1982 to 1985 by two million.

• The average out-of-pocket expenditures for the average American have increased.

• Federal health expenditures have suffered unprecedented cuts. For example, Medicare, which represents 7 percent of all federal health expenditures, has received 12 percent of all federal cuts. The percentage of federal expenditures going to the care of the elderly and disabled has declined from 7.6 to 7.1 percent while the percentage for defense has increased from 22 to 26 percent.

• Federal interventions have stimulated hospitals to discharge unprofitable cases. The National Opinion Research Center reports that 78 percent of admitting physicians report that they have received pressure from their hospitals to discharge patients.

• There has been further growth of investor-owned hospitals (the hospitals with the highest profits), stimulated by new forms of federal payment; 13 percent of all hospitals are now investor-owned. They provide care that is believed by a majority of physicians (including a quarter of those working for them) to be inferior to care by nonprofit hospitals.

• Profits for the hospital industry have increased: 81 percent of hospitals realized profits in 1985, with an average profit margin of 14.12 percent, a margin several times higher than the 3.3 percent after tax margins reported by *Business Week* for the services industry as a whole.

The US a Backward System

The U.S. is the most backward of industrial nations in dealing with this issue. While other countries have a national health insurance or a national health care system, we do not. . . .

"That is the major failure of our health system," the Gray Panthers spokesperson said. "Private enterprise in health care is keeping many people away from the care and treatment they need. Medical costs are today beyond the reach of not only the poor, but also those in the middle income bracket. There are some 37 million people in the country without medical insurance.

"The only thing to do is to make it a public system, where everyone who needs care will get it. Everyone has a right to proper care and a healthy life."

Mike Giocondo, *People's Daily World*, February 27, 1985.

The solution is to reverse the current situation that favors the greedy few over the many needy. This reversal has to be based on a popular mobilization stimulated by calls not only to compassion but also to solidarity and concern for social justice. The solution has to be rooted in a substantial change in national priorities, with a large shift of resources from the military to the health sector. As Reverend Martin Luther King, Jr. said once, "A nation that continues year after year to spend more money on military defense than on programs of social benefit is approaching spiritual death." We need to reverse this trend. . . . We need to establish a national health program.

(1) A national health program should be based on general revenues coming from income taxes rather than fees, premiums, and payroll taxes. The reason: fairness and solidarity. The current system relies heavily on payroll taxes, fees, premiums, and direct payments—all highly regressive. Moreover, when health benefits are paid by payroll funds, the size of those benefits may hinder the competitiveness of U.S. industry. Six hundred dollars for each car in Detroit is traceable to negotiated health benefits. In other countries, health is a right that does not need to be bargained for and is provided by the government. The system of payment based on general revenue dollars allows for better public accountability and the transfer of funds within the federal budget.

(2) The policy priorities should be established at the level of the federal government with the states exercising a planning authority (under federal guidelines) and the local government exercising an administrative authority (also under federal guidelines).

(3) The health institutions (e.g., hospitals and nursing homes) that are funded primarily through tax funds should be governed by boards of trustees that are publicly accountable, and representative of the communities they serve. Fifty-one percent of hospital funds and 83 percent of nursing home funds are already tax funds, but the boards of trustees—the top authority in each institution— are highly unrepresentative of the population they serve. There is a perverse quota system in which the trustees come only from the top 5 percent (in income) of our population.

(4) A major change is needed in the orientation of the health system with priorities shifted to give greater emphasis to preventive, community, environmental, and occupational and social care. This shifting of priorities will require a combination of government interventions with popular participation in which the populations affected by the health programs should play a major role in their governance. Just one example: occupational medicine. This branch of medicine is primarily controlled by management rather than labor. Most occupational doctors are paid by management, and their work shows it. We need to give a major voice to the workers and their unions in the governance of their occupational health services. Workers pay far more attention to their health and safety than bosses do.

National Health Plan Makes Sense

The major political and medical establishments oppose a national health program on the grounds that it goes against the current political mood in the country. Many liberals have abandoned their commitment to a national health program because of what is presented as an antigovernment mood in the country. Because of this reading of the popular mood the Democratic Party Platform in 1984 abandoned the party's commitment to a national health program. This is reprehensible. A basic and principled commitment cannot be abandoned because of political expediency.

The reasons for supporting a national health program are fairly straightforward: (1) it is the moral and principled thing to do— the U.S. has to join the rest of the civilized nations and recognize that health is a human right; (2) it makes sense; and (3) people want it. As simple as that.

"Countries with national health insurance invariably resort to rationing schemes which treat people in a discriminatory way and cause long waiting lines for treatment."

A Government-Run Health Care System Would Be Disastrous

J. Roy Rowland

Critics of a national health plan for the US believe such a plan would make health care less efficient and overly bureaucratic. In the following viewpoint, J. Roy Rowland agrees that a national health insurance program would be a mistake. He argues that new government-controlled programs to cut health care costs are nothing more than socialized medicine that undermine, rather than enhance, people's health care choices. Rowland is a medical doctor and in his third term as a member of the House of Representatives.

As you read, consider the following questions:

1. Why does Rowland argue that health care should not be a right guaranteed by the government?
2. What does the author believe to be the ideal system of health care?

J. Roy Rowland, "Positive Cures Needed for Health Care Ills," *Private Practice*, February 1988. Used with permission.

Many physicians, including myself, feel that the proliferation of government health regulations during the past few decades has propelled the United States toward a system of socialized medicine.

Our concern is heightened by Washington's propensity to address health problems in a knee-jerk fashion. Our politicians are quick to support proposals to meet immediate, specific needs, without regard for the long-range effects those proposals will have on physicians and patients. Neither the administration nor Congress is guided by a coordinated blueprint for the future of medicine. In a sense, our health-care system is adrift.

Our concern is also increased by the federal budget deficit. In a desperate effort to cut government spending, cost-containment measures that threaten to impose inappropriate restraints on physicians and curtail services to patients have been considered and adopted. At the same time, however, the deficit has forestalled the push for a costly nationalized system of medicine. It is money—not philosophical considerations—that has the most influence over the government's role in health care these days.

In spite of the pessimism many of us share, there is renewed hope for those who feel that government has too much control over our health-care system. For the most part, 1987 has been a hold-the-line year in Congress. This might be a reflection of a growing resistance to government interference, which has been developing among the public, as well as among elected officials, over the past several years. Only time will tell whether this change in attitude will last.

Government's Role Limited

Historians say that the conflict over government's role in health care is nearly as old as the nation itself. It dates to at least 1796, when Congress overrode the objections of some states and reacted to an epidemic of yellow fever by imposing federal supervision over state quarantine laws. Conflict continues today over a variety of proposals, including those to mandate generic drugs for Medicare patients and to extend Medicare's prospective payment system to hospital-based physicians. . . .

Government's regulatory relationship with health care has evolved primarily during the past 90 years, becoming widespread when states began adopting licensing laws at the turn of the century. Government's role in medicine increased greatly when the Medicare and Medicaid programs were introduced in the 1960s. As a result, government's share of the nation's health-care bill jumped from 25 percent to 40 percent virtually overnight. With the increase in spending came a concomitant increase in government control of our health-care system.

In addition to Medicare and Medicaid for the elderly, the dis-

Dick Locher. Reprinted by permission: Tribune Media Services.

abled and the poor, the federal government now maintains programs for military personnel, veterans and civil service employees. It funds other health activities ranging from maternal and child health-care services to research and education concerning acquired immune deficiency syndrome.

It may come as a surprise to many people, then, that millions of Americans still receive no government health benefits. The country's health-care system continues to be driven essentially by the free-market system. Physicians generally are free to exercise their best medical judgment for the benefit of their patients.

National Health Advocates' Idiocy

This would not be true if advocates of a national health insurance plan had been successful. Efforts to enact such a plan have been underway since the first decade of the 1900s. Although details have varied, the concept never has been far removed from the type of national health service that has existed in England for the past 35 years.

Proponents present an argument that, for many people, is compelling: Health care is a right of citizenship. If health care is a right, they say, it is up to government to make sure it is available to everyone. Unfortunately, the evidence indicates that too much government control diminishes the quality of care and produces even higher costs.

Medicare and Medicaid are the closest thing the United States has to national health insurance, and the expense of these programs provides the best argument against a more extensively socialized health system. In spite of spending controls—such as reimbursement based on diagnosis related groups, and physician fees freezes—federal outlays for Medicare and Medicaid increased from $4.4 billion in 1967 to $75.9 billion in 1986. The cost of these programs is expected to reach $141.2 billion by 1992.

Leading To Rationing

In a 1983 study, economist Harry Schwartz, PhD, concluded that "extending similar programs to the rest of the population would cause medical costs to skyrocket. In addition, countries with national health insurance invariably resort to rationing schemes which treat people in a discriminatory way and cause long waiting lines for treatment. In such countries, the quality of care declines and medicine becomes more impersonal, more routine and more bureaucratized."

Support for NHI plans has waxed and waned over the years. President Woodrow Wilson supported such a proposal, but opposition proved too strong. President Franklin D. Roosevelt considered adding NHI to his old-age pension and unemployment-insurance bills, but he backed down because he didn't want to jeopardize these programs. Except for Eisenhower and Reagan, every president since FDR has flirted with NHI. But so far, resistance always has been strong enough to prevent such a revolutionary step.

Because of an apparent lack of support at the present and because of run-away budget deficits, NHI probably will not be seriously considered in Congress in the foreseeable future. In fact, NHI boosters such as Sen. Edward M. Kennedy apparently have retreated and are pursuing a less dramatic strategy. Kennedy is concentrating on his Minimum Health Benefits for All Workers Act—S 1265—that would extend company health insurance coverage to many more employees. President Nixon once supported a similar plan as part of an NHI proposal introduced during his first term.

The conflict over socialized medicine will continue to focus on a wide range of issues in the coming years. Both sides can anticipate victories, as well as defeats, as they continue their long, drawn-out struggle.

One of those issues involves a proposal submitted by President Reagan that would bring radiologists, anesthesiologists and pathologists under the DRG [Diagnostic Related Groups] reimbursement system. Fortunately, it looks as if Congress has rejected the measure. Not only have the House and Senate refused to approve the proposal, but they also have written language into pending legislation that specifically precludes the extension. If it had passed, there is little doubt that the administration would have tried to force DRGs on all physicians.

Deficits Deter National Health Insurance

This is an example of how the deficit is putting conflicting pressures on the health-care system. While it is a deterrent to NHI, the deficit also prompted the president and his advisers to support a proposal that would drag our health-care system a little closer to nationalization. . . .

Health Care Problems and Government Involvement

1987 was a reasonably good year for those who feel that government should do more to assist and less to control the medical community. Resistance to a government takeover of the health-care system seems to have stiffened, and some of the more objectionable proposals introduced in Congress have fallen by the wayside. But critical problems persist.

Government Insurance a Bad Idea

In most cases, when more money becomes available for a product or a service, the price of that product or service rises. Private health insurance was the first booster of health care costs. That's because true economics is nothing more than human nature in action. If the insurance company, not the patient, is paying the bill, then neither patient nor doctor nor hospital has any incentive to keep the cost down.

It's no good to posture and moralize. That's the way it is. You know it and I know it. Patients, doctors, hospital administrators, and health insurance companies are all on an equal moral plane in this regard for not even the insurance companies cared about costs as long as they could keep upping the premiums.

Medicaid and Medicare, which are nothing more than government health insurance, acted like a match to a rocket fuse. With billions available, billions were billed.

Charley Reese, *Conservative Chronicle*, August 19, 1987.

The infant mortality rate in the United States is shameful. Rural hospitals are facing a financial crisis. Programs to combat AIDS are not well-coordinated, resulting in duplication of efforts. Long-term health care is financially devastating to many families. More effective measures must be enacted to bring health-care costs—both to the government and to private citizens—under control. Until these improvements are made, the pressure for government solutions to critical health problems will only intensify.

What is the fate of the country's health-care system? Will free-market values prevail, or is socialized medicine inevitable?

Although substantial socialization already has taken place, the medical community can stop this trend and help shape a better health-care system for the future. It is not enough, however, for those of us associated with the medical community only to oppose what we do not like. We also should take the lead in offering positive solutions. The alternative is to yield to more government control and the weakening of a system that, despite its problems, has been the best ever known by mankind.

a critical thinking activity

Distinguishing Between Fact and Opinion

This activity is designed to help develop the basic reading and thinking skill of distinguishing between fact and opinion. Consider the following statement: "A child from a black or white low-income family has only half the chance of surviving the first year of life as a child from a higher-income family." This is a fact which can be verified by checking statistical tables from a US governmental agency or a private research group. But consider this statement: "The root of our health care problem is its profit orientation with the entrenched interest groups and enormous waste that it generates." This statement expresses an opinion about the cause of a problem in the health care system. Many physicians and health care officials may attribute different causes to the same problem, and some may maintain that the health care system is not wasteful.

When investigating controversial issues it is important that one be able to distinguish between statements of fact and statements of opinion. It is also important to recognize that not all statements of fact are true. They may appear to be true, but some are based on inaccurate or false information. For this activity, however, we are concerned with understanding the difference between those statements which appear to be factual and those which appear to be based primarily on opinion.

The following statements are related to topics covered in this chapter. Consider each statement carefully. *Mark O for any statement you believe is an opinion or interpretation of facts. Mark F for any statement you consider a fact. Mark U if you are uncertain.*

If you are doing this activity as a member of a class or group, compare your answers to those of other class or group members. Be able to defend your answers. You may discover that others come to different conclusions than you. Listening to the reasons others present for their answers may give you valuable insights in distinguishing between fact and opinion.

> O = *opinion*
> F = *fact*
> U = *uncertain*

91

1. Greater reliance on market principles in financing health care is going to make it more difficult to assure health care access to all Americans.
2. The rate of inflation for medical care was about seven times greater than the rise in the Consumer Price Index.
3. Most Americans receive health care insurance coverage from their employers.
4. A commitment to two important goals—making health care available to all and ensuring a high rate of medical innovation—will mean that health care expenditures will continue to rise.
5. The challenge for health care policy is to meet the goal of cost constraint and at the same time stimulate health care innovations.
6. Most physicians dispense care without regard for the patient's amount of insurance coverage.
7. Of the 29 million Americans under 65 years of age in 1979 who lacked private health insurance, three-fourths were not below the official poverty line.
8. The struggle between 1920 and 1950 for a free-market system was won by organized medicine and the insurance industry.
9. The proportion of physicians in private practice has slowly been declining for a long time.
10. We spend at least three times as much per person on health care as other Western countries, without producing demonstrably better health.
11. Industries supplying health services responded to increased demand by rapidly developing new medical procedures which saved lives and shortened hospital stays.
12. Most medical care in the US is offered on what is called a fee-for-service basis.
13. The Reverend Martin Luther King Jr. once said a nation that year after year spends more on military defense than on social welfare is approaching spiritual death.
14. President Reagan used to work for General Electric, a major hospital supplier. He appeared in ads opposing Medicare.

Periodical Bibliography

The following articles have been selected to supplement the diverse views presented in this chapter.

Don Colburn — "Massachusetts Has Set a Course Toward Universal Health Care," *The Washington Post National Weekly Edition*, May 9, 1988.

Susan Dentzer — "Putting Money Ahead of Mission?" *U.S. News & World Report*, May 16, 1988.

Peter Downs — "Your Money or Your Life," *The Progressive*, January 1987.

Richard H. Egdahl and Cynthia H. Taft — "Financial Incentives to Physicians," *The New England Journal of Medicine*, July 3, 1986.

Martha Fay — "Why Your Family Doctor Is a Group," *The New York Times Magazine*, June 7, 1987.

Rashi Fein — "Toward Adequate Health Care," *Dissent*, Winter 1988.

Victor R. Fuchs — "The Counterrevolution in Health Care Financing," *The New England Journal of Medicine*, April 30, 1987.

Peter Fuhrman — "Go Home and Die," *Forbes*, May 16, 1988.

Nat Hentoff — "Every Canadian Has an Ace in the Hole," *The Village Voice*, June 14, 1988.

C. Wayne Higgins and Thomas R. Syre — "Competition Has Not Been Producing Desired Results," *American Medical News*, March 18, 1988.

Janet Hook — "Catastrophic Insurance for All," *The Washington Monthly*, February 1987.

Susan Hornik — "Singled Out," *Common Cause*, May/June 1988.

David Lawrence — "The Profit Epidemic in Health Care," *Political Affairs*, December 1987.

Anthony Lejeune — "Britain's Health Service: A Cautionary Tale," *National Review*, April 15, 1988.

Arnold S. Relman — "Practicing Medicine in the New Business Climate," *The New England Journal of Medicine*, April 30, 1987.

Should Government Provide More Health Care Benefits for the Elderly?

Chapter Preface

Since the enactment of Social Security in 1935 and the addition of medicare in 1955, the elderly have been guaranteed a minimum income and limited health care benefits. Now, with an aging baby-boom generation, society is facing an enormous economic burden through these programs. Will society be able to support a disproportionate number of elderly citizens and still provide care to others? How much of the health care dollar should society spend on the elderly? Should organ transplants be given as readily to a seventy-year-old heart attack victim as to a seventeen-year-old heart disease victim? What criteria, if any, should society use to determine who receives expensive medical care? These questions and others are debated in the following chapter.

> *"A universal, mandatory program seems advisable, because if all wage earners contribute throughout their working lives, the cost can be reasonable."*

Government Should Provide Universal Health Care for the Elderly

Barry T. Crickmer

Barry T. Crickmer is senior vice-president of Worldwide Information Resources Ltd., a public affairs consulting firm. In the following viewpoint, Crickmer argues that attempts to provide long-term care for the elderly by including them in a catastrophic care policy will not work. He argues that the fairest and most equitable policy would be a comprehensive health care program financed by the federal government.

As you read, consider the following questions:

1. Why would financing long-term care under catastrophic health care be insufficient, according to Crickmer?
2. Why does the author find the current proposed alternatives unacceptable?
3. Why does the author believe that long-term care for the elderly is a popular issue?

Barry T. Crickmer, "How To Handle Long-Term Health Care," *The New York Times*, January 18, 1988. Copyright © 1988 by The New York Times Company. Reprinted with permission.

The catastrophic care program is designed primarily to pay big hospital bills. But acute care accounts for less than 10 percent of the catastrophic (out-of-pocket expenses above $2,000 a year) health-care costs of the elderly. Further, two out of three people on Medicare already are protected against large hospital and doctor bills through private "medi-gap" insurance policies.

The true catastrophe is long-term custodial care, which accounts for 81 percent of catastrophic outlays. About half of those 65 and older will need some kind of long-term care. The average price of delivering this care in a nursing home is $22,000 a year.

Medicare now pays part of the cost for up to 100 days of nursing home care, if the stay follows a period of hospitalization and if the care is "medically necessary." The catastrophic bill extends this period to 150 days—still less than six months. The average stay in a nursing home is two years. Custodial care is not covered at all, because it is not considered medically necessary.

Poverty a Requirement for Care

The Medicaid program does pay for long-term custodial care, but the patient must be poor to qualify.

Of course, the middle class elderly quickly become poor when faced with $22,000 a year charges for nursing homes. According to the House Select Committee on Aging, 90 percent of single elderly patients "spend down" to the poverty level after one year in a nursing home; 70 percent after only 13 weeks. Half of the couples with one spouse in a nursing home are impoverished within six months.

Through this cruel process, Medicaid has become a de facto long-term care program, paying almost half of the nation's nursing home bills.

This arrangement is far from ideal. Those who "spend down" to qualify for Medicaid are outraged that destitution is the price of admission. Those who sacrifice to care for an aging spouse or parent at home resent the tactics—such as transfers of property to heirs and even divorce—some use to shift the burden to Medicaid. And policymakers regret that Medicaid, a program intended to serve the acute care needs of the poor, is being preempted by the demands of long-term custodial care for the elderly—the 5 percent of Medicaid recipients in nursing homes are consuming 43 percent of the Medicaid budget.

Government Fears Cost

Members of Congress are well aware of these problems. Many of them acknowledged the need to enact a program for long-term care during the debate on catastrophic care. They failed to enact one because they feared its cost.

As a result, most current proposals for long-term care are self-financing or feature other forms of cost sharing. Following are some of the leading approaches:

Using tax incentives to promote private-sector solutions. Deductions or credits would encourage either health care savings accounts or the purchase of insurance covering long-term care. Conservatives and business groups favor this program.

Paying for custodial care services delivered at home. The American Red Cross recommends such a program. Not surprisingly, people strongly prefer to remain in their homes as long as possible. Representative Claude Pepper, Democrat of Florida, has introduced legislation to provide unlimited home care, which would be financed by removing the income ceiling on the Medicare portion of the Social Security payroll tax. Individuals with incomes above $45,000 would face an increase of 1.5 percent in their tax rates.

Everybody's Problem

According to a recent survey commissioned by senior advocates, the U.S. public is uniformly concerned about the inadequacy of long-term care. Sixty percent of respondents said they had direct experience with family members or friends needing long-term care, and more than 80% said nursing home costs would be a major hardship on their families. Most significant, over 70% said they wanted a government program providing universal long-term care and would be willing to pay higher taxes to support it.

The constituent support for a comprehensive long-term care policy clearly exists. The time has come for it to be a national priority.

Dollars & Sense, January/February 1988.

Paying for nursing home care, but collecting a big co-payment. A Harvard University group has proposed offsetting part of the cost by imposing a "room and board" fee equal to 80 percent of the patient's Social Security retirement benefit. The Harvard plan also features a deductible equal to one month's care.

Paying for nursing home care, after a stiff deductible. Senator George Mitchell, Democrat of Maine, suggests establishing a Federal program that would pay nursing home costs beyond the first three years. This long deductible period would be phased in gradually, starting at about six months, to encourage the purchase of private insurance to cover the gap. Such a feature would facilitate the development of private insurance plans, because insurers fear open-ended commitments. Senator Mitchell's plan may also require a large co-payment from higher-income beneficiaries.

Can we afford a major Federal program for long-term care? Joshua Wiener, an economist and health care expert at the Brookings Institution, says that the net cost of a universal Federal program offering a minimum level of care—to be supplemented with private insurance—would be about 1.5 percent of payroll, after subtracting what is spent now through Medicaid. If split between employer and employee, like the present Social Security-Medicare tax, that would come to $150 a year for a worker earning $20,000.

Universal and Mandatory

A universal, mandatory program seems advisable, because if all wage earners contribute throughout their working lives, the cost can be reasonable. Programs that depend upon voluntary participation would leave the provident burdened both with their own care and that of the improvident, who would continue to fall back on Medicaid and other publicly financed welfare programs. Only 23 percent of the population has Individual Retirement Accounts, a voluntary program that its planners hoped would become a significant supplement to Social Security.

To establish a worthwhile long-term care program, the politicians will have to surmount the timidity that crippled the catastrophic care bill. The key: understanding that the general anti-tax mood of the American public does not rule out a new tax to fund a genuinely popular program.

One 1987 poll indicated that two-thirds of the population would pay higher taxes for Government-sponsored, long-term care. The poll discloses the reason, too. More than half of the respondents foresee a long-term care problem within their own families in the next five years. . . .

Even Senator David Durenberger, a moderate Republican from Minnesota, acknowledges: "We can no longer sidestep the issue."

"Taxpayers should not have to finance long-term care for every retiree, regardless of wealth or income."

Government Should Not Provide Universal Health Care for the Elderly

Peter J. Ferrara

Peter J. Ferrara is a former senior staff member of the White House Office of Policy Development. He teaches banking and legal writing at George Mason University School of Law where he is an associate professor. From 1981-1982, Ferrara served as special assistant at the Department of Housing and Urban Development. In the following viewpoint, Ferrara argues against a comprehensive federal long-term care policy for the elderly. Ferrara believes that while it should provide assistance to those elderly in financial need, the government should not subsidize the wealthy elderly.

As you read, consider the following questions:

1. In what cases does the author believe the government should provide long-term care assistance for the elderly?
2. What dangers does the author predict if the government implements a comprehensive long-term care policy?
3. Why does Ferrara believe it is unfair to provide long-term care assistance for all elderly?

Peter J. Ferrara, "Providing for Those in Need: Long-Term Care Policy," The Heritage Foundation *Backgrounder*, April 20, 1988. Reprinted with permission.

Many American families face the expense of assuring adequate long-term treatment and care of elderly relatives who no longer can perform basic living activities for themselves. Many of the elderly who have no relatives to help them must face these costs alone. In some cases, families also must struggle through the emotionally draining experience of a close family member's severe, long-term illness, making the financial burden even less bearable. There is broad agreement that, given the rising cost of such long-term care plus the aging of America, sound policies and institutions are required to meet such vital concerns.

This does not mean, however, that Congress should declare open season on younger taxpayers, or that family members should be free to avoid their responsibilities by shifting costs onto Uncle Sam's shoulders. What it does mean is that policy makers should begin to analyze the issue carefully and to determine the appropriate roles for the private and the public sectors, rather than engage in a buying spree for the elderly vote, leaving the tab to be picked up by future governments.

It is not the government's responsibility to underwrite the living expenses of every American who reaches a certain age. It is, however, appropriate for the government to pay for the essential long-term care expenses of those Americans who otherwise would be unable to meet such costs, or could do so only with great hardship. Federal and state governments already spend over $20 billion each year fulfilling this responsibility through Medicaid and other programs. . . .

Some propose that the government pay for the nursing home and home health care expenses of every American, even millionaires, through a universal social insurance program financed by increased payroll tax rates and possibly other tax increases. . . .

Exorbitant Costs

This social insurance program would be enormously costly. Total nursing home expenses in the U.S. this year will be close to $50 billion. Even if the program provided for some substantial contributions to expenses out of beneficiary income, the government's initial cost likely would be over $30 billion. Total expenditures on home health care this year will be well over $10 billion.

Even these figures are surely low for they assume no change in the demand for care resulting from such a program. If the government started paying nursing home expenses across the board, the number of Americans entering nursing homes almost surely would soar, sharply increasing the program's cost. It must be remembered that only 29 percent of those needing long-term care are in nursing homes. In addition, only 26 percent of the disabled elderly in care outside nusing homes receive some professional paid-for home health care services. With the government paying the expenses, many more would use such services. While advocates of home health care benefits argue that such benefits could save government funds by avoiding expensive nursing home care, studies show that such savings are unlikely to result. A study by the Institute for Research on Poverty at the University of Wisconsin, conducted for the National Center for Health Services Research, concludes that government home health care benefits result in little if any reduction in government nursing home expenses, yet lead to increases in government home health expenditures for those who would remain at home even without the expanded benefits.

With the increased demand for nursing home and home health care brought about by such a universal program, prices for such care also would soar. This is especially true since in many states the supply of new nursing home space is heavily restricted by regulation. . . .

Helping the Rich Become Richer

Expanding benefits beyond those in need, to provide free nursing home care assistance to everyone, would be highly regressive. It would mean taxing all working people to provide benefits to Americans with substantial resources. The main effect of such a policy would be to increase the estates that the wealthy can leave to their children. The true beneficiaries of such expanded benefits would be a relatively small number of Americans, mostly between 40 and 60 years old and in the middle to upper income group. This relatively small group of high income beneficiaries would receive large inheritance windfalls made possible by taxing the average taxpayer.

Minimize Government

What the nation needs is a health-care policy for the elderly that minimizes the role of government, avoids special-interest favors and gives individuals as much control as possible over their own destinies.

John C. Goodman, *The Wall Street Journal*, December 30, 1987.

A new government program to help finance long-term care expenses for those Americans who do not have the resources to meet such costs has already been recommended. Allowing the adult children of an elderly person who needs home care to qualify for the earned income tax credit also would assist families of moderate incomes. For better-off Americans, the government should promote the expansion of long-term care insurance and other private financing mechanisms to protect their assets against destructive long-term care costs. In addition, the government should encourage workers to accumulate special savings to finance long-term care insurance in retirement. The federal government could:

1) Develop better data on long-term care needs. A major concern of private insurers is the lack of solid data on which to base long-term care insurance policies. More data on the incidence, duration, and costs of long-term care is needed. The federal government should consult with private insurers and take the lead in developing a data base. This would enable the private market to grow more rapidly.

2) Extend to long-term insurance the incentives that apply to life insurance. The federal government should extend the same tax policies to long-term care insurance that it applies to life insurance. The income earned on investment reserves for long-term care policies should not be taxed, just as life insurance reserves are not taxed. Similarly, the benefits paid by long-term care policies should be tax exempt, as life insurance benefits are. The government should not be taking resources out of the funds of workers who are trying to set aside savings for long-term care, just as the government restrains itself from dipping into life insurance proceeds intended to protect widows and children.

Tax Deductions

3) Make long-term care costs and premiums eligible for the medical expense tax deduction. High medical bills and health insurance premiums can be deducted, in part, from taxable income. Expenses for long-term care and premiums for long-term care insurance should be eligible for similar medical expense deduction.

4) Allow employers to include long-term care insurance in the tax-free "cafeteria" benefit plans offered to their workers. Federal tax law should be changed to allow employers to offer long-term care insurance as one of the choices under "cafeteria" employee benefit plans. These are fringe benefit plans in which each worker is allowed to choose a package of tax-free employee benefits from a range of options.

5) Encourage employers to provide retirement nursing home care with the same tax policy that applies to pensions. The Deficit Reduction Act of 1983 bars employers from deducting most contributions to reserve funds for retirement medical benefits including long-term care coverage; it can even require tax on investment returns on such reserve funds. Contributions and returns to pension funds, however, have remained tax-free. Without a deduction for contributions and the tax exemption for reserve earnings, private employers are far less inclined to offer such retirement benefits. This 1983 tax provision should be reversed.

6) Amend corporate and individual pension plan rules to permit the purchase of long-term insurance. Workers and retirees should be allowed to use vested funds in pension plans, 401(k) plans, Individual Retirement Accounts (IRAs), and other retirement plans to make tax-free purchases of long-term care insurance. Employers should be allowed to use excess reserves in overfunded pension plans to provide long-term care health insurance benefits for their employees in retirement.

7) Stimulate the conversion of life insurance policies into long-term care protection. The government could encourage insurers to offer life insurance policies that can be converted, completely or partially, into coverage for long-term care in retirement. Life insurance needed to protect a family's earning capacity during working years generally is not needed to the same extent in retirement or when children reach adulthood. As retirement begins, death benefits under the policy could be reduced while benefits payable for long-term care could begin and be increased.

8) Encourage home equity conversion. The government should encourage insurers and other financial institutions to make it easier for the elderly to use the equity built up in their homes to finance long-term care insurance or services. Under a "reverse annuity mortgage," permitted now in several states, the elderly homeowner receives a payment each month in return for a mortgage on the home normally up to 80 percent of the home's value. The mortgage is then paid off when the home is sold. Under a "sale leaseback" arrangement, an alternative to the reverse annuity mortgage, the elderly homeowner actually sells his home but acquires an unlimited right to rent back the property for life at a predetermined rate. Through these mechanisms, the elderly could use their home equity for nursing home care insurance and expenses while retaining occupancy of the home.

9) Create health care savings accounts. Congress could adopt a comprehensive program allowing workers and employers to put aside money during their working years for retirement medical and long-term care insurance and services. . . .

Mobilize Private Resources

These measures would mobilize existing private resources to finance long-term care, increasing the ability of elderly Americans to meet such costs themselves and thereby reducing the pressure for costly and wasteful government programs.

To be sure, the government should pay for the essential long-term care expenses of those who do not have the resources to meet the cost, or could not meet it without great hardship. A new program, Long-Term Care Assistance, has been proposed to meet this need. This program would remove the current provisions for long-term care assistance from Medicaid and expand them to provide additional aid to elderly couples, who are not well served by the current system. But taxpayers should not have to finance long-term care for every retiree, regardless of wealth or income. Such a government commitment would require massive tax increases that would slow economic growth and destroy jobs.

If the government picked up the bills for everyone, the number of the elderly entering nursing homes and the price of care would soar dramatically, further increasing program costs. Moreover, free nursing home benefits to everyone would be highly regressive, since working people would be taxed to provide benefits to shield the assets of the wealthy.

Promoting Insurance and Savings

The proper policy for protecting Americans with accumulated assets is not providing them with benefits courtesy of the taxpayer, but encouraging them to protect their resources through insurance. The government thus should take steps to promote the development of private long-term care insurance to enable the elderly to obtain such protection more easily. It also should adopt policies to enable workers to accumulate savings during their careers that would be available to finance long-term care in retirement through private insurance or other means. Encouraging such prudent protection through private insurance, and not as a new entitlement program for the affluent, is the proper way to deal with the long-term care concerns of America's elderly.

"Today we find resources going inefficiently or wastefully to the elderly that are desperately needed elsewhere."

The Elderly Have Too Much Health Coverage

Richard D. Lamm

In the following viewpoint, Richard D. Lamm argues that the vast majority of the elderly do not need public assistance programs such as Medicare, Medicaid, and social security. He contends that society must restrict benefits to the elderly. Lamm is the former governor of Colorado and the director of the Center for Public Policy and Contemporary Issues at the University of Denver.

As you read, consider the following questions:

1. Why does the author argue that age should be a criterion for rationing medical care?
2. Why does Lamm find it "morally offensive" when older people demand the same health care rights as younger people?
3. How would the author put the elderly's health care needs "in perspective"? Do you agree with his plan? Why or why not?

Richard D. Lamm, speech delivered to the Eddy Foundation in Troy, NY on November 6, 1987.

America is aging—fast. Since 1900 the population of the United States has increased three times, the population of those over 65 has increased 8 times and the population of those over 85 has increased 21 times. By the year 2050 there will be as many people over the age of 80 as are today over the age of 65. Between 1986 and 2040 the population age 65 to 74 will grow by about 85 percent while the population age 80 and over will grow by about 300 percent to 400 percent and the population 90 and over will grow by an astounding 500 percent to 700 percent. We must better assess and more candidly discuss the implications of this demographic earthquake. . . .

One important public policy realization is that we have been overwhelmingly successful in raising the elderly out of poverty. Certainly not *all* the elderly. Certainly there are elderly in need. But U.S. public policy has made tremendous gains in lifting the elderly as a class out of poverty. In 1970, 24 percent of our elderly and 16 percent of our young lived in poverty; today only 14 percent of the elderly live in poverty, but 23 percent of the young live in poverty. Some studies suggest that the elderly as a demographic group have the *most* disposable income. When all forms of income, including health care programs of the federal government, are counted, the poverty rate among the senior citizens may be as low as 3 percent. We do know that families over 65 have twice the assets, on the average, as people under 30. Clearly those over the age of 65 have near the lowest poverty rate of any age group in the nation. Yet the elderly, who got 2 percent of the federal spending in 1940, today get 28 percent of the federal spending and they get well over half of all federal social spending. Now the average American working family makes *less* money in 1987 than they made in 1973; adjusted for inflation, we see the elderly have substantially improved their economic position. We thus have to insure that our policies toward the elderly do not impoverish our children, and we must make sure they do not create a burden for coming generations. . . .

Examining Elderly Programs

We simply must examine some of the programs for the elderly, not to abolish them, but to make them make sense for the next generation. . . .

I would suggest that the excesses of some of our systems are related to the inadequacies of other parts of our system. We simply must find the political courage to examine these sacred cows and streamline and amend them so that they do not steal from our children. . . .

I would suggest that we cease to use *age* as a consideration in the distribution of benefits but instead go to *need*. Age based programs set up a system whereby young people pay a significant portion of their income to seniors who are richer than they are, a system which also inadequately deals with those elderly who are desperately in need. We cannot continue to subsidize old age without regard to need. There is something terribly inappropriate about a society which doesn't even provide basic health care to millions of people and yet amends its Medicare regulations to pay for heart transplants—a number of which go to the wealthy elderly. We must stop thinking of the elderly as a monolithic group. Joseph Quinn warned us widely a few years ago not to consider the elderly a single group; they are too diverse, too variable.

"Never begin a sentence with 'the elderly are . . . , the elderly do. . . . ' No matter what dimension of the aged you are discussing, some are and some are not, some do and some do not. The central characteristic to be remembered is the diversity of the aged. The least interesting summary statistic about the elderly is their average, because it ignores the tremendous dispersion around it. Beware the mean.". . .

Use Age as a Criterion for Care

In the rationing of medicine, age should be a criterion. We already ration for age, it's just we ration for the *benefit* of the aged. Our current system gives much more generous benefits to the aged than it does to any other group in America. We are subsidizing through a number of programs, all the elderly, whether needy or not. We have for what appeared to be good, sufficient and compassionate reasons given generous benefits to the elderly.

Need and Old Age

Old age by itself doesn't make someone needy. There are many needy older Americans. But most of the elderly are relatively healthy and, like most other Americans, neither fabulously wealthy nor desperately poor. This larger group shouldn't automatically be granted tax relief or exempted from benefit cuts simply because they're over 65. . . .

Almost everyone—me included, I hope—will someday reach 65. What's really at issue here is how we overcome the mismatch between our desire for government benefits and our willingness to be taxed. We can't do that if we cling to outmoded programs or social assumptions. Decades ago, most older Americans were poor. That's no longer true, and we shouldn't pretend that it is.

Robert J. Samuelson, *Newsweek*, April 18, 1988.

There are some things that we can do easily in setting these priorities. We can certainly start to tax the medical benefits to the elderly. This is clearly one way to focus our benefits on the needy elderly, while limiting the extent of the benefit to wealthy elderly.

The second step which we must also inevitably do is to means-test entitlements to the elderly. This is not politically easy, but as a matter of distributive justice it is more than possible to reduce or eliminate the benefits we now pay the wealthy elderly in favor of programs for the impoverished young. But certainly at some point we will recognize that even these steps are not enough; that our medical genius has outstripped our ability to pay for all the procedures that are medically possible. Infinite medical needs have run into finite resources. We must develop some ways to maximize our medical resources—to get the most health for America for the money we spend.

But that in itself will not solve the problems of exploding medical costs. We must do even more. We must ask should age itself ever be a consideration in the delivery of health care?

No one "wants" to say yes to this question; but I suggest that we will have to say yes to this question.

The obligation of the government toward the elderly cannot be unlimited. No level of government can be expected to cover, without restraint, the exploding health care costs of the elderly. Government must make rational and compassionate allocations to all its citizens and it must increasingly weigh the benefits and burdens between generations.

It is marvelous idealism to say all U.S. citizens should have a "right to health care," but at this point in history that is merely rhetoric. Until that day arrives, or is imminent, we must intelligently discuss the questions of "health care priorities." We must devise a balanced health delivery system that maximizes health care for all Americans.

A Social Burden

The delivery of expensive medical miracles to the explosive growing number of elderly is creating an unsustainable economic and social burden. We are allocating our governmental benefits to those who lobby us the hardest and comprise the biggest voting block, but we are not making rational allocations. Our present policies, in face of those realities, will prevent adequate health care for other generations, especially younger generations. It is already having a distorting effect and is bound to have an increasing distorting effect.

Dan Callahan writes of a similar impact in Great Britain:

> It is understood that the consequences of a desperate struggle to save the lives of the elderly cannot fail to have a distorting consequence for health care priorities and allocations generally.

The longer I was in government, the more I realized that we are moving into an era where we shall have to make "hard choices." That there is a public policy teeter-totter where given limited resources, when we push one side up, alas another side

109

goes down. It is sad but true that we now have a system that allows the elderly to consume far more medical resources than we give to children.

I believe that we shall inevitably have to recognize age as a valid ethical consideration in the delivery of medical care. Is it not only fair, but desirable, to have a different level of care for a 10 year old than for someone who is 100? Should not public policy recognize that some people have far more statistical years ahead of them than others?

The aged are not a static group. It is a status that we all pass through. We are all locked in as males or females, all locked in as black and white. Once a white male, always a white male. But we all age daily. In a marvelously egalitarian way, time takes its toll on all of us. The elderly are the same people—at a different stage of their lives—whom we worry about when we deny prenatal care to pregnant women.

I turn 65 in the fast approaching year of 2000. I am not shooting a bullet in an intergenerational war, I'm not trying to take something from another generation. I realize that I'm arguing for new rules that I know I will have to live and die by. In fact given the normal progression of public debate, mine might well be the first generation to whom they will apply. I have a great self-interest at the age of 52 to ensure that the new considerations I argue for not be oppressive or hard-hearted. I will be their beneficiary or their victim.

Hypocritical Elderly

The immediate task is to meet the elderly's genuine needs without overburdening workers. Perceptions are changing. A wealthier older population is properly being asked to do more. For example, Medicare recipients would pay the added costs of catastrophic coverage—for big doctor and hospital bills, but not for long-term care—under a plan being considered by Congress. . . .

As older people have become more energetic, they've also become more organized to defend their group interests. They insist (rightly) that age alone doesn't rob them of vitality and independence, while also arguing (wrongly) that age alone entitles them to special treatment. It's hypocrisy.

Robert J. Samuelson, *Newsweek*, March 21, 1988.

I care a great deal about myself, but I care also for my children. Economists tell us that "capital is the stored flexibility" that we have to build a better life for our children. I feel it is morally repugnant if I use $100,000 or $200,000 of our kids' limited resources as I'm on my way out the door.

I want to be valued as a senior citizen but I don't want to unnecessarily impose on my children and spend massive resources for a few more months of pain-racked existence. I fear death in the forgotten corner of a nursing home, caught in the twilight zone between life and death, with technology giving me not a longer life but a longer death. I do not want the same standard of medical care that you would give someone who was in their 20's. I have lived my life—experienced joy and sorrow. I believe that technology has replaced God as the author of death and I don't like one bit what I see going on in treatment of the elderly. I am immensely impressed at how many of the elderly see medical treatment as "the enemy." I'm impressed at how the elderly fear pain, suffering, loss of autonomy, and degradation, much more than they fear death. They recognize, as Shakespeare did, that "we all owe God a death."

A Normal Life Span

All cultures distinguish between deaths after a normal life span and a death which is a premature death. Death due to age is universally accepted and understood. Death before a normal life span is universally distinguished and is usually invested with elements of tragedy as it is in our society.

We shrug and call pneumonia an "old man's friend" and yet rage with Lear at the death of the young. We understand with an atavistic wisdom that we cannot live forever and that death in old age is natural and inevitable. At some point to fight against death is not only useless, but unseemly.

One doctor writing in the *New England Journal of Medicine* states: "My personal experience in the practice of neurology for over twenty years is that there is widespread refusal to acknowledge the suffering and degradation experienced by helpless people permanently maintained with life support systems. The American health care system breeds a mentality of turning away from this consideration, perhaps because it does not acknowledge the reality that there is a time to die."

I find it morally offensive at the age of even 52 to demand the same level of medical treatment as someone who has their whole life ahead of them.

Yet there is reason to pause. The ghost of the English system hangs over this debate, a system that seems cruel to our eyes because it rations certain scarce resources on the basis of age. I do not argue for a such a system.

We have other ethical options between massive oppressive technology imposing a slow painful death on us, and an arbitrary rationing using age as the criteria. I do not argue that age should be the criteria, but a criteria.

I find it hard to believe that the health care system should consider a person's blood pressure, whether or not they smoke, how much alcohol they drink, and what their cholesterol count is, but not consider their age. I believe age should not be the consideration, but a consideration along with many others in the allocation of medical resources. It should not dictate, but it should be considered. That doesn't give anyone license to abandon me, or to treat me as superfluous. Far from it. But I should not and will not object if age is laid on the scale in deciding medical treatment.

I consider it relevant in how I treat me—why shouldn't the health care system? I no longer climb trees or play Rugby. I do not lower myself in my own self-esteem that I realize that I have an older body. I treat it with more care. I recognize that my time is limited. I spend more time smelling the flowers.

Now, if I consider it relevant, why shouldn't my doctor? Dan Callahan makes a similar point:

> The elderly have already lived out a full life. They have not been denied (at least because of their age) the opportunities of living a life; and their death deprives them of less than a child or young person who has had no such opportunity. Not only does it seem justifiable to work harder, and to take more chances, to save and rehabilitate the life of a sick child, but also to allocate more resources to those conditions that bring premature death than to those that bring death after a long life.

To maximize our health care dollars we not only ethically can, but ethically must, set some priorities. In setting those priorities we must recognize that some reform of the health treatment of the terminally ill is possible. It will help, but not solve the problem of exploding health care costs.

But to do justice to all Americans, we must do more. We must recognize that age is a valid and ethical consideration in the delivery of health care. We must do so not to abandon the elderly, but to put their needs in perspective with other health care demands of our society. . . .

In summary, let me tell you of the old Middle East proverb, "that the beginning of wisdom comes when a person plants trees, the shade under which he knows he will never sit." I reflect deeply on that proverb. The ultimate question of an aging society is how do we do justice to *all* sectors of the economy, including the elderly, but not only the elderly. Today we find resources going inefficiently or wastefully to the elderly that are desperately needed elsewhere.

"We must protect our senior citizens from further health cuts and urge the rapid development of a long term insurance program."

The Elderly Need More Health Coverage

Timothy Norbeck

A central argument over health care for the aged centers on two disparate pictures of senior citizens. One group holds that seniors are often poor, with limited savings, while another group believes seniors are disproportionately well-off compared to the younger segment of the population. In the following viewpoint, Timothy Norbeck, executive director of the Connecticut State Medical Society, argues that recent threats to cut medical benefits for the elderly that are based on their comparative wealth are mean-spirited and dangerous. The elderly need more coverage, not less, he believes.

As you read, consider the following questions:

1. Why does the author believe we should rejoice about the large elderly population?
2. Why is it natural for the elderly to account for one-third of the health care costs, according to the author?

Timothy Norbeck, speech delivered before the New Haven Rotary Club, New Haven, CT, August 12, 1986.

When Mark Twain was asked what he thought of Richard Wagner's music, he said that "It's not as bad as it sounds." Close examination of the national debate on aging America, which is about to intensify, would indicate that things are as bad as they sound. Up to now, we have heard smatterings of statistics cast about which lead us to the conclusion that we, as a nation, have not properly addressed the elderly's financial ability to meet their health care needs. The plain and simple truth is that we are facing a bona fide crisis in every sense of the word.

Around the time of the great depression in the early 1930s, America's population was considered young. In the past fifty years, however, we have shifted to the opposite end of that spectrum. We cannot deny this trend. Quite simply, no other nation has aged so rapidly in the history of the world. Also obvious is that the national debate on aging is, and will continue to be, one of the most important issues of our time. Unfortunately, we have not prepared ourselves for the aging phenomenon, and the debate lends itself to emotional outbursts and threatens to polarize our people.

Today there are 28 million Americans 65 years of age and older (more than the entire population of Canada), and that number will increase by 18 percent in the next decade. Between 1970 and 1984, the number of very old people—those 85 and over—rose by nearly 90 percent, from 1.4 million to 2.7 million people. The 85 and over group, a most significant part of our population in several respects, is the fastest growing segment of our population. This rapid growth is expected to continue through the end of this century when in a period of only 14 years, their numbers will have almost doubled. Today there are 35,000 Americans over 100 years of age and that number will triple by the year 2000.

Medicine's Accomplishments

All of us can and should rejoice at those numbers and projections, and American medicine can take particular pride in its contributions to this notable achievement. This aging phenomenon attests to medicine's accomplishments over the past 50 years along with its abilities to greatly enhance the quality of life for all citizens. But for all the joy that its success has wrought, there is a downside, too. Lost in the shuffle of statistics and demographics is the realization that our nation has not prepared itself for such an eventuality.

Although constituting slightly less than 12 percent of our population (11.9 percent nationally and 12.9 percent in Connecticut), the 65 and over group accounts for one-third of our health care costs. While this should be expected, there are some critics who claim that this is too disproportionate a figure. Pointing to the 10.6 percent of our Gross National Product spent on health care in the United States, they rail against any further increases. We should remember, however, that the GNP is really nothing more than an indication of a nation's wealth. Is 10.6 percent too much for a people who clearly demand the best possible health care? Besides, as Benjamin Disraeli once noted, if "The health of the people is really the foundation upon which all of their happiness and power as a state depend," how much is too much?

Still others express concern about the high cost of dying and cite the almost 30 percent of the Medicare budget which goes to pay for medical bills for those in their last six months of life. Many raise the question of life-prolonging machines which seem to have replaced God as the author of death, and suggest that we stop treating death like it's an option. There remain numerous legal and ethical obstacles before this question can be resolved.

Elderly Face High Costs

The continuing high health-care costs of the elderly are themselves cause for concern in any attempt to accurately assess the income adequacy of the elderly. Even excluding costly long-term care, for example, the elderly's out-of-pocket health-care costs today are over $1,000 per year—3½ times higher than that of other age groups, and higher proportionately than the amount they spent prior to the enactment of Medicare and Medicaid more than two decades ago. Contrary to popular myth, Medicare pays only about 45 percent of the elderly's medical-care bills, and recipients have experienced huge increases in cost sharing (e.g., a 141 percent increase in the Part A deductible) under the Reagan Administration. Inflation in health care at a rate roughly double that of the consumer price index further suggests that the *de facto* income adequacy of many elderly may be significantly less than the crude figures imply. . . .

The scapegoating of the elderly as a primary cause of the fiscal crisis has deflected attention from the more compelling and deep-seated causes of the current economic crisis. At the same time, and wittingly or unwittingly fueled by recent mass media . . . , it has been used as a political tool to stoke resentment of the elderly and to create perceptions of a forced competition of the aged and younger members of society for limited resources.

Meredith Minkler, *Social Policy,* Winter 1987.

Some critics claim that the elderly are well off and that government programs are already too heavily skewed toward our senior citizens. Members of the Americans for Generational Equity complain that the Social Security program is nothing more than a massive transfer of wealth from the young (many of them struggling) to the old (many of them living comfortably). Others cite figures indicating that the over 65 poverty rate of 12.4 percent and which becomes 2.6 percent after non-cash benefits are considered, is lower than any other age group. But this tells only part of the story.

While the elderly are slightly less likely than other groups to be poor, they are more likely to be near poor. For example and according to the U.S. Senate Committee on Aging, senior citizens are poorer than the younger population at 125 percent of the poverty level—23.7 percent for persons over 65 as compared to 19.8 percent for those under 65. It may be that Irish poet and playwright William Butler Yeats's opinion that "old age is nothing but a tattered coat upon a stick" does not apply to the elderly as a group but the description is not so far off for increasing numbers of senior citizens.

At the same time that all statistics confirm a population boom among our elderly, programs such as Medicare are being cut. The Medicare program has undergone reductions of $40 billion over the past five years, reductions that amount to a full 12 percent of the total federal cuts to the budget even though Medicare accounts for only 7 percent of all total federal budget outlays. Additional slashes of equal magnitude are being considered and planned for the next five years. Compounding these difficulties is the rapidly escalating hospital deductible paid by Medicare patients. Senior citizens have experienced a 200 percent increase in that deductible since 1977 and a 23 percent rise in 1986 to $492. . . .

Although the ranks of our 85 and over elderly are swelling faster than any other age group in America, the growth in the number of new nursing home beds available to care for them has lagged. Some forecasters estimate that we may have to double our current bed capacity by the year 2000 in order to accommodate that need. At this time, nursing home bed capacity is increasing at a little better than half the rate of growth of the groups most likely to need nursing home care—that is, those 85 and over. The odds are something like 1 in 100 that one aged 65-74 will have to enter a nursing home. Those odds become 7 in 100 for senior citizens between 74 and 85. At the 85 and over level, however, the odds change considerably. Some 23 in 100 in this latter group will find themselves candidates for nursing home care.

A Gap in Long Term Care

We as a people should also be concerned about an American Association of Retired Persons (AARP) poll which indicates that 79 percent of the elderly mistakenly believe that Medicare will cover long term nursing home care when, in fact, the program only covers 100 days—and then, only in a low percentage of cases due to its many restrictions. To my knowledge, only 125,000 to 150,000 long term care policies have been marketed to a senior citizen population of 28 million plus countless millions more who will join the ranks of the elderly in the next few years.

Long term nursing home care has exacted a horrendous toll on senior citizens and their families alike. The average individual requiring long term nursing home care uses up his or her accumulated life savings within just one year. Then Medicaid takes over. A great majority of our elderly have been characterized over the years as taking great pride in paying their own bills. Losing their life savings and their dignity in the same process as they are forced on the burgeoning rolls of the Medicaid program is a very bitter pill for them to swallow.

Support Congressional Plans

The elderly, medicine, business and industry must work together to fight reductions in the Medicare and Medicaid programs and be more visible in standing up for the poor.

We must call on the insurance industry, with all its power, influence and ingenuity to support both congressional long term care plans and to develop and aggressively market its own program at a cost within the means of the American people.

Timothy Norbeck, *Vital Speeches of the Day,* February 2, 1987.

Another major concern related to long term care is that 50 percent of all those covered by Medicaid in nursing homes were not on that program upon entering that home. Officials talk of cutting back on Medicaid budgets, but how can that possibly be achieved when it represents the last hope for so many to receive help?

We should be concerned about the 63 percent of our elderly in Connecticut who are women, many of them living alone and in need of help—and whose problems are different and incomes less than those of men. Some 40 percent of all single women over 65 in the United States have incomes less than $5000 a year. Half of all elderly women in this nation live within $800 of the poverty line. Poverty remains at a crisis level for widows, minorities, and those who live into their 80s. It is clear that over 65 women are one of the most disadvantaged groups, and the fact that more than 71 percent of the elderly poor are women certainly attests to that!

Elderly Suicide Rate Rising

Another major concern deals with the overall effects of these problems and other pressures on the mental health of our senior citizens. Do you realize that the suicide rate for those over 65, after dropping for years, has risen dramatically over the past few years to the extent that it is now 50 percent above that of the general population? Cutbacks in Medicare, Medicaid, food stamps and pensions along with forced retirements have made poverty an increasingly common feature of old age for growing numbers of senior citizens.

But the problem doesn't even end there. The General Accounting Office and the Senate Special Committee on Aging suggest that under the DRG [Diagnostic Related Groups] prospective payment system in hospitals, some senior citizens are being discharged too early from hospitals with nowhere else to go. As the Senate Committee chairman puts it, these elderly fall into a "no-care" zone where nursing homes reject them either because the homes are too full or the patients are too sick. Thousands of complaints have been directed from elderly patients to the U.S. Department of Health and Human Services.

Many should be eligible for home health care benefits under Medicare, but once again our senior citizens have drawn the short straw. Federal government policies restrain benefits by invoking vague, confusing and unpublished guidelines—thereby denying help to the very people who need it the most. It has become increasingly difficult for Medicare beneficiaries to appeal denials. These denials, not so incidentally, numbered almost 50,000 in the first quarter of 1986 alone. We are fortunate in Connecticut that the State Department on Aging and the Commission on Aging have recognized these federal deficiencies and taken steps to alleviate them by providing a grant program which will offer help to those who have been denied Medicare payments for home health services. Denials of essential home health services serve as another example to remind us that elderly health problems have far too low a priority with the federal government.

What can we do about this litany of problems directly afflicting our senior citizens and indirectly affecting the rest of us? Congress is wrestling with a catastrophic insurance plan, and others favor expanding the Medicare program to include such benefits. Obviously we must address the issue of long term care for the elderly. Perhaps you may remember Linus from the "Peanuts" comic strip saying to Charlie Brown that "There's no problem too big that we can't run away from it." This is of such magnitude, however, that we cannot any longer run away or ignore it.

Expand Benefits to the Aged

Even in its best light, long term care can only be viewed as the greatest threat to financial security to the aged. As the odds for living past age 85 increase, that threat only intensifies. If we do not resolve it, we may reach a sad point in our history where long term care will be available only to the wealthy who can afford it, or to the poor who will be covered by Medicaid.

The insurance industry, with all its power, influence and ingenuity, must develop benefit plans that can be expanded to the elderly. They must be affordable and must be marketed nationally. People must be educated so that they understand that Medicare is not their long term care salvation—in fact, that Medicare will only provide a very restrictive 100 days of coverage. All citizens, young and old alike, must plan for living longer lives. Medicare should be expanded to include catastrophic coverage for acute health care needs.

We must protect our senior citizens from further health cuts and urge the rapid development of a long term insurance program. Let us not, in the rush to cut costs and balance budgets, forget our elderly who helped build this state and nation and who spent a lifetime working and paying taxes.

"Provision of medical care for those who have lived out a natural life span will be limited to the relief of suffering."

Health Care for the Elderly Should Be Rationed

Daniel Callahan

Daniel Callahan is director of The Hastings Center, an organization devoted to the exploration of ethical issues related to health care and public education. In the following viewpoint, excerpted from his highly controversial book, *Setting Limits*, Callahan discusses his plan to ration health care. Callahan argues that health care costs demand that society no longer employ expensive medical technology to prolong the lives of the aged.

As you read, consider the following questions:

1. Why should age be taken into consideration for medical treatment, according to the author?
2. What benefits does Callahan see in rationing health care for the aged?
3. What three criteria does the author contend must be taken into account when limiting care for the aged?

Death, we are told, is no longer a hidden subject. That is at best a half-truth. The aged constitute the majority of those who die, some 70 percent, but a specific discussion of their dying is remarkably scant in legal, ethical, and medical writings. That omission is probably not accidental. The modernization of aging induces a sharp separation between aging and death. The latter is often treated as if it had little to do with the former, a kind of accidental conjunction. In medicine, the long-standing tradition of treating patients regardless of their age works against an open discussion, even though many physicians admit it is a consideration in their actual practice. The courts appear to follow a similar tradition. Despite the large number of decisions in recent years bearing on cases of elderly patients, that fact is typically not mentioned, though it is an obvious feature of the cases.

These inhibitions against explicit discussion of the elderly dying doubtless serve a valuable function. They reflect a sensible fear that the aged might be singled out for unfairly discriminatory treatment. They are a way of acknowledging the difficulty of sharply differentiating the medical conditions of the aged from those of other patients. Yet the pervasiveness of backstage debate about the care of the elderly dying among physicians and nurses, jurists and legislators, and the elderly themselves makes it imperative now to deal explicitly with the issue. There are also other reasons for having such a discussion. What is the proper goal of medicine for those who have already lived out a natural life span, by which I mean a full biographical, not a maximum biological life? That goal is, I believe, the relief of suffering rather than the extension of life. What are the practical implications of that position for the care of the critically ill, or elderly dying? If the goals of the aging ought to be service to the young and coming generations, what follows for their way of thinking about death? How does the ready availability of technology sway the making of decisions about the dying? I want to start with that last question.

Medical Technology: A House Divided

One of the hardy illusions of the past few decades has been the belief that with a few changes in law and attitudes, the dying can be spared excessive medical treatment and be allowed to die a "death with dignity." Yet the termination of treatment seems to remain almost as hard, if not harder, in practice now than in earlier times. That is true with the old as much as with the young. Despite the public debate and soothing words, both the public and physicians remain profoundly ambivalent about stopping the use of life-sustaining medical technologies. It is often and accurately said that the elderly do not want excessive and useless treatment. They greatly fear a death marked by technological oppressiveness, wrapped in a cocoon of tubes and machines. Yet they have also no less come—as we all have—to expect medicine whenever possible to extend their lives as well as alleviate or cure their diseases. These are not logically incompatible impulses, but they can be psychologically at odds.

More Costs for the Elderly?

Do we really want to pay more to cover medical costs of the elderly? Samuel H. Preston, a demographer, calculates that we spend 10 times more per capita of the Federal budget on the elderly than on our children. If we have idle assets, why not do something about the 37 million Americans who were refused even basic health care [in 1986]? Or about the 20 percent of our children who haven't yet been given polio shots? Or about the one-third of all pregnant women who have had no health care in their first trimester?

The Federal Government pays 50 percent of the health care costs of the elderly. This may not be enough, but it is far more than for any other demographic group, and the elderly have the highest disposable income. While the nation's borrowing costs are soaring, is it fair to put a new entitlement program for the elderly on the national credit card?

Richard D. Lamm, *The New York Times*, February 19, 1987.

Two fears seem to compete with each other among the elderly: on the one hand, that they will be abandoned or neglected if they become critically ill or begin to die and that few will care about their fate; or, on the other hand, that they will be excessively treated and their lives painfully extended. Death after a long, lingering illness marked by dementia and isolation in the back room of a nursing home similarly competes as a vision of horror with that of death in an intensive care unit, a dying constantly interrupted by painful and unwanted interventions. There is reason for such fears. Medicine steadily extends to the elderly the use of drugs, surgery, rehabilitation, and other procedures once thought suitable only for younger patients. Ever-more-aggressive technological means are used to extend the life of the elderly. On the whole, the elderly welcome that development—even as they fear some of its consequences. They want, somehow, that most elusive of all goals: a steadily improving medical technology that will relieve their pain and illness while not leading to overtreatment and to a harmful extension of life.

Diagnosing Terminal Illness

The difficulty of making accurate prognoses is part of the problem. In all too many cases, technology is used because it is not known that a patient is dying or in irreversible decline. The prognosis of a terminal illness is always difficult to achieve. The problem is even greater, a recent Office of Technology Assessment (OTA) study concluded, when immediate decisions must be made about initiating treatment. Only for patients who have been fully diagnosed can estimates of survival probability be made. Even then, the probabilities are very likely to be insufficient for guiding decisionmaking about withholding or withdrawing treatment for an individual patient.

The ordinary, almost instinctive, tendency of physicians faced with that uncertainty is then to use technology, to treat with vigor. For his or her part, the patient—who will ordinarily want to live, but may also be fearful of useless overtreatment—will be faced with a no less highly uncertain situation. How sick am I? What are my chances? Both patients and families are likely to have the same inclination as the physician, to treat. Given a normal desire to preserve life and to use available technologies, those impulses of both patients and physicians are understandable. The hard question, therefore, is not why technology is used so much by physicians, or why patients want it no less than doctors. We have to ask instead why it is so hard to *stop* using it, even when patient welfare and plain common sense appear to demand just that. . . .

Age as a Criterion

Could we not, however, turn to age as a criterion in order to know when to stop, when to say that no more should be done? I want to look first at one great source of confusion: the common failure to distinguish between age as a medical or technical criterion, pertinent to prognosis, and age as a person- or patient-centered criterion. By age as a medical criterion, I mean treating chronological age as if it were the equivalent of other physical characteristics of a patient—that is, as the equivalent of such typical medical indicators as weight, blood pressure, or white-cell count. Just as those characteristics would be reasonable considerations in treating a patient, so also would age if it could be treated as a reliable technical consideration. Age as a person-centered characteristic, by contrast, would be understood as the relevance of a person's history and biography, his situation not as a collection of organs but as a person, to be taken into account when that personal situation could legitimately be considered. . . .

Age as a biographical standard. If we know someone's age, but nothing else about him, what do we know of significance? If the person is old—say, in his seventies (and certainly by his eighties)— we would know that most of his chronological life is in his past rather than his future, would not expect to find him playing football or climbing trees for recreation, might not be surprised to find that most of his friends are older rather than younger people, and might expect him to have two or more physical impairments, minor or major. Certain "age-associated" traits would almost invariably be present. . . .

His age would, in other words, surely be a part of our overall understanding of him—not the whole story, but hardly of no consequence either. While many "age-associated" traits will bear on the functioning of an elderly person, age as a biographical trait does not reduce to that. Age encompasses a relationship to time—less time statistically remains for an old person than a young person, and there is more personal history behind him as well. It encompasses a relationship to self-consciousness—life and its prospects will usually be thought about differently. And it encompasses a relationship to the passing of the generations—the old are next in line to pass as individuals. The old know they are old, and so does everyone else. Age is not an incidental trait of a person. Might the combination of age and other characteristics then be allowed to have a bearing on medical treatment, and particularly termination decisions? . . .

Denying the Elderly Access to Care

What do we owe each other as we grow old? I think we would be justified in saying that beyond a certain age we will simply not provide expensive, life-extending care. We will always relieve your pain and suffering, but we will not give you organ transplantations, we will not give you access to open-heart surgery, or even possibly access to an intensive-care unit. We will really say: "Look, we have already done justice to you in our society by getting you this far. And we cannot be asked to indefinitely extend your life."

Daniel Callahan, *U.S. News & World Report*, February 22, 1988.

Age as a biographical standard for terminating treatment. How can a combination of age and other characteristics be allowed to have a bearing on the termination of treatment? How, I respond, can it not any longer? If "medical need" is too indeterminate and elastic a concept to be used by itself, then some use of age will be *necessary* to make a judgment about terminating care of the elderly. Since age is an important aspect of the patient as a person, someone who is not just a collection of organs, it falsifies the reality that is part of a person in his fullness to set it aside as irrelevant. Moreover, in addition to being a necessary part of a full and proper medical-moral judgment, age is a valuable and illuminating part, telling us where the patient stands in relation to his own history. There are a large and growing number of elderly who are not imminently dying but who are feeble and declining, often chronically ill, for whom curative medicine has little to offer. That kind of medicine may still be able to do something for failing organs; it can keep them going a bit longer. But it cannot

124

offer the patient as a person any hope of being restored to good health. A different treatment plan should be in order. That person's history has all but come to an end, and medical care needs to encompass that reality, not try to deny it.

For many people, beginning with the aged themselves, old age is a reason in itself to think about medical care in a different way, whether in forgoing its lifesaving powers when death is clearly imminent, or in forgoing its use even when death may be distant but life has become a blight rather than a blessing. The alternative is not, as some would have it, respect for life but an idolatrous enslavement to technology.

The Whole Person

We should want to know not just what chronological age may tell us about the state of a person's body (as a technical criterion), but also what it morally and psychologically signifies for a person to have an old rather than a young body; or what it means for a person to be old rather than young when considering the prospect of painful treatment; or what it signifies to live life as an old person—or as a sick old person—who cannot expect to recapture the vitality of youth, or even of an earlier old age. When considered in those ways, age becomes a category of evaluation in its own right, something reasonable and proper to wonder and worry about. It bears not only on physical characteristics, but on a person's self-understanding, as something intrinsic (with varying degrees of intensity, to be sure) to a person's individuality and life story. The whole person—and it is that whole person who presents himself or herself for treatment—is a person of a certain chronological age: that determines many characteristics, and much of the coloring, of a person's life. That is the importance of the biographical point of view.

Principles for the Use of Age

How, from a biographical vantage point, should we formulate age as a criterion for the termination of treatment and make use of it in termination decisions? I will begin by proposing some general background principles for the termination of treatment of the aged, each meant to articulate themes developed earlier.

After a person has lived out a natural life span, medical care should no longer be oriented to resisting death. No precise chronological age can readily be set for determining when a natural life span has been achieved—biographies vary—but it would normally be expected by the late seventies or early eighties. While a person's history may not be complete—time is always open-ended—most of it will have been achieved by that stage of life. It will be a full biography, even if more details are still to be added. Death beyond that period is not now, nor should it be, typically considered premature or untimely. Any greater precision than my "late seventies or early eighties" does not at present seem possible, and extended public discussion would be needed to achieve even a rough consensus on the appropriate age range. That discussion would also have to consider whether, for policy purposes, it would be necessary to set an exact age or a range only, and that would pose a classic policy dilemma. Too vague a standard of a "natural life span" would open the way for too great a flexibility of application to be fair or workable, while too specific a standard—one indifferent to the unique features of individual biographies—would preclude prudence and appropriate room for discretion.

Accept Aging and Death

As it confronts aging, medicine should have as its specific goals the averting of premature death, that is, death prior to the completion of a natural life span, and thereafter, the relief of suffering. It should pursue those goals so that the elderly can finish out their years with as little needless pain as possible—and with as much vitality as can be generated in contributing to the welfare of younger age groups and to the community of which they are a part. Above all, the elderly need to have a sense of the meaning and significance of their stage in life, one that is not dependent on economic productivity or physical vigor. . . .

The indefinite extension of life combined with an insatiable ambition to improve the health of the elderly is a recipe for monomania and bottomless spending. It fails to put health in its proper place as only one among many human goods. It fails to accept aging and death as part of the human condition. It fails to present to younger generations a model of wise stewardship.

Daniel Callahan, *The Nation*, August 15/22, 1987.

Problems of that kind, however difficult, should not be used as an excuse to evade the necessity of setting some kind of age standard, or to conclude that any age standard must necessarily mean denying the value of the elderly. The presumption against resisting death after a natural life span would not in any sense demean those who have lived that long or suggest that their lives are less valuable than those of younger people. To come to the end of life in old age does not diminish the value of the life; that remains until the very end. This is not a principle, in short, for the comparison of lives. It reflects instead an acceptance of the inevitability of death in general and its acceptability for the individual after a natural life span in particular. Death will then take its proper place as a necessary link in the transition of generations.

Provision of medical care for those who have lived out a natural life span will be limited to the relief of suffering. Medicine is not in a position to bring meaning and significance to the lives of the old. That only they can do for themselves, with the help of the larger culture. Yet medicine can help promote the physical functioning, the mental alertness, and the emotional stability conducive to this pursuit. These remain valuable goals, even when a natural life span has been attained. The difference at that point is that death should no longer be treated by medicine as an enemy. It may well be, of course, that medical efforts to relieve suffering will frequently have the unintended but foreseeable consequence of extending life expectancy. That is to be expected. A sharp line between relieving suffering and extending life will be on occasion difficult to draw, and under no circumstance would it be acceptable to fail to relieve suffering because of the possibility of life extension. The bias of the principle should be to stop resisting death after a certain age, but not when the price of doing so is unrelievable suffering. At the same time—as the success of the hospice movement proves—it is perfectly possible to relieve suffering while not seeking to extend life.

The Aged and Technology

The existence of medical technologies capable of extending the lives of the elderly who have lived out a natural life span creates no presumption whatever that the technologies must be used for that purpose. The uses of technology are always to be subordinated to the appropriate ends of medicine: that is, to the avoidance of premature death and to the relief of suffering. The alternative is slavery to the powers of technology—they, not we, will determine our end. Medicine should in particular resist the tendency to provide to the aged the life-extending capabilities of technologies developed primarily to help younger people avoid premature and untimely death. The use of those technologies should be subordinate to what is good for the elderly as individuals, good for them as members of society, good for them as a link in the passing of the generations, and good for the needs of other age groups.

The three principles detailed above are not so radical as they may first appear. They come close to actually articulating what many elderly express as their fears about aging and death. They indicate a wish that their life not be aggressively extended beyond a point at which they still possess a good degree of physical functioning and mental alertness, a life that has value and meaning for them; they are asking not for more years as such (though some would want just that), but for as many *good* years as possible; and that medical technology be limited in its use to those situations in which it will maintain or restore an adequate quality of life, not sustain and extend a deteriorating one.

"People without resources in need of certain kinds of care will die sooner than old folks who do not have to depend on the government."

Health Care for the Elderly Should Not Be Rationed

Nat Hentoff

Nat Hentoff has been a board member for the American Civil Liberties Union and is the author of *The First Freedom: The Tumultuous History of Free Speech in America*. Hentoff is also a prolific writer who takes a strong stand against euthanasia and abortion. In the following viewpoint, he uses Daniel Callahan's book, *Setting Limits*, as a starting point to discuss rationing health care for the aged. Hentoff believes limiting life-saving procedures for the aged is discriminatory and immoral.

As you read, consider the following questions:

1. What does the author believe is the current attitude toward the aged?
2. Why does the author compare limiting treatment of the aged to Nazism?
3. Why does Hentoff believe rationing health care for the elderly is unconstitutional?

Nat Hentoff, "The Pied Piper Returns for the Old Folks," *The Village Voice*, April 26, 1988. Reprinted with permission of the author and the Village Voice © 1988.

In 1983, the [New York] *Times* ran an Op-Ed piece, "Our Elderly's Fate," by Northeastern University sociology professors Jack Levin and Arnold Arluke. The lead paragraph was, to say the least, compelling:

"American society may be heading toward a *de facto* 'final solution' to the problem of a growing elderly population. This trend raises the unthinkable prospect of the elderly one day being exterminated as a matter of law."

Having seized the elderly reader by the throat, the authors backed off a little. The deliberate massing of the old to take their last showers was not quite what they saw ahead. But already, "there is strong evidence that increasing numbers of frail, disabled, and financially dependent elders, most of whom are over 78, are even now, as a result of our social policies, being isolated from society and dying prematurely."

You don't need to rebuild Auschwitz to send a message to the old that it is time for them to enter eternity. The signals are everywhere. "Self-help manuals," wrote Levin and Arluke, "are showing the elderly how to commit suicide. Studies show that emergency room personnel tend to spend less time and effort to resuscitate elderly heart attack victims than their younger counterparts.

"There is also a growing tendency in medical circles to *emphasize quality over quantity of life*. 'Death with dignity' may in some cases be a euphemism for extermination." (Emphasis added.)

The two professors were also astute enough to look at the auguries in the popular culture. *Logan's Run*, a science fiction movie, starred Michael York as a man in the future who, at 30, had reached the age at which he must be executed by the state. The book *Triage* "conjectures that the Government would solve the problems of old age by burning all nursing homes and their inhabitants."

Not in America. It can't happen here. Not that way. But five years ago, there was no way Jack Levin and Arnold Arluke could imagine that a distinguished, widely respected bioethicist would come forth with what his admirers call a "humane" way, a "morally courageous" way, of solving the problems of old age.

Socially Responsible Death

The method: persuading the elderly that they can be socially responsible by having the government take away from them certain forms of costly, life-extending medical care.

After all, the kind of medical care he has in mind—heart bypass operations, for instance—would only make them live longer, vainly dreaming of immortality. But the Pied Piper would show old folks how to leave us with grace by being content with a "natural life span."

129

The Pied Piper, in his autumnal colors, has brought the news of his gentle proposal in magazines, on television, and in a widely praised book.

By having their medical care rationed, he says, the aged will learn to savor the meaning and significance of their final years, for they will *know* they are final. And since the rest of society will no longer be spending so much on the health care of the old, the money saved can be used for the vast numbers of the population who are not old but need more care they they can afford—single or widowed women, members of minority groups.

This benefactor of the elderly is Daniel Callahan, director of the Hastings Center—a pacesetter in medical ethics—in Briarcliff Manor, New York. His book is *Setting Limits* (Simon and Schuster), and it has been respectfully received in just about every important periodical in the nation. He has been asked to speak about his solution to all kinds of groups. Some disagree with him, but they all take him seriously.

I confess that when I first heard distant word of this notion of the elderly going gently into that good Callahan night, I thought he was putting us on. (I should have realized that the Hastings Center—where he and other bioethicists labor to tell us how to

Dan Wasserman. © 1987, *Boston Globe*. Reprinted with permission.

fit our lives and deaths into their designs—long ago found humor far too spontaneous and certainly too personal for its religion of utilitarianism.)

Still, I expect that the sardonic Dean of Dublin's Saint Patrick's Cathedral, Jonathan Swift, would appreciate Daniel Callahan's *Setting Limits*—though not in the way he would be supposed to. Swift, you will recall, at a time of terrible poverty and hunger in Ireland, wrote *A Modest Proposal*. Rather than having the children of the poor continue to be such a burden to their parents and their nation, why not persuade the poor to raise their children to be slaughtered at the right, succulent time and sold to the rich as delicacies for dining?

What could be more humane? The children would be spared a life of poverty, their parents would be saved from starvation, and the overall economy of Ireland would be in better shape.

So, I thought, Callahan, wanting to dramatize the parlous and poignant state of America's elderly, as described by Jack Levin and Arnold Arluke, had created his modern version of *A Modest Proposal*.

I was wrong. He's not jiving.

So let us look at the Callahan way of ordering the future of America's elderly.

Government Moves In

First, Callahan sees "a natural life span" as being ready to say good-bye in one's late seventies or early eighties. He hasn't fixed on an exact age yet. Don't lose your birth certificate.

If people persist in living beyond the time that Callahan, if not God, has allotted them, the government will move in. Congress will require that anybody past that age must be denied Medicare payments for such procedures as certain forms of open heart surgery, certain extended stays in an intensive care unit, and who knows what else.

Moreover, as an index of how humane the spirit of *Setting Limits* is, if an old person is diagnosed as being in a chronic vegetative state (some physicians screw up this diagnosis), the Callahan plan mandates that the feeding tube be denied or removed. (No one is certain whether someone actually in a persistent vegetative state can *feel* what's going on while being starved to death. If there is sensation, there is no more horrible way to die.)

What about the elderly who don't have to depend on Medicare? Millions of the poor and middle class have no other choice than to go to the government, but there are some old folks with money. They, of course, do not have to pay any attention to Daniel Callahan at all. Like the well-to-do from time immemorial, they will get any degree of medical care they want.

So, *Setting Limits* is class-biased in the most fundamental way.

People without resources in need of certain kinds of care will die sooner than old folks who do not have to depend on the government and Daniel Callahan.

I am aware that there are more limits—in all respects—to the lives of the poor than to the lives of the comfortable. But there is something almost depraved about so brazenly discriminatory a plan coming from the director of a place that derives all its income and its considerable prestige from its reputation as a definer of ethical behavior—in the healing arts particularly.

Prorated Aging

To assume that the elderly may use up only that percentage of medical costs that is equal to their percentage of the total population is a misuse of statistics. We don't insist the entire education budget be prorated over all cohorts in the population.

Does [Callahan's] projection of future health costs take the expense of fighting acquired immune deficiency syndrome into account? AIDS is not a disease of the elderly, yet we do not begrudge that expense.

Ruth Sperber, *The Nation*, October 10, 1987.

Callahan reveals that once we start going down the slippery slope of utilitarianism, we slide by—faster and faster—a lot of old-timey ethical norms. Like the declaration of the Catholic bishops of America that medical care is "indispensable to the protection of human dignity." The bishops didn't say that dignity is only for people who can afford it. They know that if you're 84, and only Medicare can pay your bills but says it won't pay for treatment that will extend your life, then your "human dignity" is shot to hell.

What does Daniel Callahan say about this—uh—imbalance of justice? In the course of an appearance on the *MacNeil Lehrer News Hour*, Callahan said:

". . . After the age of 80 or 85, wherever we might set it [the age of limiting medical care], then I agree injustice might set in. However, it seems to me in the nature of the case, it would not be for a very long time."

There's a logical man. It would indeed not be for a very long time, and all the shorter for the intervention of Mr. Callahan.

He noted on the same program that his is not an ideal proposal, "but I think the hard choice of that injustice at a later age is well worth the kinds of gains we would get in a more rounded, coherent health care system."

Again, this is naked utilitarianism—the greatest good for the greatest number. And individuals who are in the way—in this case, the elderly poor—have to be gotten out of the way. Not murdered, heaven forfend. Just made comfortable until they die with all deliberate speed.

It must be pointed out that Daniel Callahan does not expect or intend his design for natural dying to be implemented soon. First of all, the public will have to be brought around. But that shouldn't be too difficult in the long run. I am aware of few organized protests against the court decisions in a number of states that feeding tubes can be removed from patients—many of them elderly—who are not terminally ill and are not in intractable pain. And some of these people may not be in a persistently vegetative state.

So, the way the Zeitgeist is going, I think public opinion could eventually be won over to Callahan's modest proposal. But he has another reason to want to wait. He doesn't want his vision of "setting limits" to go into effect until society has assured the elderly access to decent long-term home care or nursing home care as well as better coverage for drugs, eyeglasses, and the like.

Even if all that were to happen, there still would be profound ethical and constitutional problems. What kind of a society will we have become if we tuck in the elderly in nursing homes and then refuse them medical treatment that could prolong their lives?

And what of the physicians who will find it abhorrent to limit the care they give soley on the basis of age? As a presumably penitent former Nazi doctor said, "Either one is a doctor or one is not."

On the other hand, if the Callahan plan is not to begin for a while, new kinds of doctors can be trained who will take a utilitarian rather than a Hippocratic oath. ("I will never forget that my dedication is to the society as a whole rather than to any individual patient.") Already, I have been told by a physician who heads a large teaching institution that a growing number of doctors are spending less time and attention on the elderly. There are similar reports from other such places.

Will You Be Ready?

Meanwhile, nobody I've read or heard on the Callahan proposal has mentioned the Fourteenth Amendment and its insistence that all of us must have "equal protection of the laws." What Callahan aims to do is take an entire class of people—on the basis only of their age—and deny them medical care that might prolong their lives. This is not quite *Dred Scott*; but even though the elderly are not yet at the level of close constitutional scrutiny given by the Supreme Court to blacks, other minorities, and women, the old can't be pushed into the grave just like that, can they?

Or can they? Some of the more influential luminaries in the nation—Joe Califano, George Will, and a fleet of bioethicists, among them—have heralded *Setting Limits* as the way to go.

Will you be ready?

Ranking Health Care Concerns

As the authors in this chapter indicate, leaders in government and health care must make tough decisions in allocating limited funds to competing health care concerns. When confronting an issue such as health care for the elderly, officials must not only weigh the costs and benefits of each proposal, but must consider ethical questions of which group is more deserving of funding. To make the decision, leaders apply their own values as well as the values of their constituency.

This activity will allow you to discover your own, your classmates', and America's values relating to care for the elderly while you make the hard choices of a health care official.

PART I

Step 1. Working individually, each student should develop a personal list of health care priorities by ranking the following health care concerns in order of importance; the number 1 for the most important concern, the number 2 for the next most important concern, and so on until all the concerns have been ranked. The higher the issue ranks on the list, the more it deserves government or health care institution funding.

_____ medical research on disease causes and prevention

_____ life-extending care for the elderly

_____ life-sustaining technology for "vegetative" patients

_____ long term health care for the aged, such as nursing homes

_____ health care benefits for the young, such as those with leukemia or organ failure.

_____ comprehensive health care benefits for the poor

_____ home health care for the aged

_____ profits for health care institutions

_____ development of treatment technology

_____ granting equal health care support for all elderly, including the wealthy

Step 2. Students should form groups of four to six and compare their rankings with others in the group, giving reasons for their rankings.

PART II

Step 1. Each group should rank the issues according to what they believe most Americans find important. The health care issue most deserving of government or health care institution funding, in the opinion of the American majority, receives the number 1, the second most important the number 2, and so on until every concern has been ranked.

Step 2. Groups should compare these rankings in a classwide discussion.

Step 3. The entire class should discuss the following questions:

1. What noticeable differences do you see between personal rankings in Part I and the perceived rankings in Part II?

2. As America ages, how do you think the priorities of the American majority will change, and how do you think this will affect the decisions of health care officials?

3. Imagine yourself as an elderly person. What would be your priorities, and which health care concerns would you most want to be funded?

4. In light of your priorities, do you think America's health care system today is effective?

Periodical Bibliography

The following articles have been selected to supplement the diverse views presented in this chapter.

Henry J. Aaron — "When Is a Burden Not a Burden? The Elderly in America," *The Brookings Review*, Summer 1986.

American Medical News — "Financing Long-Term Care for the Elderly," January 15, 1988.

Dave Andrusko — "Daniel Callahan: Death and the 'Natural Life Span,'" *National Right to Life News*, April 21, 1988.

Jerry Avorn — "Benefit and Cost Analysis in Geriatric Care," *The New England Journal of Medicine*, May 17, 1984.

David Blumenthal — "Health Care for the Elderly: How Much Is Too Much?" *The Washington Post National Weekly Edition*, October 26, 1987.

Ronald Blythe — "In the Long, Late Afternoon of Life," *Hastings Center Report*, August 1987.

Daniel Callahan — "A Better Life—Not a Longer One," *U.S. News & World Report*, February 22, 1988.

Daniel Callahan — "Allocating Health Resources," *Hastings Center Report*, April/May 1988.

Dollars & Sense — "Common Futures: Aging in a Changing Economy," special issue, January/February 1988.

Amitai Etzioni — "Spare the Old, Save the Young," *The Nation*, June 11, 1988.

Peter J. Ferrara — "Providing for Those in Need: Long-Term Care Policy," The Heritage Foundation *Backgrounder*, April 20, 1988. Available from The Heritage Foundation, 214 Massachusetts Ave. NE, Washington, DC 20002.

Milt Freudenheim — "The Elderly and the Politics of Health Care," *The New York Times*, May 22, 1988.

John Heinz — "A Sword Hangs Over Us," *Los Angeles Times*, June 10, 1987.

Nat Hentoff — "'Life Unworthy of Life,'" *The Village Voice*, May 3, 1988.

Are Health Care Costs Too High?

Chapter Preface

Every year society spends more money on health care. Curiously, there are almost as many different causes for rising health care costs as there are interests involved in the health care system. Doctors blame government, government blames doctors, and almost everyone involved blames the new, expensive, and frequently-used medical technology. How can society reduce these ever-increasing costs? Or, perhaps more importantly, do we need to reduce them?

Some doctors and others believe it is immoral to discuss health care as an economic issue. They believe that no matter how expensive medical technology and care may be, every patient deserves the most aggressive and innovative care available. Others contend that this goal, while admirable, is impossible to achieve. Society must impose limits on health care costs. As shown by the authors in this chapter who debate the causes and solutions to high costs, the moral dilemma has no easy solution.

"In less than 10 years we can have a health care system efficient enough to provide higher quality care for all."

Cutting Costs Will Improve Health Care

Joseph A. Califano Jr.

Joseph A. Califano Jr. is a lawyer and the former Secretary of the US Department of Health, Education, and Welfare. He is chairman of the health care committees of the Chrysler Corporation and American Can Company and the author of *America's Health Care Revolution: Who Lives? Who Dies? Who Pays?* In the following viewpoint, Califano expresses enthusiasm for the changes in American health care. He believes that great potential exists for a more efficient and less costly health care system in the near future.

As you read, consider the following questions:

1. According to the author, what factors are contributing to the American health care revolution?
2. What problems does the author recognize in the current health care system?
3. In spite of its problems, Califano expresses great hope for the American health care system. Are his predictions more, or less, believable than Dieter von Oettingen's forebodings in the opposing viewpoint?

Joseph A. Califano Jr., "A Revolution Looms in American Health," *The New York Times*, March 25, 1986. Copyright © 1986 by The New York Times Company. Reprinted by permission.

The revolution in the American way of health will be as profound and turbulent as any economic and social upheaval our nation has experienced. At stake are not only billions of dollars but who lives, who dies—and who decides.

Science serves up biomedical breakthroughs that hold the promise of miraculous cures and the threat of unacceptable costs. The aging of the population—in the first quarter of the next century 60 million Americans will be over 65—signals the dawn of the four-generation society, in which it will soon be common to have two generations of the same family in retirement, on Medicare, receiving Social Security and nursing care. In law and religion, a confounding mix of issues bewilders our judges and theologians.

At the same time, the spirited air of competition is for the first time swirling through the health industry. Fed up with years of waste, the big buyers of care—governments, corporations and unions—are demanding the facts, changing the way doctors, hospitals and other providers are used and paid, and reshaping financial incentives that have encouraged patients to seek unnecessary care. And a host of new health care providers is scrambling to get their business.

Encouraging Signs

The early signs are encouraging: hospital admissions, lengths of stay, and occupancy rates dropped in 1984 and again in 1985. Medicare, which many feared would go bust by the early 1990's, looks solvent until late in that decade. Cigarette consumption has been going down.

But the facts make it clear that the health care revolution is just beginning. And the facts are startling enough to shake up even the most complacent purchaser of health care.

Item. When doctors don't have to get advance approval, 20 percent to 25 percent of the patients they admit to hospitals shouldn't be, and those who should are kept there for too many $500 days. Largely by requiring that all non-emergency, nonmaternity hospital stays be approved in advance by a second medical opinion, the Chrysler Corporation cut $100 million from its health care bills [from 1982-1985] and provided its employees with better care.

Corporate Health Programs

Item. Corporate and government health programs are paying as much as $60 billion for medical procedures that are unrelated to the health needs of patients. With no apparent difference in health status, residents in three Massachusetts communities—Fairhaven, Fitchburg and Framingham—are 15 times more likely to have their tonsils removed than residents of other areas in the state where antibiotics are used to treat tonsillitis at far less cost. The rate of major cardiovascular surgery is twice as high in Des Moines as in Iowa City for patients with the same symptoms—and with no noticeable difference in health results. A comprehensive study of 4.4 million Medicare beneficiaries has further documented the erratic geographic variations in medical practice.

Item. Those who go to fee-for-service doctors are twice as likely to have coronary bypass surgery as those who belong to health maintenance organizations—and four times more likely than their European and Canadian counterparts—for no apparent reason except that fee-for-service doctors receive payments to make repairs rather than payments to keep us healthy.

Item. A relatively small number of patients account for a large proportion of health costs. More than 30 percent of Medicare's money goes to patients with less than a year to live. In 1984, a mere 3.4 percent of Chrysler's insured accounted for 43.5 percent of the company's health care payments. These high cost cases often involve chronic or terminal illnesses and more often than not are related to life styles. Millions of dollars can be saved, and pointless anguish avoided, by using home health and hospice care and by promoting healthier life styles.

Item. The cockeyed malpractice system costs far more than the $4-plus billion in premiums [of 1985]. Billions more are wasted on tests by doctors anticipating possible lawsuits.

Item. Medical technology makes it possible to provide, at home

HEALTH CARE COSTS

The Miami Herald

Jim Morin. © 1987, *The Miami Herald.* Reprinted with permission.

and in the doctor's office, diagnosis and treatment (for example, chemotherapy, dialysis, intravenous therapies and feeding) that once could be delivered only in a hospital. Today, nurses can perform many tasks once reserved for doctors, such as examining, diagnosing and treating many wounds and sprains and common ailments. Early results of a Memorial Sloan-Kettering program indicate that many cancer patients can be treated just as effectively on an outpatient basis as in the hospital.

Item. Each of us can do more for our own health than any hospital, doctor, medicine or drug. Smoking has killed and maimed more Americans than all our wars and automobile accidents combined. Alcoholism and alcohol abuse is the No. 4 disease in America. More than half of the dramatic 25 percent decline in deaths from heart disease over the past 15 years is attributable to changes in diet and quitting smoking. A program at Johnson & Johnson encouraging employees to quit smoking and eat and exercise properly has slashed absenteeism by 20 percent and hospitalization by 35 percent, recapturing three times the cost of the company's effort.

A Better System

If the big buyers of health care act on these facts, in less than 10 years we can have a health care system efficient enough to provide higher quality care for all, at the same price we are paying for a "sick care" system that leaves 33 million Americans without adequate care.

Half the hospital beds can be closed down in less than 10 years. The number of doctors, particularly specialists, can be sharply curtailed. Their monopoly over the practice of medicine can be eased to allow paraprofessionals to provide many medical services just as competently and far less expensively. Government and private insurance programs can cover more care in the home and the doctor's office.

Instead of paying doctors a fee for each service to treat us after we are sick, corporate and government purchasers can pay doctors an annual fee to keep us healthy or a pre-set fee-for-illness if we do get sick. Individuals can be given financial incentives to pursue healthy life styles. Those who smoke, don't keep their weight and cholesterol levels in acceptable ranges, and miss periodic medical or dental checkups, can be charged more.

The medical malpractice system can limit recovery to a modest amount for pain and suffering, and to the amounts necessary to pay medical bills, replace lost income or compensate for the inability to function because of disability. Lawyers' contingent fees can be sharply cut. For doctors, malpractice reform can begin at home with strengthened disciplinary systems that clean out incompetents.

Lots more information can be given to purchasers of health care: how much hospitals and doctors charge, how often they treat different ailments and perform various medical and surgical procedures, what their drug-dispensing practices are, how often doctors put patients in hospitals and how long they keep them there.

At this stage in the revolution, the private sector holds the key to success. Politicians who must pander for private contributions for their election campaigns can't stand up to the clout and money of the hospitals, medical equipment manufacturers and physicians. But corporate America has discovered that the health industry takes a huge bite from profits. It has also discovered that it can offer employees better care at far less cost.

If we fail to create an efficient health care system, we will also find ourselves involved in a debate over death control—who lives and who dies—far nastier than the controversy over abortion, and end up with government bureaucrats deciding who gets the next heart or kidney, hip or knee operation, and who is entitled to expensive anticancer therapy. The debate over death control could pit sons and daughters against parents and grandparents. And unlike fetuses, the old can speak and vote.

Finish the Revolution

The uncertainties are not in knowing what to do, not in science, not in economics. The uncertainties lie in our ability to discipline ourselves and in our will to act with courage and compassion. A health care system as efficient and fair as it is miraculous is at long last within our reach, if we have the daring and persistence to finish the revolution.

"If the trend continues, doctors will no longer be physicians but will become merely 'health-care providers.'"

Cutting Costs Will Harm Health Care

Dieter von Oettingen

Health maintenance organizations and third-party reimbursement in health care have wrought massive changes in the traditional fee-for-service system. In the following viewpoint, Dieter von Oettingen, a surgeon in private practice in Virginia, greets these changes with trepidation. By searching for ways to cut costs, von Oettingen contends, the health care industry is eroding the sacred one-on-one relationship of doctor and patient. He places blame on doctors, patients, and lawyers for the deterioration of American health care.

As you read, consider the following questions:

1. How does von Oettingen characterize the medical profession of the past?
2. In what ways are doctors, patients, and lawyers at fault for undesirable changes in health care, according to the author?
3. Do you think the author's predictions for American health care are realistic? Why or why not?

Dieter von Oettingen, "Medicine's Future and Physicians' Roles," *The Washington Times*, August 11, 1986. Reprinted with the author's permission.

Huxley's "Brave New World" seems to have caught up with us.

Consider the medical profession: recent changes have been depressing, even alarming. If the trend continues, doctors will no longer be physicians but will become merely "health-care providers." The personal doctor-patient relationship will become a nostalgic afterthought, if not forgotten altogether. And it might well be the patient who loses and suffers most.

Not all was perfect in the past. Yet, there was a time not long ago when physicians were respected, often admired, and generally trusted. Most of them enjoyed their work, were proud of their profession, and cared about the ill, who in turn believed in the capability and goodwill of the medical men and women they depended upon. Indigents were treated in community hospitals and clinics free of charge, usually by house doctors who were supervised by staff physicians, rotating voluntarily and without payment for their services.

It wasn't an ideal system, but it usually worked.

The Heavy Hand of Government

The heavy hand of state and federal government lay only in the future. Third-party reimbursement was inconsequential and malpractice suits were rare indeed. Liability insurance rates were minimal, and many physicians did not feel the need to carry such insurance at all.

Since then, malpractice has become a monstrous nightmare. Insurance rates have climbed to obscene levels, driving many physicians out of their fields of specialization and out of the states they live and work in. A case in point is Maryland, where an increase of 50 percent in insurance rates was approved by the state, sending yearly premiums for obstetricians up to $60,000. How young physicians or rural practitioners can afford such payments, nobody seems to know or, worse, even care.

Only the other day, a Pennsylvania insurance company said it would cancel malpractice insurance for 1,300 physicians in the Washington area alone. Included are all solo practitioners and partners in groups smaller than 10 physicians. To practice without liability insurance would be reckless and is quite impossible, as most states and hospitals require appropriate insurance prior to granting license and staff privileges.

What are the 1,300 doctors to do? Again, nobody seems to care.

Serious Consequences

A serious consequence of the malpractice madness has been the evolution of "defensive medicine," meaning the use of too many, often unnecessary, and almost always expensive tests and procedures in order to avoid all possibility of an oversight which could result in a malpractice suit.

As long as lawyers get contingency fees, with no sensible limits of payments for damages established by law, the number of suits will expand, and insurance rates will climb higher and higher, eventually destroying what is left of the profession.

Other problems have caused deterioration of old standards. Third-party reimbursement is to a large extent controlled by non-medical bureaucrats, whose concern is cost containment rather than quality of care. Every aspect of medical management is interfered with and dictated by insurance and government agencies, eventually putting physicians in the role of employees, who get the message that they had better fall in line, or fall out.

The solo practitioner is nearly extinct and small partnerships will follow, to be replaced by large health organizations that will in time offer medical care as impersonal as a rubber stamp.

Shaken Confidence

Meanwhile, the physician's self-confidence and pride have been shaken by these trends, which would have amazed and disgusted physicians a generation ago. Marketing, for example, has become a way of life. Hospitals advertise in newspapers and on television like health spas, and a good number of doctors join the action with the enthusiasm of used-car dealers. Commercialism intrudes on a profession that once took pride in being precisely that: a profession, not a business.

Who is to be blamed for the sorry state we find ourselves in? We don't have to look very far:

• Doctors, because they allowed some of their colleagues to practice sloppy medicine, overtreat, or overcharge, thus inviting ever-tighter outside control. Earlier and more effective self-policing might have kept such third-party interference and the number of malpractice suits in check.

• Patients, because they learned all too quickly how to sue, regardless of whether there was fault or even damage inflicted. Without doubt some suits and settlements are justified, but a far greater number are not, and have become a clever way to chase big money, something of a national lottery.

• Last, but certainly not least, the lawyers, who often encourage and pursue questionable or totally unfounded claims, fully aware that the defendant physician and/or hospital was not at fault, and no real damage existed. (Just as doctors once looked with a contemptuous eye on colleagues who turned their professional practices into a commercial business, so lawyers once took a tougher line on barratry, the inciting of litigation.)

Brave New World

Can, or should, anything be done to influence and at least slow the decline of our profession? It would take a tremendous effort by everyone. Not much hope of that, I fear. More likely the evolution will continue to favor large organizations that have more clout to deal with the malpractice dilemma. Physicians will become dependent members of such corporations and will have to learn to do what they are told.

You might wonder whether that would be all that bad. Maybe I am just getting old and sentimental. Maybe modern man will not care about personal relationships any longer, and will be content to be diagnosed by computers and treated by a conglomerate of highly specialized and compartmentalized "health-care providers." Maybe the physician of the future will prefer to work under the tutelage of big brothers, rather than struggle on his own against disease and death.

If so: welcome, brave new world.

"Technology by its very nature offers us the opportunity to reduce costs."

Medical Technology Reduces Health Care Costs

Robert A. Schoellhorn

One of the most heated debates in health care relates to the usefulness of expensive medical technology. The following viewpoint is excerpted from a speech to a group of health care executives. In it, Robert A. Schoellhorn argues that, while initially expensive, new medical technology reduce costs in the long run. Medical technology can detect diseases much earlier, he believes, and this in turn means a higher chance of inexpensive treatment. Schoellhorn is the chairman and chief executive officer of Abbott Laboratories.

As you read, consider the following questions:

1. Why does the author believe cutting health care costs is dangerous?
2. In what two ways does Schoellhorn argue that medical technology reduces health care costs?
3. How does the author believe cost containment will threaten medical research and development?

Robert A. Schoellhorn, speech delivered at the SMS Health Executives Forum, Palm Desert, CA, October 14, 1987.

I believe everybody in this room appreciates the tremendous contribution medical advances have made to improve the quality of health care—and most of us appreciate to some degree how technologies can help control spiraling health care costs.

But what hasn't been aired publicly is the pending crisis medical technology now faces under the weight of today's simultaneous and somewhat contradictory demands for higher quality care and rigorous cost controls. The crisis is inconspicuous, but ominous. Important advances in medical technology face the threat of being sacrificed in the name of cost control. . . .

Most of today's medical advances came about in an era driven by untethered patient demand for more and better health care with virtually unlimited access. Today's environment is a very different one.

Few industries have changed so dramatically over such a short time. In just two decades, we've built a health care delivery system in this country that is second to none. A vast majority—80 percent—of Americans now have access to a system which includes the best in medical technology, most of it developed by U.S.-based manufacturers and providers.

This kind of expanded access has had its costs. Between 1966 and 1986, health care expenditures grew tenfold from $42 billion a year to $425 billion annually. It took a while, but these huge outlays did not go unnoticed by a government footing 42 percent of the bill. . . .

Cost-Effective Systems

The name of the game today is creating incentives that direct health care utilization towards the most cost-effective systems and technologies. Much of the private sector's way of doing this is through a variety of "managed care" approaches. While providers traditionally emphasized quality, "managed care" focuses more on cost.

In the process, a new set of decision makers has been created. Medical care decisions are no longer the domain of only the physician. Insurance companies, employers and utilization review coordinators are now acting as the gatekeepers to health care—and I might add, to new medical technologies. . . .

I believe that our system's responses to demands for cost controls are now on a collision course with the new medical technologies being developed in response to public demands for more and better health care. This brings us to a critical crossroads in deciding the value we want to place on protecting medical innovation. . . .

Inherent in our new competitive environment is a substantial yet largely unrecognized risk of seriously damaging the innovative process that produces so many important medical advances for us.

Why do I believe this? As we have debated solutions to the cost of health care, two words have become synonymous: technology and expensive. New drugs, new medical devices, new diagnostic tests and new procedures are often criticized for their price and rate of utilization.

According to a study done by Lewin Associates for the National Committee for Quality Health Care, "Under the sometimes misleading label of 'intensity,' technology has been charged with responsibility for 20 to 50 percent of the growth in health care costs." In a recent *Forbes* magazine article, Professor William Schwartz of Tufts University says, "Unless we are willing to forgo the introduction and diffusion of innovative diagnostic and therapeutic measures, they will add billions to medical costs."

If we accept this kind of reasoning, we are allowing technology to become identified as the major factor in increasing the cost of health care. Nothing could be further from the truth.

Reducing the Costs of Health Care

Technology can reduce the costs of health care in several inter-related ways. New technology can reduce hospital recovery time, it can reduce the costs of the procedure or treatment used, or it can reduce the costs of diagnosis. For example, a relatively new procedure, coronary angioplasty, can be used as an alternative to coronary bypass surgery in some patients. This new procedure not only reduces the costs associated with the surgical procedure, but also reduces the hospital recovery period.

National Committee for Quality Health Care, *Critical Condition*, 1988.

Technology by its very nature offers us the opportunity to reduce costs. This can occur in two basic ways. First, technology can produce something that does the job better, more accurately or faster even though the specific technological element may cost more. Examples of this include premixed I.V. solutions that improve hospital productivity and less invasive surgical procedures, such as arthroscopic surgery that allows outpatient treatment instead of inpatient care. Most managed care systems recognize the effectiveness of these kinds of technologies.

There is a second type of technology whose primary quality and economic benefits do not immediately accrue to the system, but are realized in longer terms. This type also can lead to the development of cures or procedures that are not possible today.

A couple of quick examples come to mind. One is the continuous measurement of oxygen saturation with a catheter. While this new catheter technology is initially more expensive than the standard thermal dilution catheter, its superior ability to detect cardiac output problems early helps avoid complications which, of course, reduce longer-term costs.

Another example is the cochlear implant that offers a stone-deaf person a rather crude but nevertheless important advance in his or her ability to hear. This is an expensive technology. But it's an advance that is clearly the first generation of an increasingly sophisticated range of products—products with long-term economic benefits that can allow a person to be more productive in the workplace.

Unfortunately, these kinds of advances that do not produce clear, immediate cost savings are much less likely to be reimbursed by the government or purchased by providers. I can tell you—this doesn't offer a medical products manufacturer much incentive to invest in the development of such technologies. R&D [Research & Development] decisions, after all, reflect the reality of the marketplace. . . .

Cost Containment—A Challenge

In conclusion, the new competitive environment and its twin driving forces of cost control and quality will have a significant impact on future medical technologies. Some of the impacts will be good. The search for cost reductions has forced many major health care players together. From these new partnerships will come significant efficiencies in the way health care is delivered as well as some important cost and quality improvements in medical technology.

However, the impact of cost-driven systems with myopic approaches to containment could seriously damage incentives to discover and develop new advances. All of us should be concerned about these incentives. We should be concerned about industry's ability to invest in R&D that is going to yield important advances with long-term economic efficiencies—not just those that help cut costs immediately.

So all of us have a stake in protecting continued medical innovation and we need to work together to achieve this goal. . . .

We have worked hard to make our system of health care the best in the world. Let's do everything we can to keep it that way.

"High-tech medicine is nothing more than institutionalized hypochondria."

Medical Technology Increases Health Care Costs

Hugh Drummond

Those who object to high-tech medical advances argue that this technology results in exorbitant costs to patients. In the following viewpoint, Hugh Drummond agrees with this position and encourages readers to question their doctor's use of technology. He contends that scientific advances have only raised costs and decreased quality in patient health care. Drummond is a psychiatrist in a mental health clinic in a low-income urban industrial community.

As you read, consider the following questions:

1. According to Drummond, why do doctors use high-tech medical machinery?
2. Why does the author argue that high-tech advances are like hypochondria?
3. Where does high technology belong, according to the author? Why?

Hugh Drummond, "Take Two Echocardiograms and Call Me in the Morning," *Mother Jones*, November 1986. Reprinted with permission from *Mother Jones* magazine, © 1986, Foundation for National Progress.

Now look, I know very well that you all want a few good laughs about dumb doctors, but the minute you feel a twinge in your chest you will run to the emergency room of General Hospital. You are living in a Woody Allen movie with sight gags and glitzy shots of Manhattan on the outside, while inside there is an ecstasy of hypochondria. You are terrified of getting sick, and when you are sick you go zero at the bone and pray to a suddenly remembered god that your doctor be in a good mood so that he or she will pat you on the head and say, "There, there."

Nothing Sacred About Medicine

I will not suggest that your go down the street to a chanting charismatic who also wants to be called "doctor." And I am not going to suggest that in the middle of describing your complaints to a physician you murmur in an offhand sort of way that Melvin Belli is your uncle. All I want you to do is feel a little less powerless and passive when the great god Aesculapius walks into the room and tells you to drop your pants. You ought to learn that there is nothing sacred about medicine, and that if your doctor cannot tolerate some straightforward questions and even some challenges about his or her assumptions, then you should find a new doctor.

This is not just a matter of good medicine. As long as our health care remains the province of a priesthood, there will never be justice. It will not matter how much progress the world makes toward economic and social equality (and it's happening, it's happening!). If we are made to feel like children when we are ill and we entrust our health to an esoteric elite, the root and fruit of fascism will stay alive.

Since knowledge is power, I am going to continue to report some things about my business so it can become yours, and at least you will know what kind of wall you are up against. Much of this will center on the self-serving charades behind the curtain at the altar of medicine. You will forgive me if at times I seem like Toto barking at the heels of the Wizard of Oz.

Explaining High-Tech Medicine

I am going to start by explaining high-tech medicine. No, not the physics and engineering of it. For me, even a vacuum cleaner is an adorable mystery. I am going to try to explain the why and wherefore of technology in medicine—its purposes, presumptions, consequences, and economics.

You should understand at the outset that the alleged causal link between necessity and invention does not apply to medical inventiveness. The inventions come first, spawned in the depths of engineering and computer companies for the sole purpose of profit. A machine is thought up that might possibly have some utility in the medical marketplace. They probably tried to turn it into a weapon first, but hospitals are almost as profitable as battlefields

153

and a lot closer to home. It is no coincidence that such giant companies as Hewlett-Packard and General Electric serve both medical and military markets.

First, the company lends the expensive machine to a few big-shot doctors who call it "research" when they play with it. Next, the National Institutes of Health and the National Science Foundation (that's our money) are asked to give grants so that more doctors can play with the machines.

"WE DID IT! FOUND A CURE FOR THOSE POOR HELPLESS SOULS LIVING IN TORMENTING AGONY WITHOUT HOPE...IF, OF COURSE, THEY CAN AFFORD IT!"

Wayne Stayskal. Reprinted by permission: Tribune Media Services.

Soon, articles describing the "research" begin to appear in medical journals. These journals, not surprisingly, are supported by advertisements for the companies that make the machines. Before long, every medical center insists on having a machine of its own, even if there is another one a mile away. To justify having the machine, doctors use it as much as possible, and when the grants run out, the cost is passed on to the patient. This means that insurers, Medicaid, Medicare, and our friendly neighborhood HMO [Health Maintenance Organization] pass the cost on to the rest of us.

Eventually, within a couple of years at most, what started out as an expensive toy becomes a routine, and everybody is unhappy if the machine is *not* used. There may even be a lawsuit or two because the machine wasn't used and, as sometimes happens, the patient died.

Ten years later, some smart-ass epidemiologists do some counting and calculating and figure out that not only does the machine play no part in improving the quality of care, but it may actually make things worse. By then it's too late.

An Example

Some time ago I took a look at the case of electronic fetal monitoring, an array of gadgetry routinely used to "watch" the progress of labor. Word is now getting around that EFM may play little or no role in lowering the rate of perinatal death or handicap. It serves only to justify a cesarean delivery earlier than would have been the case with the old-fashioned stethoscope attached to a human being who measured the pulse rate of the fetus every few minutes.

Think of it like this. Having a high-tech thermometer that measured body temperature to a thousandth of a degree would not help a parent decide when to call the doctor, nor tell the doctor when to perform a lumbar puncture.

A feedback system that is too precise can be self-defeating. The thermostat of your furnace has to be designed with a certain lag, an inaccuracy, a kind of screw-off factor. If it were too precisely set for a certain temperature, the furnace would shut off as soon as it turned on and turn on as soon as it shut off. The temperature would be accurately maintained at a precise level, but the machine would soon burn itself out or drive you crazy turning itself on and off.

Too Much Feedback

Much of the neuroticism of contemporary urban industrial life seems tied to a too finely tuned emotional feedback system. We focus too much on "how we are doing," and we do not process feedback in a neutral way. Most of us carry a sensor that anticipates, looks for, and defends against negative information. Failures are more finely etched in our minds than triumphs, and success is an elusive, if not mythic, goal in our demanding society. So, the more feedback we get, the more negative feedback we experience.

This is true of our bodies as well. After many years of listening to hypochondriacs, I have concluded that they merely focus more attention on bodily sensations than the rest of us. The same feeling of fullness in the stomach or muscular cramp in the shoulder will be ignored by some and experienced as agony or a harbinger of death by others. Pain is physiological, but suffering is psychological and has to do with the focusing and framing that, for whatever reason, the cerebral cortex performs on the information carried by nerve fibers to the thalamus, deep in the brain.

155

High-tech medicine is nothing more than institutionalized hypochondria. It is neurosis writ large with everyone living in an overfedback world. The machines simply amplify physiological information. They do not help us interpret the information because it is not seen in proper scale, and as the feedback is quickly and profitably translated into grounds for intervention, it often does harm. . . .

Defining Normal

One of the myths of high-tech medicine is that anything that deviates from "normal" is "sick," and that the more astute we are in identifying the deviations, the better the health care that may follow. It may be, however, that there are as many different "normal" hearts as "normal" noses. One anatomical variation in the human heart is the extent to which the mitral valve balloons a bit into the left auricle during contraction of the left ventricle. When it does so, the stethoscope can detect a little "click" between the lubb and the dupp of the heartbeat. In the absence of other signs or symptoms of heart disease, we used to pay no attention, until about 25 years ago some cardiologists decided that this might be associated with sudden death from an arrhythmia (an irregular heartbeat). Before long the little "click" came to be associated with a whole variety of problems, including chest pains and panic attacks.

Technology Desensitizes the User

Excessive use of technology has a way of desensitizing the user, and especially the young, impressionable medical student, intern, resident, or new practitioner. The technology itself becomes the object of attention, of respect, of value. Test results take on a life of their own, and, in composite, can become the proxy of the patient. Thus the intentions and decisions about what is and what needs to be done are between the physician (or team) and the technology.

Charles B. Inlander and others, *Medicine on Trial*, 1988.

So "mitral valve prolapse" became a disease and anyone with the condition was thought to bear watching—and might even be placed on a medicine like propranolol, which prevents arrhythmias. Never mind that later studies found that the incidence of MVP was as high as 21 percent in apparently healthy people, and the actual risk of sudden death was so low as to be virtually nonexistent; once a disease is discovered it is not easily undiscovered.

Then along comes a new diagnostic tool, echocardiography, a

kind of Superman's X-ray hearing that can hear a "click" inaudible to the naked ear. Thousands more cases of MVP will be diagnosed, thousands more people told they have heart disease and put on medicine for the rest of their life. Can you imagine a whole generation of worrywarts being told they have a potentially fatal disorder of the heart—a prolapse of the mitral valve (as if it were going to drop out of the rectum or something)? And then they are told they have anxiety *because* of the prolapse, and the panic may go away if the dosage of propranolol is increased.

Making Patients Sick

Of course, there are some really sick people, a lot of them in hospitals. Have you ever wondered how they got there? A 1981 study in the *New England Journal of Medicine* concluded that of all the admissions to a reputable Boston medical center, 36 percent were there for complications ("untoward events," as the study so delicately puts it) caused by previous medical treatment. Nine percent of these were major problems, 2 percent of them fatal. At least one-third of the hospital beds in this study, then, are occupied by really sick people who were made really sick by me and my colleagues.

Perhaps you might think that if modern medicine is making people sick, with all that pocketa-pocketa machinery, it can at least find out *how* it is making them sick. In the last 20 years there has been a bumper crop of new diagnostic devices, including ultrasound, computerized tomography, magnetic imaging, and radioisotope labeling—which is, incidentally, one of the major sources of low-level radioactive waste in the world.

Well, it seems that the only way of making a really certain diagnosis is to wait for the patient to die and then perform a postmortem examination—although by then the diagnosis is not terribly useful. In 1983, also in the *New England Journal of Medicine,* a group of pathologists grimly assessed the accuracy of clinical diagnoses over a span of 20 years compared with the correct ones from the morgue. And guess what? The rate of major misdiagnoses actually went up rather than down. Between 1960 and 1980 there was a 20 percent *decline* in the accuracy of diagnoses made on live patients.

Unnecessary Technology

One of the interesting findings of their study is that the use of old-fashioned diagnostic tests such as simple X-rays, endoscopies, biopsies, and surgical exploration did not change over the course of time. The only change was the addition of the newfangled stuff that doctors choose to trust.

5

"Physicians use resources in order to protect themselves, to satisfy patient demand for service, and to make more money."

Physicians Are Responsible for Higher Health Care Costs

J.H.U. Brown

Physicians have been accused of using expensive medical technology and diagnostic equipment not to benefit patients but because these tools allow them to make more money. Some people argue that this irresponsible disregard for health care costs places too large a burden on the health care system. In the following viewpoint, J.H.U. Brown agrees with this view and argues that physicians should stop hiding behind the curtain of patient advocacy and start taking responsibility for unnecessary health procedures. Brown is a professor of biology at the University of Houston and adjunct professor of health care administration at the University of Texas Health Science Center in Houston.

As you read, consider the following questions:
1. Why does the author believe physicians use worthless technology?
2. Why does the author think competition should be encouraged?
3. Why has the image of the physician changed in the last twenty years, according to Brown?

J.H.U. Brown, *The High Costs of Healing: Physicians and the Health Care System.* New York: Human Sciences Press, 1985. Used with permission.

The costs of a medical education are miniscule compared to the costs to society after the physician graduates. Current estimations are that the average physician will cost society about $300,000 per year during the rest of that doctor's life. This includes charges to patients out of which must come office expenses, assistants, and personal income. The average physician in private practice nets about $75,000 per year. Furthermore, the doctor may increase this income by specialization which adds about 35 percent to the total. The physician may decide to become a surgeon, which multiplies the base income two to three times. And it is clear that this additional training does not enhance performance as a practitioner in that up to 40 percent of the practice is usually general practice which could be performed by a much less well trained individual. [In 1984] physicians had about 600 million office visits for which they received about $11.4 billion under Medicare, while surgeons had only 15 million operations for which they received $4.6 billion.

The average physician has little information on the costs of care. The general assumption is that the physician will provide everything which in this doctor's opinion is best for the patient, and the question of payment may not arise. Third-party payment and the payment of bills retroactively both tend to isolate the physician from the actual costs of services, especially those services rendered in the hospital where most of the costs are incurred.

The retrospective payment method also encourages the protectionism surrounding the average physician. The insurance company will pay for most tests ordered. In the case of Medicare only about 20 percent of bills are refused payment on the basis of overcharges. The physician can order more tests for personal protection rather than for the good of the patient and know that most bills will be honored.

In this regard, it should be pointed out that the physician usually represents about 20-25 percent of the total health care costs in the country and also represents about 80 percent of hospital costs or another 35 percent of the total bill. This occurs because the physician determines who will enter the hospital, the type of care to be provided, the number and type of tests given, and the time which will be spent in the institution. It has been estimated that the hospital contributes about 20 percent of the total amount usually charged to the hospital for services, cleaning, administration, etc.

How the Physician Uses the System

Many practices of the physician have been under scrutiny. . . . There is a strong possibility that the physician overuses drug prescription orders. In about 75 percent of all ambulatory care visits at least one prescription is provided. In addition, of the drugs prescribed, 75 percent were brand names despite the clear demonstration that generic drugs save money for the patients and are equally effective. Most of the prescriptions were for antihistamines, antibiotics, central nervous system depressants or stimulants, or drugs to control water or calorie intake or loss. Some questions have been raised about how many of these drugs were necessary and how many were to alleviate America's hypochondria. When we realize that 580 million outpatient visits were made [in 1984], there is good reason for the nation's drug bill of $25 billion.

Seymour Joseph. BUMPS, *People's Daily World.*

Physicians have been indicted by many economists because of a direct conflict of interest. Many physicians own hospitals, laboratories, drug stores, apparatus manufacturing companies, and the like. Ethicists have proposed that no physicians should own such businesses because the more drugs, lab use, or apparatus required, the more profit the physician makes. It is not difficult to reconcile the dilemma of a highly moral physician treating a patient who could resist one more test which might clinch a diagnosis and at the same time double the profit of a visit. . . .

Worthless Technology

Studies on the use of technology indicate that physicians, in their concern for patient care, often use, at the patient's expense, technology which is worthless. The use of thermography to detect cancer is only about 50 percent effective and has a high number of false positive results yet was used extensively for years. Inhalation therapy may actually do more harm than good to many patients but is a part of the hospital armamentarium ordered by many doctors. E.J. Carels has stated that 25 percent of all procedures performed in the care of a patient are unnecessary. The use of radical rather than partial mastectomy, the use of radiotherapy in the treatment of cancer of many types, and the use of clinical laboratory services are other indications of overuse of technology without benefit and perhaps with harm to the patient. . . .

The problem of overordering tests is not confined to the laboratory. J.D. Patrick found that only 7 percent of the lumbar spine x-rays taken in emergency rooms were positive and that in most of those the physical examination revealed tenderness, contusions, or other abnormal physical findings which made the diagnosis. Barium enemas are routine orders in many cases of cancer of the cervix or endometrium but to date there has been a zero correlation between x-ray results and extension of the cancer. Of all abdominal x-rays following injury, 98 percent are negative and revised protocols for x-rays of patients with extremity injury would save $140 million per year in the country, with a less than 0.5 percent chance of missing a fracture. These incidences, which could be multiplied many times, suggest the overuse of facilities for no gain to the patient and little protection for the physician. Other data point up further problems. In one study, 27 out of 55 patients were given antibiotics when there were no indications for the drug. Among patients who have lab tests before entering the hospital, 71 percent have those tests repeated in the hospital. While there may be good reason to repeat suspect tests, it is doubtful that this frequency of repetition is necessary. Such examples could be repeated endlessly. These few demonstrate the lack of discretion in choosing the kind and number of tests ordered by the physician.

One of the newer technologies is the PET (Positron Emission Tomography) scanner which requires the expenditure of $3-4 million in a cyclotron or other generator of high energy particles. The estimated cost to operate the system is about $1,000 per hour. The usual charges may be about $2,500 per hour but some administrators estimate that $8,000 would be a more realistic figure. The scanner is postulated to be able to detect Alzheimer's disease, a degeneration of the brain cells, for which there is no cure. Is this a reasonable investment in technology?

We must remember that in spite of the advances in technology the dreams of long life may not be realized. Given the rate of cell degeneration especially in the irreplaceable nervous system, it is doubtful that we can hope to have a life span of more than 100 years.

Cut Physicians' Salaries

Medical costs in this country are indeed high. In recent years, spending has risen 5.5 to 6 percent annually, after adjustment for inflation. The costs are fueled by open-heart surgery, organ transplants, CAT scans and other scientific advances. They are inflated by greedy profit-taking of private hospital chains and giant pharmaceutical companies. Policy-making leaders of the American Medical Association (AMA) do all they can to keep fees and or salaries of physicians unconscionably high.

Julia Barnes, *People's Daily World*, April 19, 1988.

From another viewpoint, it can be argued that physicians take the easy way for themselves and not for the patients. Some 80 percent of deaths occur in the hospital at the present time. It can be argued that many of these individuals would die happier and easier in the home or in a hospice.

The physician, to many, as revealed by numerous polls, is more of a technician than a psychologist. The doctor spends very few minutes with patients, uses technology in the form of lab results rather than ears, eyes, and hands to make diagnoses, and is unaware of the costs of care or of the alternatives to care. More than 80 percent of physicians are unaware of community resources for home care and rely upon the hospital as the almost sole source of patient support. D.P. Connelly states that the physician now uses more than twice as many tests as 7 years ago for the same diseases and virtually the same treatment. This raises again the question of reliance upon testing to solve problems. . . .

Patients should have confidence that when they enter the doctor's office the charges will be appropriate to the treatment. Nationwide ranges of fees should be established and insurance companies and the government should pay no more than the average for any procedure. By the same token, such rates would be of great advantage to the rural physicians who traditionally make much less than the urban practitioner and this might attract more doctors to rural areas.

Competition should be encouraged. E. Ginzberg says that competition in which rates are published and patients have the right to choose the physicians of their choice might broaden choices of Medicare patients and restructure the whole system toward lower rates. Competition does not exist in the health care industry at the present time. The expanding supply of physicians does not lower costs. It leads to more specialization and higher costs and results in competition for hospital space, which results in more building of unnecessary beds. It may also reduce the use of ancillary cheaper personnel and adversely affect the quality of care offered. . . .

Physicians' Beliefs

As we look across the medical field several general principles come to light. On the whole, physicians believe that the use of more resources will improve service, whereas the contrary may actually be true. Physicians use resources in order to protect themselves, to satisfy patient demand for service, and to make more money. The demand for service and the surplus of physicians and surgeons, together with the payment by retrospective charges and through third-party payers has increased costs of care. These factors suggest that some changes are possible. The most logical steps to rearrange the system would be to publish the fees and costs of care, to use the prospective payment system, to refuse to pay for unnecessary tests, to place an absolute ceiling on costs by paying all physicians the same for equal work and to provide an educational service for the physicians. One suggestion is that the physicians be provided with a copy of the patient's bill with all charges clearly stated. Another step in the right direction would be a refusal to pay for a specialist unless needed and requested by a general practitioner.

These maneuvers are not likely to be accepted by the medical profession within the foreseeable future. And that is too bad, for in these measures lies one method of controlling health care costs.

Burnham, writing in *Science*, pointed out that medicine went through a golden age in the 1960s when the image was Dr. Kildare and Marcus Welby. Physicians were heroes in the movies and on the battlefield. In the 1970s and to the present, that picture has changed. The physician is pictured as charging excessive fees, indulging in unethical acts, performing unnecessary procedures, and running a business rather than a profession. Lists of criticisms in-

163

clude failure to take a personal interest in the patient, unavailability in an emergency, long waiting times in offices, and failure to communicate. In addition to these social criticisms, we are now beginning to hear greater complaints about incompetence in the actual practice of medicine. The physician must be aware of the attitudes and work to change them.

"Physicians are required to do everything that they believe may benefit each patient without regard to costs or other societal considerations."

Physicians Must Disregard Health Care Costs

Norman J. Levinsky

In the fight over the causes and remedies of health care costs, physicians are often the focus. Many people argue that physicians are to blame for high health care costs because they order too many unnecessary tests, overuse the hospital when home-care should be used, and overprescribe expensive drugs. Should physicians worry about the costs of health care? In the following viewpoint, Norman J. Levinsky argues no. He believes the physicians' loyalty must be to patients, not to costs. Physicians must aggressively treat every patient, and society must worry about the costs, he concludes. Levinsky is a medical doctor at Boston University Medical Center.

As you read, consider the following questions:

1. How is a doctor like a lawyer, according to the author? How does this analogy relate to health care?
2. Why does the author argue that basing decisions on "probable outcome" is unworkable?

Norman J. Levinsky, "The Doctor's Master," *The New England Journal of Medicine*, vol. 311, pages 1573-1575, 1984. Copyright © 1984 by the Massachusetts Medical Society. Reprinted with permission.

There is increasing pressure on doctors to serve two masters. Physicians in practice are being enjoined to consider society's needs as well as each patient's needs in deciding what type and amount of medical care to deliver. Not surprisingly, many government leaders and health planners take this position. More remarkably, important elements of the medical profession are promoting this view.

I would argue the contrary, that physicians are required to do everything that they believe may benefit each patient without regard to costs or other societal considerations. In caring for an individual patient, the doctor must act solely as that patient's advocate, against the apparent interests of society as a whole, if necessary. An analogy can be drawn with the role of a lawyer defending a client against a criminal charge. The attorney is obligated to use all ethical means to defend the client, regardless of the cost of prolonged legal proceedings or even of the possibility that a guilty person may be aquitted through skillful advocacy. Similarly, in the practice of medicine, physicians are obligated to do all that they can for their patients without regard to any costs to society.

Society benefits if it expects its medical practitioners to follow this principle. As C. Fried has eloquently argued, in any decent, advanced society there are rights in health care, in that "one is entitled to be treated decently, humanely, personally and honestly in the course of medical care. . . ." In such a just society "the physician who withholds care that it is in his power to give because he judges it is wasteful to provide it to a particular person breaks faith with his patient." A similar position has been stated by H.H. Hiatt: "A physician or other provider must do all that is permitted on behalf of his patient. . . . The patient and the physician want no less, and society should settle for no less." A just society must have a group of professionals whose sole responsibility as health-care practitioners is to their patients as individuals.

Ethics of Discontinuing Treatment

The issue is not whether physicians must do everything technically possible for each patient. Rather it is that they should decide how much to do according to what they believe best for that patient, without regard for what is best for society or what it costs. I do not argue, as some have, that doctors are obligated to prolong life under all circumstances or that they are required to use their expertise to confer technological immortality on dehumanized bodies. Actual practice is infinitely complex and varied. Caring and experienced doctors will differ about what to do in individual cases. In my opinion, ethical physicians may discontinue life-extending treatment if their decisions are based solely on what they and the patient or his or her surrogate believe to be the patient's best interests. (The legal issues surrounding such decisions are beyond the scope of this paper.) They are not entitled to discontinue treatment on the basis of other considerations, such as cost. This distinction may become blurred if physicians are pressed to balance the needs of their patients with societal needs. The practitioner may make decisions for economic reasons but rationalize them as in the best interest of the individual patient. This phenomenon may be occurring in Britain, where physicians "seem to seek medical justification for decisions forced on them by resource limits. Doctors gradually redefine standards of care so that they can escape the constant recognition that financial limits compel them to do less than their best."

Doctors and Cops

Blaming hospitals and physicians for the increasing costs of health care makes about as much sense as blaming the police for the cost of crime. Hospitals and physicians treat disease; they do not cause it!

John C. Braun, *American Medical News,* March 11, 1988.

A similar danger lurks if physicians attempt to conserve resources by using probabilities of success or failure to make decisions about the care of individual patients. Estimates of the probable outcome of a clinical condition in a given patient are almost invariably based on "soft data": uncontrolled studies, reports of cases of dubious comparability, or the physician's anecdotal clinical experience—all further devalued by rapidly changing diagnostic and therapeutic techniques. The standard errors of such estimates are undefined but undoubtedly large. Yet leading physicians advise doctors to practice probabilistic medicine—i.e., to withhold expensive treatment if the probability of success is low. How is the practitioner to define "low" in everyday practice—2, 5, 10, or 20 percent likelihood of survival with a good quality of life? Even if the dividing line were defined and the requisite precision in estimating outcome could be achieved, the role of the doctor as patient advocate would be subverted by probabilistic practice. This point should not be blurred by using the phrase "hopelessly ill." If there is no hope for a patient, then there is no problem for the doctor in discontinuing treatment. In practice, doctors can rarely be certain who is hopelessly ill. This problem is not resolved by redefining the phrase to exclude consideration of the "rare report of a patient with a similar condition who survived . . ." in deciding whether to continue aggressive treatment. Physicians cannot discharge their responsibility to their individual patients if they try to conserve societal resources by discontinuing treatment on statistical grounds.

167

An example may indicate the possibilities for disregarding the best interests of a patient in an attempt to conserve societal resources by probabilistic practice. A gerontologist has suggested that we may rapidly be approaching a time when the majority of people will live until the end of a maximal life span to the point of "natural death" at about 85 years of age. Even if the argument is correct as applied to populations, what is the individual doctor to do when caring for a desperately ill 85-year-old patient? Should advanced treatment be withheld, because [as J.F. Fries argues,] "high-level medical technology applied at the end of a natural life span epitomizes the absurd"? In terms of probability, the practitioner may be correct in predicting that the patient will not respond to treatment, but how is the physician to know that this person was not destined for a life span of 90 years? On what grounds can the physician withhold maximal treatment?

Society's Decisions Biased

Another consideration weighs against any dilution of the mandate to doctors to consider solely the needs of their individual patients. Societal decisions about the proper allocation of resources are highly subjective and open to bias. For example, J. Avorn has argued that cost-benefit analyses in geriatric care tend to turn age discrimination into health policy, because they depend on techniques for quantifying benefits that have a built-in bias against expenditures on health care for the elderly. A large part of the recent increase in overall health-care costs is due to the growing expense of care for older people. Negative attitudes toward aging and the elderly may influence our willingness to meet these costs. Society may encourage physicians to withhold expensive care on the basis of age, even if such care is likely to benefit the individual patient greatly. In Great Britain, persons over age 55 who have end-stage renal disease are steered away from long-term dialysis.

None of the foregoing implies that in caring for individual patients doctors should disregard the escalating cost of medical care. Physicians can help control costs by choosing the most economical ways to deliver optimal care to their patients. They can use the least expensive setting, ambulatory or inpatient, in which first-class care can be given. They can eliminate redundant or useless diagnostic procedures ordered because of habit, deficient knowledge, personal financial gain, or the practice of "defensive medicine" to avoid malpractice judgments.

However, it is society, not the individual practitioner, that must make the decision to limit the availability of effective but expensive types of medical care. Heart and liver transplantation are current cases in point. These are extraordinarily expensive procedures that may prolong a life of "good quality" for some people. Society, through its elected officials, is entitled to decide that the resources required for such programs are better used for other purposes. However, a physician who thinks that his or her patient may benefit from a transplant must make that patient aware of this opinion and assist the patient in obtaining the organ.

Physicians and the Bottom Line

The business community deals with the "bottom line." As a physician, if I deal with the "bottom line" and forsake my primary obligation to the health care needs of my patient, I am abandoning the central focus of what it means to be professional: "Will I get paid more if I send my patient home a day or two earlier?" "What if I follow that breast mass just one or two months more? That specialist may charge quite a bit for his evaluation, and just maybe the mass will go away." "This procedure can be done as an outpatient, the patient can take pain pills, and besides, it's cheaper." "And that patient with the lung mass, he's worried, and frightened, and lives 30 miles from town, but I can work this up as an outpatient (during the next two weeks). After all, that won't come out of my pocket!"

James P. Weaver, *American Medical News,* April 17, 1987.

The continuous increase in the costs of medical care is a difficult social issue. However, it is not self-evident that expenditures for health care should be limited to any arbitrary percentage of the gross national product, such as the current 11 percent figure. Moreover, if physicians and others make concerted and effective attempts to eliminate health-care expenditures that do not truly benefit patients, it is not a given fact that the proportion of the national wealth devoted to health care will increase indefinitely. It certainly is not self-evident that resources saved by limiting health care will be allocated to other equally worthy programs, such as preventive medicine, health maintenance, or improved nutrition and housing for the needy. In the United States, the societal decision to limit potentially life-saving health care will not easily be made or enforced, nor should it be, in my opinion. Officials who press for the rationing of medical resources must be prepared for a public outcry, since unlimited availability of useful medical care has been perceived as a right in American society. Governor Richard Lamm of Colorado was the target of such a response. Concerned that society cannot afford technological advances such as heart transplants, he quoted favorably a philosopher who believes that it is our societal duty to die. If society decides to ration health care, political leaders must accept responsibility. David Owen, who is both a political leader in Britain and a physician, believes that "it is right for doctors to demand that politicians openly acknowledge the limitations within which medical practice has to operate." I agree and would add that doctors are entitled to lobby vigorously in the political arena for the resources needed for high-quality health care.

Doctors Cannot Serve Two Masters

Through its democratic processes, American society may well choose to ration medical resources. In that event, physicians as citizens and experts will have a key role in implementing the decision. Their advice will be needed in allocating limited resources to provide the greatest good for the greatest number. As experience in other countries has shown, it may be difficult for doctors to separate their role as citizens and expert advisors from their role in the practice of medicine as unyielding advocates for the health needs of their individual patients. They must strive relentlessly to do so. When practicing medicine, doctors cannot serve two masters. It is to the advantage both of our society and of the individuals it comprises that physicians retain their historic single-mindedness. The doctor's master must be the patient.

a critical thinking activity

Locating Scapegoats

During World War II the Nazis in Germany systematically killed millions of Jews. The Nazis continually propagandized the outrageous lie that Jews were responsible for many of Germany's social problems. Jews became the victims of irrational leaders who glorified force, violence, and the doctrine of racial supremacy. One of the principal propaganda weapons used against the Jews by Germany's leaders was the tactic of scapegoating.

On an individual level scapegoating involves the process of transferring personal blame or anger to another individual or object. Most people, for example, have kicked their table or chair as an outlet for anger and frustration over a mistake or failure. *On a group level, scapegoating involves the placement of blame on entire groups of people or objects for social problems that they have not caused.* Scapegoats may be totally or only partially innocent, but they always receive more blame than can be rationally justified. Unfortunately scapegoating is still a common practice.

Because societies are so complex and complicated, problems are often not completely understood by any single citizen. Yet people always demand answers and there exists a human tendency to create imaginary and simplistic explanations for complex racial, social, economic, and political problems that defy easy understanding and solution. America's health care system falls into this category. Accompanying the evolution in medical technology have been increases in malpractice suits, insurance premiums for doctors, and the costs of treatment. These problems provide fertile ground for scapegoating.

Examine the statements below and mark them in the following manner: *Mark S for any statement which you feel is an example of scapegoating. Mark NS for any statement which you feel is not an example of scapegoating. Mark U if you are unsure.*

> S = *an example of scapegoating*
> NS = *not an example of scapegoating*
> U = *unsure or undecided*

171

1. A relatively small number of terminally ill patients use up federal health care dollars, thus forcing millions of Americans to do without proper treatment.

.2 Patients, because they learned all too quickly how to sue regardless of whether any damage was inflicted, brought about the demise of the personal doctor and patient relationship.

3. A gerontologist has suggested that we may rapidly be approaching a time when the majority of people will live until the end of a maximal life span; a point of "natural death" at about 85 years of age.

4. Lawyers often encourage and pursue totally unfounded claims, well aware that the defendant physician was not at fault. The result: malpractice madness and the evolution of "defensive medicine."

5. Rather than helping patients prolong their lives through nutritional changes, the medical managers of diabetes focus solely on control of blood sugar levels, causing many diabetics to die of blood vessel complications or go blind from retina damage.

6. Some have argued that doctors are obligated to prolong life under all circumstances without regard for the extraordinary costs of such care.

7. Patients who don't pursue healthy lifestyles are responsible for their own illness and should be charged more for their health care.

8. Society may encourage physicians to withhold expensive care on the basis of age. In Great Britain, persons over age 55 who have end-stage renal disease are steered away from long-term dialysis.

9. Physicians should eliminate redundant or useless diagnostic procedures ordered because of habit, deficient knowledge, or personal financial gain.

10. Ignorant officials who press for the rationing of health care had better be ready for a public outcry since they are the ones who approved wasteful policies in the first place.

Periodical Bibliography

The following articles have been selected to supplement the diverse views presented in this chapter.

Amanda Bennett	"Firms Stunned by Retiree Health Costs," *The Wall Street Journal*, May 24, 1988.
Otis R. Bowen	"Shattuck Lecture—What Is Quality Care?" *The New England Journal of Medicine*, June 18, 1987.
Robert H. Brook	"Will We Need To Ration Effective Health Care?" *Issues in Science and Technology*, Fall 1986.
Joseph A. Califano Jr.	"The Health Care Chaos," *The New York Times Magazine*, March 20, 1988.
Janice Castro	"Critical Condition," *Time*, February 1, 1988.
Gregg Easterbrook	"The Revolution in Medicine," *Newsweek*, January 26, 1987.
Victor R. Fuchs	"The 'Rationing' of Health Care," *The New England Journal of Medicine*, December 13, 1984.
Nat Hentoff	"Saving the Most Lives for the Buck," *The Village Voice*, May 31, 1988.
Richard D. Lamm	"America's Inefficient Health Care: One Possible Cure Could Be Rationing," *Los Angeles Times*, February 1, 1987.
Boris Odynocki	"Corporate Cost-Containment Strategy and Employee Health Care," *Social Policy*, Winter 1988.
Alan Sager	"Condition: Critical," *Dollars and Sense*, January/February 1988.
William B. Schwartz	"The Inevitable Failure of Current Cost-Containment Strategies," *Journal of the American Medical Association*, January 9, 1987.
William B. Schwartz and Henry J. Aaron	"A Tough Choice on Health Care Costs," *The New York Times*, April 6, 1988.
Lester Carl Thurow	"Learning To Say 'No,'" *The New England Journal of Medicine*, December 13, 1984.

Is a Holistic
Lifestyle Healthier?

Chapter Preface

Many people are disillusioned with medical technology and have turned to holistic medicine as an alternative. Proponents of holistic medicine argue that the world has become an unnatural and polluted place where one must keep a constant vigil over food, air, and water. Only by returning to the world of our ancestors, who grew their own food, drank from clean streams, and breathed fresh, outdoor air, can Americans improve their health significantly. Since this kind of lifestyle has become almost impossible, these advocates suggest a regimen of special foods, purified water, and home air filters.

Opponents argue that holists are hopeless romantics who don't really understand the components of health. The past that they believe in so ardently was fraught with disease, and a lack of pesticides caused the food to be riddled with insects and impurities. These people contend that holistic believers are victims of health frauds, ranging from so-called organic food to self-help diets that could be more harmful than the impurities they seek to avoid.

Whether or not the holistic approach can truly improve health is the subject of this chapter.

"Holistic . . . medicine has come to denote both an approach to the whole person in his or her total environment and a variety of healing and health-promoting practices."

Holistic Medicine Is Better than Traditional Medicine

James S. Gordon

Advocates of holistic medicine claim it is superior to traditional medicine in that it takes into account the whole person—body, spirit, and mind. In the following viewpoint, James S. Gordon supports this view. He believes the holistic approach to medicine is more personal and ultimately more beneficial to the patient because it considers psychosocial factors that may be affecting recovery from illness. Gordon is a research psychiatrist and consultant on alternative forms of medicine at the Center for Studies of Child and Family Mental Health, National Institute of Mental Health in Rockville, Maryland.

As you read, consider the following questions:

1. Why is "treating people in the context of family and culture" important, according to Gordon?
2. Why does the author argue that taking responsibility for disease and self-care are important?
3. How does the author define holistic medicine?

Reprinted by permission of Westview Press from "The Paradigm of Holistic Medicine," by James S. Gordon, in *Health for the Whole Person*, edited by Arthur C. Hastings, James Fadiman, and James S. Gordon. © Westview Press, Boulder, Colorado, 1980.

The concept of "holism" was first introduced by the South African philosopher Jan Christian Smuts in 1926. To Smuts holism was an antidote to the analytic reductionism of the prevailing sciences. It was a way of comprehending whole organisms and systems as entities greater than and different from the sum of their parts.

In the last several years holistic (sometimes spelled wholistic) medicine has come to denote both an approach to the whole person in his or her total environment and a variety of healing and health-promoting practices. This approach, which encompasses and is at times indistinguishable from humanistic, behavioral, and integral medicine, includes an appreciation of patients as mental and emotional, social and spiritual, as well as physical beings. It respects their capacity for healing themselves and regards them as active partners in, rather than passive recipients of, health care. Such an approach has always been an integral part of the healer's heritage. It is named and emphasized now to correct our tendencies to equate medicine and health care with the treatment of disease entities; to ignore the shaping force of familial, social, and economic contexts on health and disease; and to confuse the patient with his illness. . . .

The Biomedical Background

In the last several centuries Western civilization has been shaped by a system of thought and a world view we variously call rational, scientific, or mechanistic. Emphasizing analysis, action, and achievement, it has helped to create a technology that has brought enormous material advances to a significant sector of the developed world. This technology has made it possible for people in any part of the world to be in instantaneous communication with one another, it has enabled us to move for considerable periods of time beyond the gravitational pull of the earth, and it has helped us to resolve matter into particles so small that even our most sophisticated instruments can observe them only indirectly. It has produced telephones and television, satellites and space programs, nuclear medicine and nuclear weapons.

The medicine we practice reflects this method of thought and relies on the technology it has produced. Since the philosopher Descartes separated a transcendent nonmaterial mind from the material and mechanical operations of the body, science has been concerned with ever more accurately resolving that body into its component parts. From Harvey's physiological observations to modern biochemistry, from Vesalius's gross anatomy through Leeuwenhoek's microscopic researches to the ultrastructural anatomy revealed by the electron miscroscope, science has honed in ever more finely on the irreducible forms and functions that sustain our physical being. . . .

The paradigm or model of holistic medicine has evolved in tandem with the critique of modern biomedicine. Each informs, stimulates, enlarges, and tempers the other. This model is, at least potentially, a corrective to the excesses of biomedicine, a supplement to its deficiencies, and an affirmation of its deepest and most enduring strengths. It sets our contemporary concern with the cure of diseases in the larger frame of health care, enlarges and enriches the roles of both health care providers and patients, and provides a framework within which many techniques—old and new, Western and non-Western—may be used.

Doctors vs. People

In this modern era of medical specialization, doctors are trained to concentrate on specific organs or physical systems. Their expertise is narrow and intense, and thus it is not surprising that they may fail to look at each patient as a whole person who is part of a larger environment that might have contributed to his or her illness. They see each patient only once or twice, typically when he is seriously ill, and often don't gather information about his living situation. Medicine has become separated from the community. It exists primarily in hospitals. Too often, organs and diseases, not people, are the objects of treatment.

Dennis T. Jaffe, *Healing from Within*, 1980.

The outline of characteristics that follows is my own synthesis. It is probably both larger and less distinct than any individual practice and undoubtedly omits features that some practitioners would consider essential. It does, I think, provide some sense of the form, content, and spirit of the holistic medicine that is evolving. . . .

Holistic medicine addresses itself to the physical, mental, and spiritual aspects of those who come for care. The practitioners of holistic medicine are concerned with helping their patients heal the split that has stripped the mind of its power to experience and control the body, that has stripped the body of its wisdom and intentionality, and that has ruptured the bond between these two and the spirit that gives them both meaning. In the language of science, human beings . . . may be addressed at a variety of levels, the psychosocial and spiritual as well as the biochemical and physiological.

Mood, Psychological Factors

Holisitic practitioners are as interested in the coloring of the mood that preceded an attack of chest pain and the meaning it had for the patient as in the dimensions of the electrocardiographic changes that followed it. Their therapeutic approach may include a meditative technique; dietary changes and exercise to improve cardiovascular functioning; psychotherapy to mitigate the depression and rage that predispose a person to myocardial infarctions; or pastoral counseling to help someone confront the despair that can be as lethal as any anatomic pathology.

On a professional level holistic medicine recalls the healer's physical, psychological, and spiritual functions from the specialist—internists, mental health professionals, and clerics—to whom they have been parceled out, reuniting them in each practitioner as well as in the teams of health care workers—physicians and nurses, psychotherapists, ministers, acupuncturists, chiropractors, nutritionists, health educators, and others—who jointly staff and run holistic health centers and clinics.

Although it appreciates the predictive value of data based on statistical studies, holistic medicine emphasizes each patient's genetic, biological, and psychosocial uniqueness as well as the importance of tailoring treatment to meet each individual's needs. Medical schools today recognize that the majority of their graduates' future patients will suffer from a small number of chronic debilitating psychophysiological conditions. Nonetheless they emphasize—in their grand rounds and in the readings they assign—the exotic disease, the rare tumor, the vital importance of the single finding that distinguishes one slightly different pathological condition from another. Holistic medicine, by contrast, emphasizes the uniqueness of each *person*, the complex socioeconomic and psychological factors that in addition to biochemical and psychological factors characterize each person's health or illness. It encourages students and practitioners to spend considerable time with their patients, to explore and appreciate the minute particularity of the new world that each patient brings to them, to become sensitive to the complex psychology and uncommon life of people with common diseases.

Each Person Unique

Each person will require a different approach—different forms of exercise, a different diet, a different pharmacological treatment, and different kinds of psychotherapeutic intervention. One asthmatic adolescent may best be treated in a group that runs several miles a day. Another may be seen in the context of a systems-oriented family therapy. The first may work out her anger and improve her vital capacity through daily running. The second may diminish her anxieties and increase her self-confidence through biofeedback techniques. One may be able to distincontinue antiasthmatic medication almost immediately, the other may have to continue occasionally to use it.

A holistic approach to medicine and health care includes understanding and treating people in the context of their culture, their family, and their community. A holistic perspective respects the ways culture shapes pathophysiology and distinguishes between the anatomical lesions that constitute a "disease" state or diagnostic category and the individual's experience of "illness" (Arthur Kleinman et al., 1978). This kind of perspective leads to a respect for culturally sanctioned views of illness and its treatment and to the incorporation of indigenous healers where their services are appropriate. It also provides a theoretical basis for including families and communities in the therapeutic process, for working to change as well as to understand their dynamics.

The Holistic Principle

The most valuable contribution that the practitioners of alternative therapies have made is not the technique they practice, but their insistence upon the holistic principle: the principle that it is *you* who is being considered, not just your symptoms. But this in turn requires a willingness on your part to abandon entrenched attitudes and habits, largely derived from the assumption that specific symptoms have to be treated by specific drugs. Any one of a score of different therapies may be capable of banishing your headaches or indigestion, not by acting on your forehead or your gut, but by removing the stresses, physical and psychological, that give rise to these symptoms.

Brian Inglis and Ruth West, *The Alternative Health Guide*, 1983.

Some practitioners have discovered that they can alter the biochemistry and psychology of some asthmatic, diabetic, and anorectic children by helping their families change the patterns of relating that precipitate acute attacks and maintain chronic illness. Others have learned to augment their individual treatment by mobilizing the family's capacity for emotional support. . . .

Health: A Positive State

Holistic medicine views health as a positive state, not as the absence of disease. Holistic practitioners tend to measure well-being on a continuum that ascends from clinical disease through the absence of disease to the World Health Organization's definition of "complete physical and mental well-being" to a state of extraordinary vigor, joy, and creativity that some are beginning to call "super health" and "high level wellness." This perspective allows practitioners to work constructively to improve the health of those who do not feel well but have no obvious organic disease (by some estimates, 75 to 80 percent of those who come to primary-care physicians) and to help those who are functioning well to make still greater use of their faculties, as well as to treat those who have clinical illness.

Holistic medicine emphasizes the promotion of health and the preven-

tion of disease. Only a few physicians—notably John Travis—restrict their attentions to the "well," but virtually all holistic practitioners would agree that health—not just the cure of illness—is the goal and that a preoccupation—whether personal or professional—with illness may itself be debilitating.

The histories that holistic practitioners take include extensive inquiries about their patients' goals and the obstacles in meeting them as well as about their past and present illnesses and "chief complaints." They want to know how the people who come to them live and feel, what they eat and smoke, how much they exercise, what kind of stress they have at work and at home, whether they are satisfied with their achievements and their relationships to other people. Some practitioners use standardized tests—health hazards appraisals, social readjustment rating scales, and wellness inventories to help them and their patients determine whether or not they are likely to become ill. Much of their therapeutic work consists of helping people to see how their habits, attitudes, expectations, and the way they live, work, think, and feel affect their physical and emotional health and then assisting them to take steps not only to prevent disease but also to feel better.

Taking Responsibility

Holistic medicine emphasizes the responsibility of each individual for his or her health. The practitioners of holistic medicine feel that we have the capacity to understand the psychobiological origins of our illness, to stimulate our innate healing processes, and to make changes in our lives that will promote health and prevent illness. . . .

Many of the therapeutic techniques that holistic practitioners use rely primarily on the patient's rather than the physician's efforts. Inspired by the examples of the yogis and aided by contemporary psychological techniques and modern instrumentation, they have taught their patients to use biofeedback, autogenic training, meditation, and self-hypnosis to control blood pressure and flow, heart rate, and intestinal motility; to relieve migraine headaches and chronic pain; to reverse abnormal electroencephalographic patterns; and to stimulate an immune response.

Self-Healing

Holistic medicine uses therapeutic approaches that mobilize the individual's innate capacity for self-healing. Practitioners view themselves as midwives to the body's own resources. Their job is to help restore what Hippocrates called the *vis medicatrix naturae,* the healing force of nature (the Chinese call it *chi* and the French philosopher Bergson labeled it *élan vital*), not primarily to relieve symptoms or combat disease. Instead of suppressing symptoms, holistic practitioners regard them as indicators of disharmony and

181

arrows to the origins of distress. Instead of trying to eradicate an illness, they may attempt to strengthen the body so that it can rid itself of disease. . . .

Understanding the Illness

Though none would deny the occasional necessity for swift and authoritative medical or surgical intervention, the emphasis in holistic medicine is on helping people to understand and to help themselves, on education and self-care rather than treatment and dependence. Holistic practitioners tend to believe that each person is his or her own best source of care, that their job is to share rather than withhold or mystify their knowledge, to become resources rather than authorities. . . .

Holistic medicine makes use of a variety of diagnostic methods and systems in addition to and sometimes in place of the standard laboratory examinations. Practitioners are particularly concerned with reviving and extending the kind of clinical observation that has always been the hallmark of great diagnosticians. They watch the way their patients stand, sit, and walk, attend to the fear or anger that a sunken chest or hunched shoulders may reveal. They listen carefully to the tone of voice their patients use to describe their symptoms and observe the color, feel the texture, and smell the odor of their skin. . . .

Illness as Discovery

Holistic medicine views illness as an opportunity for discovery as well as a misfortune. Holistic practitioners help their patients understand the psychosocial stresses—loss, unemployment, or simply change—that may have precipitated an illness and the relationship between particular forms of organic pathology and particular emotional problems. They may help a patient to see the connection between feeling overburdened and having a bad back, between chronic genito-urinary or gynecological problems and fear of or aggressive use of sex. They may use the overwhelming trauma of a heart attack as a lever to help the middle-aged man reevaluate the killing pace of his life and the destructiveness of some of his habits and attitudes. Some have even been able to help terminal cancer patients wrest an understanding of lifelong patterns of behavior and a sense of personal meaning from the illness that threatens to soon kill them. . . .

The Medical Center

Holistic medicine emphasizes the potential therapeutic value of the setting in which health care takes place. . . .

The small centers that holistic practitioners have created for general health care are built on a more human scale and substitute respectful and responsive personal attention for a large, impersonal bureaucracy. Some are free standing, others occupy parts of such existing community institutions as churches or schools. All offer an opportunity for education and socializing as well as care in health and illness. Though holistic practitioners would of course use the personnel and technology of the hospital for a high-risk delivery or an acute life-threatening illness, they prefer to attend those who are giving birth or dying in the familiarity and intimacy of their own homes or in special birthing centers or hospices where family members are encouraged to participate in care.

An understanding of and a commitment to change those social and economic conditions that perpetuate ill health are as much a part of holistic medicine as its emphasis on individual responsibility. A holistic medical practitioner cannot consider individuals in isolation from their social, economic, and ecological context. Treatment of a lead-intoxicated child with chelating agents is doomed to failure unless the child's physical surroundings change; administration of vitamins is absurd in the face of a poverty that continues to make proper nutrition impossible and is inadequate in a society whose media daily encourage children to subsist on processed junk food. . . .

A Combination of Old and New

The holistic approach to medicine and health care that I have described synthesizes the ecological sensitivity of ancient healing traditions and the precision of modern science, techniques whose effectiveness has already been extensively documented and techniques we are just beginning to explore, our contemporary concern with personal responsibility and spiritual and emotional growth, and our urge to democratic cooperation and social and political activism. . . . The future of our medicine and our health as a people will in part be determined by the ways this approach comes to shape the larger health care system, the training of the professionals who will work in that system, and the education of the citizens who must ultimately learn to take care of themselves.

"The holistic medical movement constitutes both a deliberate attempt to substitute a magical for an engineering conception of the physician and an attack on scientific understanding."

Holistic Medicine Is Bogus

Clark Glymour and Douglas Stalker

In the following viewpoint, Clark Glymour and Douglas Stalker take issue with the precepts of holistic medicine. They argue that all physicians take into account psychosocial factors in treating disease. The authors contend that by arguing that spiritual and mental factors are paramount, the practitioners of holistic medicine are really advocating superstition and magic. Glymour is professor of philosophy at Carnegie Mellon University of Delaware. Stalker is associate professor of philosophy at the University of Delaware.

As you read, consider the following questions:

1. Why do Glymour and Stalker take issue with the idea that one's health is affected by "everything"?
2. How does holistic medicine attack reason, according to the authors?
3. What do the authors believe would be an appropriate role for holistic advocates?

Clark Glymour and Douglas Stalker, "Engineers, Cranks, Physicians, Magicians," *The New England Journal of Medicine*, vol. 308, pages 960-964, 1983. Copyright © 1983 by the Massachusetts Medical Society. Reprinted with permission.

Medicine in industrialized nations is scientific medicine. The claim tacitly made by American or European physicians, and tacitly relied on by their patients, is that their palliatives and procedures have been shown by science to be effective. Although the physician's medical practice is not itself science, it is based on science and on training that is supposed to teach physicians to apply scientific knowledge to people in a rational way.

The practice of medicine in the United States and in other industrialized nations is a form of consultant engineering. The subjects are people rather than bridges, but in many respects the professions of medicine and engineering are alike. We expect skilled engineers to be able to learn from experience and to get better at building bridges, because we believe that their training has subjected them to a rational discipline that has made them good learners about such matters. Sometimes, of course, we are disappointed. It is entirely the same with physicians, who must apply both explicit scientific principles and also a great deal of tacit knowledge to the treatment of their patients. Medical training is supposed to make physicians good at applying scientific knowledge to sickness, and it is also supposed to make medical doctors good at acquiring through practice an abundance of tacit knowledge useful to their craft.

Physicians' Training

There is no reason, either historically or logically, to conceive of the science used by physician engineers as necessarily physical science. Engineers need not care in principle whether the generalizations on which they rely are psychological, physical, or psychophysical; what they care about is that the generalizations be applicable and that their reliability be scientifically demonstrated. A great deal of what physicians learn consists of biologic and biochemical generalizations, broadly construed, but they also learn a substantial body of psychophysical generalizations which can be regarded as bridging the crevasse between mind and body. For example, generalizations concerning the effects of drugs, correlating the location of pain with other physical symptoms of disease, and positing the causal factors in dizziness and senility connect the mental with the physical and are thus useful for medical engineering. If physicians learn relatively fewer generalizations that are entirely psychological or social in nature or that posit psychological mechanisms for physical effects, the reason is not that such generalizations are alien to the "medical model" but that relatively few of them are applicable and scientifically warranted.

There are alternative conceptions of the physician. Some of them play a dominant part in the understanding of medicine in other societies, and some serve to qualify the conception of the physician as engineer even in our own society. One such conception is that physicians are consolers. Another is that they are magicians who exercise occult powers to bring about healing. As magicians, they possess magical powers either because of the occult knowledge they possess or simply because of who they are—for example, because they stand in some special relation to gods or demons. Again, the physician may be understood to be someone who applies a reliable body of knowledge that is not warranted

Berke Breathed. © 1988, Washington Post Writers Group. Reprinted with permission.

by science or by magic but is simply known and, so far as the community is concerned, always has been known. The warrant behind this conception of the healer is tradition and "common knowledge."...

Is there another, holistic, conception of medicine distinct from those described above? Certainly, many people seem to think so. In 1978 a group of medical and osteopathic physicians formed the American Holistic Medicine Association, which now publishes a journal and whose meetings have been recognized for educational purposes by the American Medical Association. Popular bookstores are filled with works on "holistic medicine," many edited by medical doctors and some recommended by such political eminences as Edward Kennedy and George McGovern. The same shelves boast best-selling books on holistic medicine authored by professors at distinguished medical schools, and, in at least one case, by a physician administrator at the National Institutes of Health. The therapies described and recommended in a typical book of this genre include biofeedback, hypnosis, psychic healing, chiropractic, tai chi, iridology, homeopathy, acupuncture, clairvoyant diagnosis, human auras, and Rolfing. One of the larger books of this kind was even subsidized by the National Institute of Mental Health.

What ties together the diverse practices described in such books as *Health for the Whole Person, Ways of Health,* and *The Holistic Health Handbook*? In part, a banal rhetoric about the physician as consoler; holistic dentists, for example, promise to take account of the spiritual factors affecting their patients' teeth. In part, familiar and rather useless admonitions about not overlooking the abundance of circumstances that may contribute to one condition or another. Such banalities are often true and no doubt sometimes ignored, with disastrous consequences, but they scarcely amount to a distinctive conception of medicine. Holistic therapies can be divided into those that are adaptations of traditional medical practices in other societies—Chinese, Navaho, and so forth—and those that were invented, so to speak, the week before last by some relatively successful crank.

Returning to Superstition

Insofar as it extends beyond banality, the holistic medical movement constitutes both a deliberate attempt to substitute a magical for an engineering conception of the physician and an attack on scientific understanding and reasoning. Although the holistic movement does not contain a conception of medicine distinct from those we have discussed, it does contain a reactionary impetus to return the practice of medicine to the practice of magic and to replace logic and method with occultism and obfuscation.

Several conceptions of "holism" have been developed in the

writings of holistic practitioners and their advocates. Most of them are vacuous; they are banalities of orthodox medicine, or they have no medical content and no applicability to any possible practice of medicine; they merely sound nice. Some are patently false. A much-repeated and trivial thesis, and moreover one that is said to characterize the sense in which holistic medicine is "holistic," amounts to no more than this: mental and physical properties are interdependent. Mental states affect physical states and physical states affect mental states. No one doubts it. To make such a claim seem somehow profound, holistic writers invariably conjoin it with a discussion of Cartesian dualism, insinuating that modern medicine follows Descartes in postulating an impassable chasm between the mind and the body. Modern medicine does no such thing, and could not even if it wanted to, since Descartes held no such view.

Crank Therapies and Diagnoses

Holist advocacy blends a plausible request for preventive medicine and a reasonable concern for behavioral, environmental, and social causes of illness, with all sorts of crank therapies and diagnostics. Well-intentioned people may fail to realize that in endorsing these pleas in the name of holism, they also give comfort to the darker side of holistic medicine. Thus Edward Kennedy and George McGovern wrote forewords to two different compendia of holistic cures. Presumably they did so in the thought that preventive medicine is a good thing and that care for the social and environmental causes of illness is also good. Yet most of the therapies and diagnostics they implicitly endorsed are without any scientific basis, and several of them have been proven to be impotent. The philosophies of the books that Kennedy and McGovern endorse caricature or disparage scientific, rational testing of medical procedures, and the reasoning they exhibit is typically inadequate, even woefully so.

Douglas Stalker and Clark Glymour, *Examining Holistic Medicine*, 1985.

Another doctrine said to be holistic is that one's state of health is affected by everything. Whatever this means, it has nothing to do with any possible practice of medicine, for no one can attend to everything. If physicians cannot distinguish relevant from irrelevant factors, important from unimportant causes, then they can do nothing. A variant of this doctrine is not vacuous but merely vapid: [as Kenneth Pelletier says in *Holistic Medicine*] "Fundamental to holistic medicine is the recognition that each state of health and disease requires a consideration of all contributing factors: psychological, psychosocial, environmental, and spiritual." This is not a new revelation about medicine. Insofar as such multiple factors are known and believed to be important, they are routinely addressed in conventional medical practice. Patients who suffer from coronary heart disease may be treated with beta-blockers and antiplatelet drugs, and they may also be advised to change their work, their diet, their smoking habits, their exercise habits, and their living conditions.

A stronger thesis, also presented by the writer quoted above, is that "all states of health and all disorders are considered to be psychosomatic," which is to say that psychological conditions are major causal factors in every illness and in all morbidity. So understood, the claim does not present an alternative conception of medicine, only a patent falsehood. Psychological states are not in any ordinary sense causal factors in Down's syndrome, cholera, nephritis, or a host of other disorders. Of course, psychological states may affect how an affliction is endured, even if they do not cause the affliction, but that is a different matter. Even if we believed (albeit mistakenly) that psychological conditions were an important causal factor in every disorder, this imagined fact would not itself require a change in the conception of the physician as engineer. It would require that scientists try to identify such factors so that physician engineers might apply the additional knowledge.

Balance and Harmony a Hoax

These rhetorical flourishes fail to constitute a distinct conception of the physician's role, of medical knowledge, or even of nature. However, an extraordinary vision of the functioning of the body and mind that runs through much of the holistic literature is utterly different from the scientific viewpoint. The holistic claim is this: the entire body (and psyche) can be treated or diagnosed through the treatment or observation of a special part of the anatomy. However much this notion of holism may be at odds with the themes that seem to run through the holistic doctrines, it characterizes many of the treatments described in the literature on holistic medicine. Chiropractors, iridologists, reflexologists, tongue diagnosers, zone therapists, and many others all claim to treat or diagnose the whole from some anatomical part. Of course, they differ about which part, but that does not seem to bother either them or the editors of holistic books. Almost invariably, this rhetoric claims that manipulating a part of the body somehow restores an inarticulated "balance" or "harmony" to the whole.

At the base of the litany that each person must be treated as unique, that every part of the body is interdependent on every other part, and that body and mind are inseparable is the claim that holistic practitioners are absolved from demonstrating causal relations between their treatments and alleged therapeutic gains. They are under no obligation, they believe, to reconcile their claims about therapy with what is known about the causal pathways of the body. Their emphasis on the power of the mind is part theme and part tactic: the mind is supposed to be able to exert its power on parts of the body without regard to the laws of nature. The holistic practitioner sees the body in much the same way that magicians of old viewed the universe. The body becomes the last bastion of magic.

A magical view of the mind and body is antithetical to the scientific viewpoint, however much holistic therapists may parade what they take to be the trappings of science. Consequently, they make every effort to disparage rational assessments of their practices. A magical view of nature and mind and a mystical conception of knowledge are opposed not just to scientific conclusions but to scientific reasoning. Beyond disparaging the sort of rational assessment of their wares made by, say the Consumers Union, holistic advocates attack reason itself. . . .

Inspecting Holistic Medicine

We are repeatedly told that holistic medicine has not really been investigated, that funds ought to be made available for conducting tests of holistic practices, and that meanwhile we should keep our minds open about holistic techniques. Although it might be interesting to know more about the physiological pathways that are correlated with such processes as the placebo effect, this has nothing to do with taking seriously the claims advanced by iridologists or zone therapists or even chiropractors. The claim to diagnose by examining the eye or to cure by massaging the foot is completely bogus; we know more than enough about the workings of the body to be reasonably certain that geometric features of the iris, for instance, do not provide the specific information about disorders that iridologists claim they do. And if a test is really necessary here, it can be and has been run cheaply: iridologists have been shown to fail as diagnosticians. Chiropractors and zone therapists could readily devise rigorous tests of their therapies if they wished to, but they don't. Of course, it is conceivable that the beliefs of scientific medicine are in error about one or another of these matters, but that is no reason for using public funds to investigate holistic claims. One cannot justify spending other people's money simply because one can imagine something to be true. The mere fact that holistic medicine is widespread and enduring is no reason to take its claims seriously; superstition, self-deception, stupidity, and fraud are ubiquitous and always have been.

It is unlikely that the lack of evidence concerning the specific curative powers of holistic therapies is the result of a conspiracy of disinterest. There are enormous rewards, financial and otherwise, for scientific demonstrations that new and inexpensive therapeutic procedures are effective. Holistic practitioners know these rewards full well. If they have been unable to produce sound scientific evidence of the efficacy of their therapies, we are not being closed-minded in concluding that the therapies probably have no specific effects of the kinds advertised. Certainly we should leave our minds open, but not, in the words of an eminent philosopher, the late Alan Ross Anderson, so open that our brains fall out.

Attacking Reason Itself

The most fundamental attack made by advocates of holistic medicine is on reason itself: since science will not warrant holistic medicine, they imply that we should abandon science and the claims of reason. One common line of argument is derived from a radical misunderstanding of the contemporary philosophy of science. Some years ago, Thomas Kuhn claimed that scientific work in any particular field is normally governed by a "paradigm"—that is, by some concrete piece of work done in the past that is used as a model for subsequent scientific work. Newton's celestial mechanics provided a paradigm, as did Dalton's chemistry, Darwin's biology, and Einstein's electrodynamics. . . .

Holistic advocates repeatedly cite Kuhn and claim that holistic medicine is an alternative paradigm with its own standards, one that cannot be understood or assessed by the practitioners of orthodox medicine. If the claim were valid, holistic practice would have to constitute a scientific tradition, albeit one in competition with the tradition of orthodox medicine. However, holistic medicine is not a scientific tradition. It has no paradigmatic work, no recognized set of problems, and no shared standards for what constitutes a solution to those problems; it also lacks the critical exchange among its practitioners that is characteristic of the sciences. Cranks have been common throughout the history of science, as Kuhn, a distinguished historian of science, knew well. The work of cranks does not constitute a scientific revolution, and no cranks appear among Kuhn's many examples. . . .

Pabulum and Nonsense

If holistic-health advocates were content with encouraging sensible preventive medicine or with criticizing the economic organization of American medicine, we might be enthusiastic, but they are not. If the movement were without influence on American life, we would be indifferent, but it is not. Holistic medicine is a pabulum of common sense and nonsense offered by cranks and quacks and failed pedants who share an attachment to magic and an animosity toward reason. Too many people seem willing to swallow the rhetoric—even too many medical doctors—and the results will not be benign.

191

"The healthiest, strongest, and most disease resistant [societies] . . . ever known lived on natural foods—fish, meat, fowl, vegetables, fruits, and sometimes grains and unprocessed dairy products."

Natural Foods Are Best

Ronald F. Schmid

Ronald F. Schmid is licensed to practice as a naturopathic physician in Oregon, Washington, and Connecticut. A graduate of the Massachusetts Institute of Technology, he holds degrees in design, education, human biology, and naturopathic medicine. In the following viewpoint, Schmid argues that studying less technically-advanced but healthier societies shows that poor health and processed foods are linked. Only by returning to a more natural, unprocessed diet, he concludes, can people be truly healthy.

As you read, consider the following questions:

1. What does the author believe is the only path to good health?
2. What kinds of animals does the author recommend eating?
3. Why does Schmid contend that raw foods are better than processed foods?

Ronald F. Schmid, *Traditional Foods Are Your Best Medicine*. Stratford, CT: Ocean View Publications, 1987. Reprinted with permission.

Confusion reigns when the subject turns to nutrition. Every popular diet book presents a different expert's opinion on food. What should we eat and how much? What are the effects of meat, cholesterol, fruit, animal fats, vegetables, vegetable oils, fish, eggs, milk, cheese, grains, raw foods? How much damage does sugar do? Refined flour?

Which experts are right—those who say cholesterol is killing us, or those who tell us it is not the real culprit in heart disease?

Do food additives and pollutants cause cancer? Sweets and fats? Or might modern foods lack nutrients protective against cancer?

What foods help prevent chronic disease?

What foods will enable us to enjoy the robust good health we sense has been partly lost to modern living and modern foods?

These questions have no simple answers.

Questions To Ask

In seeking answers, several other questions might first be asked:

What was the health of people in traditional and primitive cultures existing into the early twentieth century, people eating only their traditional foods? What about isolated traditional cultures still surviving, and the three hundred thousand remaining hunter-gatherers still living and eating primitively?

If the health of such people is superior to ours, could this be directly related to their foods? If so, what foods did and do such people eat? What differences exist between their foods and modern foods? How do their meats, fish, milk products, fruits, vegetables, and grains differ from the foods we use? Do the differences help explain our modern problems?

What is the effect of traditional kinds of foods on people with chronic diseases? What evidence has been published in the medical literature?

Facts from historical records and recent medical research provide answers to these questions. With the understanding the answers provide, confusion about nutrition can be clarified. Answers to many seemingly unanswerable questions become clear.

The healthiest, strongest, and most disease resistant cultures ever known lived on natural foods—fish, meat, fowl, vegetables, fruits, and sometimes grains and unprocessed dairy products. . . .

Vegetables, and in some cases grains and fruits, were important foods for most of these cultures, and for many provided more calories than animal source foods. Invariably, however, the latter were considered of prime importance and great efforts were made to secure them. . . .

Our genes and the structure of our enzymes have been passed down through thousands of generations. The building-block molecules of genes are identical in all living things. Biological laws unite all life forms.

Laws of physics govern the movement of planets, the changing of seasons, the coming and going of tides; biological laws govern the ways the human body reacts to different foods. People once argued the earth was flat, that blood did not circulate in the human body . . . some now argue that our ills are not intimately connected with food.

Illness weighs heavily, but those willing to give nature's methods an honest try can be helped to help themselves. To be frank at the outset: traveling a path to good health requires disciplined eating. The body requires natural foods in order to function well. Most are readily available. Some shopping in special places may be needed—seafood markets, natural foods stores, places with high quality fresh vegetables, and if possible, stores with naturally raised beef and fowl. Refined foods must be largely avoided.

By making an effort and accepting elements of a natural diet and lifestyle, one may rebuild one's birthright—good health. Notice the words "elements of"; this is not an all or nothing proposition. A willingness to work on change will yield results. Understand the principles, and apply what is reasonable now. The foundation is commitment and disciplined application; benefits follow proportionately. . . .

Diets of traditional groups immune to dental and degenerative

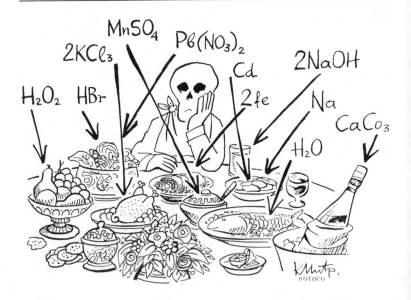

© Mitro/Rothco

disease had several characteristics in common (these people will be referred to as immune groups). Nearly all foods were whole, unrefined, and unconcentrated. The only modification was cooking, often minimal; many were eaten raw. Major exceptions to this whole-foods generality were the use of butter and cheese in the Loetschental Valley of Switzerland and of seal oil and other concentrated animal and fish oils by Eskimos.

The foods of each immune group had been used by the group for centuries or longer and were indigenous to the group's region. No imported foods were used. Customs dictated the importance of eating certain foods at specified times in life. Specific foods were known to prevent specific problems. Certain special foods believed to insure the birth of normal, healthy offspring were particularly valued and were included in the pre-conception diet of both parents.

None of the diets contained large amounts of fruit, which was used when available, though in limited quantities. Even where large quantities of fruit were available, fish and shellfish, animals, and vegetables were preferred.

Immune groups used none of many foods commonly used today. The obvious include sugar, white flour, canned goods, and other supermarket standards. Less obvious are vegetable oils and fruit juices, both commonly used by health-conscious people. Nor did they use significant amounts of honey, the only sweetener sometimes available. Alcohol was used moderately if at all, in raw fermented beverages rich in enzymes and minerals. They took no vitamin pills.

Sea Foods

Fish and shellfish were used in quantity by immune groups near the sea, supplemented by sea mammals or land animals or both. Freshwater fish, animals, and sometimes milk and cheese were the most important protein foods for inland groups. Seaweed was used by every immune group living near the sea. Inland groups traded for it or, in the case of certain African tribes, used special iodine-rich freshwater plants. Green vegetables and plants, in many groups gathered wild, were staples for all. Most used at least some fruit. Organs of animals or fish or both were considered vital.

Given these common characteristics, we will now consider specific fat-soluble nutrients, fiber, minerals, and raw food proteins and enzymes. These biochemical and structural elements, abundant in primitive diets and lacking in modern, help explain why the foods of traditional people largely protected them from disease.

Foods rich in fat-soluble vitamins and the essential fatty acid eicosapentaenoic acid formed substantial parts of traditional diets. These foods fall into three categories:

1) Sea foods, especially fatty fish such as salmon.
2) Animal and fish organs, especially liver.
3) Dairy products from animals feeding on fresh green pasturage, particularly cheese and butter, which concentrate fat-soluble nutrients.

Vitamin D is richly supplied in these foods. Vitamin D is a complex of several vitamins; one, Vitamin D_3, is produced in humans by action of ultraviolet light on skin. Vitamin D_3 helps regulate the absorption and utilization of calcium and other minerals, and other members of the D-complex appear to play similar but complementary roles.

Sunlight does not stimulate production of these other members of the D-complex; they are supplied in the above foods. This may be a reason these foods proved essential for building immunity to dental and degenerative disease, for these other members of the D-complex may play crucial roles in maintaining health. Indeed, why would they be present in animals' bodies if each did not serve a function?

Food Can Save Your Life

I'm talking about organic food. Grains, vegetables and fruits grown without the use of synthetic fertilizers or pesticides. Food that also has the fresh, wonderful taste you remember from the days of your childhood.

Can such totally natural food *really* save your life?

Yes it can, if you look not just at organic food itself, but also at *how other kinds of food are grown*. In organic food you'll see purity of product. And farms rich in wildlife that don't pollute the environment. Look beyond to the regular farms that produce most of America's food and you'll see something else entirely.

Robert Rodale, *Prevention*, August 1987.

Weston Price found when patients with active decay eliminated refined foods and ate sufficient protective foods, the decay process often ceased. This was the case in young people of the Loetschental Valley who experienced decay only while outside the valley. The decay ceased without fillings, and photographs in his book detail this. Present-day dentists occasionally observe cavities that have ceased to be active; this relates to dietary changes.

Price's chemical analyses of dairy products from all over Europe and America showed the fat-soluble vitamin content much higher in those made from milk from animals fed fresh green pasturage. It was highest when grass was growing most rapidly. Dairy products from animals not eating fresh grass did not contain significant amounts. In Pottenger's experiments, milk from cows fed fresh greens had a significantly healthier effect on animals than milk from cows fed hay, perhaps because of the presence of EPA [a fatty acid] in the former.

Fish fats are rich in EPA. Wild grazing animals have small but significant amounts, yet domestic beef fattened on grains contains almost undetectable amounts. EPA is similar in structure to a fatty acid found in domestic animals, arachadonic acid, and to one found in vegetable oils, linoleic acid. All are precursors of different prostaglandins, each of which has subtly different effects.

Desirable prostaglandins are formed from EPA; some seem responsible for keeping arteries optimally dilated and platelets from clotting abnormally (platelets are small particles in the blood which aid in clotting). Other prostaglandins made from EPA seem to enhance the functioning of the immune system, and many other effects are being studied by medical researchers. Evidence indicates high EPA consumption is one reason Eskimos and other primitive people (consumers of large amounts of fish and wild game) rarely suffer from heart disease and other chronic and acute diseases.

Health and Dairy Products

An assumption was made above in stating that dairy products from animals feeding on fresh pasturage contain EPA. Analysis of wild African grazing animals found significant amounts of EPA, and we may assume milk from such animals contains EPA. Analysis of domestic beef found almost no EPA; such animals are fattened on grains and fed little or no fresh grass the last few months of life, likely explaining the lack of EPA in their fat (for reasons later to be explained). We may assume fat in animals fed a diet similar to that of wild animals—fresh pasturage—contains significant amounts of EPA; so too would cheese and butter made from milk from animals so fed. However, to the author's knowledge no analyses of such foods for EPA content have yet been made. Price did his work before EPA was identified and understood.

The health of people in the Loetschental Valley lends credence to the assumption. This immune group alone ate little meat or fish, instead using large amounts of cheese and butter made from milk from animals kept at pasture. Protective nutrients supplied by animals and fish in other immune groups were likely supplied by these dairy foods.

Sea foods, organ meats, or raw dairy products of the proper quality are, in the author's experience, essential for full recovery from chronic disease and maintenance of optimal health. Experiences of traditional cultures when these foods were displaced by refined foods indicate they are essential also to insure normal development, birth, and growth of the fetus and child.

Most people benefit from more fiber, for typical diets are low in fiber. Meat and foods made from refined flour have little; sugar, fats and oils, and alcohol, none. Foods high in fiber—whole grain foods and vegetables—may greatly benefit the digestive tract.

Fiber's Essential Role in Health

Diets high in fiber nearly always end constipation. Individuals with chronic stomach or intestinal problems must use vegetables and fruits cautiously, however; especially eaten raw, they may initially worsen symptoms. Well-cooked vegetables and whole grains rarely aggravate such problems.

The traditional diets were high in fiber. Plants, roots, and fruits were widely used, and in some places, whole grains. In northern Canada, Alaska, and the Outer Hebrides, few land vegetables were available, but much seaweed was used. Seaweed holds considerable water in passing through the digestive tract, forming a gel which increases the bulk of the stools and the speed at which they move through the bowels.

What Price Purity?

Most consumers pay the hefty hikes for organic produce in order to avoid eating chemical residues which accumulate on food; some are also consciously supporting an alternative agriculture that is ecologically based and does not dump toxins into the environment.

The shopper who chooses organic raisins will avoid not only pesticide and herbicide residues, but also traces of methyl bromide, a fumigant applied to raisins in storage to kill insects. (Organic raisins are frozen instead—the only legal alternative to fumigation.) Scientific literature tells us little about what effect chemical residues have on our bodies. So buying organic is an indirect form of life insurance.

Michael Rozyne, *The New Holistic Health Handbook*, 1985.

People eating traditional diets led active lives. Because their caloric needs were greater than those of most Americans, they ate more food and thus more fiber. This also provided greater amounts of essential nutrients.

Higher cancer rates occur in countries with high fat, high meat, low fiber diets, such as America, where the typical diet is mostly meat, fats, and refined carbohydrates. Lower cancer rates, especially colon cancer, occur in countries with high fiber diets, as in rural areas of Africa, where native people eat mostly natural foods. But low cancer rates, to the point of near absence, occurred among certain cultures with diets high in fiber and also rich in animal and fish fats, as shown by Price. . . .

Every primitive culture Weston Price studied ate many foods raw; tradition often dictated which. The milk, cheese, and butter of Swiss villagers and African herdsmen were seldom heated. Organs everywhere were often eaten raw or lightly cooked. Eskimos of Arctic regions, where no plants were available much of the year, ate some fish raw. This practice prevented scurvy; the vitamin C in meat and fish is destroyed by cooking. Much meat was eaten raw, lightly cooked, or smoked. Salmon eggs were important for coastal people; uncooked eggs were dried in fall for use in winter.

In the South Pacific, islanders and coastal Australian Aborigines ate much fish and shellfish raw. When shellfish were cooked, native people arranged them circularly about a small fire, with the animals' valve ends toward the flames. Just enough heat was used to open the valves, saving much work.

Dried raw seaweed was used by coastal people everywhere. Many vegetables and other plant foods were used raw, especially young greens. Fruits were nearly always eaten raw. . . .

Foods of the highest quality are more expensive and may be difficult to find. The financial reward is considerable, however, if one succeeds in building health to the point where visits to a physician are no longer a regular affair. This is a reasonable goal. Intangible rewards are even greater; nothing equals the feeling of a smoothly functioning body.

"There is no food other than mother's milk that can be considered as natural for human beings, and even that suits only babies."

Natural Foods Are a Hoax

Arnold Bender

Arnold Bender is a retired professor of nutrition and dietetics from the University of London. A world authority on nutrition, Bender is the author of several textbooks and a popular lecturer and broadcaster. He is vice-president of the International Union of Food Science and Technology. In the following viewpoint, he argues that the recent trend of eating so-called "health foods" is bogus. There is no nutritional difference between processed and raw foods, he believes, and consumers are merely being fooled by health food producers into buying more expensive items.

As you read, consider the following questions:

1. What are the four ways advertising works to make consumers think that "natural" foods are better, according to Bender?
2. Why does the author argue that there are no foods that are more appropriate than others for humans?
3. Why does the author believe unprocessed foods can be harmful?

Reprinted from HEALTH OR HOAX? THE TRUTH ABOUT HEALTH FOODS AND DIETS, by Arnold Bender, © 1985, with permission of Prometheus Books, Buffalo, New York.

The word 'natural' is used in so many connotations by the advertisers of traditional as well as health foods that it has lost all meaning and ought to be banned. Indeed, there have been suggestions from time to time to control its use.

In a *Report of the British Food Standards Committee (Claims and Misleading Descriptions 1966)* it was recommended that the word natural should only be used without qualification in two senses. First, to indicate that ingredients (such as colours and flavours) were extracted from biological material as distinct from being synthetic. Second, to mean unprocessed and without any additions.

'Pure' was also discussed and it was recommended that its use should be restricted to products which contain no additive of any kind. (It is difficult to see where chemically impure sea salt fits here compared with chemically purified salt from salt mines.)

In 1983 the Canadian Department for Consumer and Corporate Affairs suggested guidelines pertaining to the use of the term 'natural' to describe a food or its ingredients (*Communique No. 38*). This was considered necessary to safeguard the significance of the term 'since it is deemed important to consumers'.

It was suggested that the term should be restricted to foods 'which have been submitted to a minimum of processing and which have undergone a minimum of physical, chemical or biological change'. Such a definition differs with the opinions of different manufacturers, retailers and consumers, and the guidelines have not met with general approval. Baking, for example, was listed as non-significant despite the major changes in physical properties and nutritional damage to protein quality and vitamin B1 that inevitably accompany baking of any degree or type. Degerming was also listed among the insignificant changes but many consumers would certainly not accept that.

The guidelines did not permit use of the word for a food that had been simply enriched with vitamins and minerals. Presumably milk straight from the cow is a natural food, but what if the diet of the cow has been manipulated? It is possible to increase the vitamin A in milk by feeding extra to the cow, and it is possible to increase the vitamin D by exposing the milk to sunshine.

Ban the Word

With such difficulties it might be more advisable to ban any use of the word.

The appeal of the term natural to the consumer is obvious but it can be misused unintentionally or innocently. For example a book of 'natural cooking' (if cooking itself can be considered natural), extolled 'natural brandy'—made by fermenting grape juice and then distilling it—but said that fortified wines—made by fermenting the grape juice and then adding previously distilled brandy—are 'unnatural and bad'.

201

The term natural is used in advertising in four different ways. The first means a food taken from the ground, sea or farm and not processed in any way. So all raw fruits, vegetables, farm crops, meat, fish and milk would fall into this category. Such definitions would seem to be in the minds of health food purveyors when they describe ordinary foods as refined, tinned, frozen, freeze-dried, excessively packaged (which is in some way a derogatory term) and 'otherwise tampered with'. This is to distinguish unprocessed foods from those to which colours, flavours and preservatives have been added, or which have been subjected to any treatment listed above. It is not made clear at what temperature a food ceases to be regarded as natural—in the above description of processed foods, processing is clearly denigrated but it is not clear whether cooling in a refrigerator or exposure to cold weather is equally deprecated.

Organic Foods and Pesticides

If you buy "organic" labeled foods in the hope of avoiding pesticides, you are unlikely to be successful. But don't let this trouble you. Government agencies keep watch on our food supplies to be sure they are safe to eat. The pesticide content of today's food is not a threat to our health. The amounts of pesticides found in our foods are extremely small. They would not even be detectable if it were not for the exquisite sensitivity of modern measuring equipment which can measure some substances in parts per *trillion!* Moreover, pesticides have a greater margin of safety than many other substances found naturally in foods which we eat all the time without worrying about them.

Victor Herbert and Stephen Barrett, *Vitamins and "Health" Foods: The Great American Hustle*, 1982.

A speaker on BBC Woman's Hour once discussed how she would never have a refrigerator, but was living in Scotland and had a north-facing larder. In her mind it was clear that artificial cold differed from natural cold.

A second use of the word is simply for the commercial purpose of making a product appear superior to that of a rival. Butter, for instance, is advertised as being natural while margarine adverts say it is made from natural ingredients. Both, of course, are equally true. Butter is made from a product, milk, that must, under all headings, be considered as natural, but it has to be manipulated by separating the cream, churning, often adding salt and colouring matter (which can come from a plant extract or even be synthetic). Whether or not it can still be called natural is arguable. Similarly margarine is made from oils extracted from natural sources such as nuts, fish and animal carcasses, hardened with hydrogen in the presence of a nickel catalyst, salted, coloured and enriched with vitamins.

In the public mind butter is regarded as the more natural product although nutritionally margarine may be the same as, or, as I will explain later, even superior to butter. Both are claimed as natural for advertising purposes.

A third use of the word is again for commercial reasons when the food has been processed to a lesser degree than its rival. So brown sugar, which has been highly purified from the starting material, whether beet or cane, is labelled natural compared to white sugar which is fractionally more refined. Sea salt, 98 per cent pure sodium chloride, is labelled 'natural sea salt' and sometimes 'pure, natural sea salt' as distinct from the very pure recrystallized product which is 99 per cent sodium chloride. The difference between the 98 per cent and 99 per cent is largely debris from the sea such as particles of shrimp, fish and seaweed. These will provide a trace of mineral salts but too little to be of any nutritional interest. The 'dirt' is not harmful but is invariably costly. . . .

Man's Natural Food

There is yet another use of the term natural in the context of a food that is natural for man to eat. Such a food is even more difficult to define. Many articles have been written to explain why man is naturally a vegetarian because of the construction of his intestines, just as many others have argued that he is a carnivore because primitive man was a hunter. It is not possible to prove either argument and in practice human beings are omnivores— we eat almost everything.

In the context of what is natural food, the term is often applied to whole foods as distinct from processed or refined foods. Compare wholemeal bread with white bread for instance. Certainly wholemeal bread contains more nutrients, but what is natural about separating the wheat grain from the rest of the plant, grinding it, adding a strange living substance called yeast, usually together with salt, mixing it with water and leaving it to ferment, then subjecting it to so high a temperature that a great deal of the vitamin B1 and the amino acid lysine are destroyed?

There is no food other than mother's milk that can be considered as natural for human beings, and even that suits only babies. While there is no doubt that breast milk is best for babies it is not always realized that its nutrient composition can vary with the mother's diet, especially in its vitamin content. There is even a report in the *New England Journal of Medicine*(Vol. 29, 1978) of anaemia developing in a breast-fed infant because the mother was a strict vegetarian who consumed no vitamin B12. So what can be called man's natural food?

Since most of our foods are pasteurized, sterilized, canned, bottled, homogenized and otherwise processed, as well as being chemically preserved, coloured and flavoured, it is quite understandable that people are often concerned. We are entitled to ask whether such foods are safe to eat and whether 'natural' unprocessed foods are not better.

In fact, food laws take care of the safety of manufactured foods and no chemical aids are permitted unless they are considered to be safe. So far from unprocessed foods being safer than factory products, the opposite is true because processed foods have to satisfy certain standards while raw fruit, vegetables, fish and meat do not.

An interesting example which would test the lawyers is the case of the fruit from Scandinavia known as cloudberry. This fruit, rather like a yellow raspberry in appearance but sharply acid in taste, is so rich in the natural preservative benzoic acid that it cannot ferment and does not go bad. It will keep fresh—if that is the right word—for years.

Chemical Phobia

What most people fail to realize is that *all* foods are composed of chemicals. You might easily be repulsed by the offer of a hot, steamy solution containing, among other things, caffeine, tannin, geraniol; and butyl, isoamyl, phenyl ethyl, hexyl and benzyl alcohols—yet what we have just described is a simple cup of tea, organically grown or otherwise. And what about those supernatural apples and oranges? Apples contain fascinating compounds like phlorizin and isoflavones; and those vitamin C-laden oranges also give us tangeretin, tyramine, synephrine, and citral. Natural grape flavoring contains at least nineteen different chemical compounds. Artificial grape flavoring contains only five, yet the public is led to believe that only the natural version is "safe." If every item in any given food market were to be labeled with a list of all the chemicals it contained, many people would apparently end up eating nothing at all.

Elizabeth M. Whelan and Fredrick J. Stare, *The One-Hundred-Percent Natural, Purely Organic, Cholesterol-Free, Megavitamin, Low-Carbohydrate Nutrition Hoax*, 1983.

Benzoic acid is a permitted preservative for fruit juices in Great Britain but in strictly limited amounts. Fruit squashes and cordials which are to be diluted with water before being served may contain not more than 800 parts per million of benzoic acid. If the fruit juice preparation is ready-to-drink without adding water, then it must not contain more than one-fifth of this amount, i.e., 160 parts per million, which is 0.016 per cent.

In their natural state, cloudberries contain as much as 0.8 per cent benzoic acid which is eight thousand parts per million or fifty times the legal limit!

There is no law to stop anyone selling cloudberries because they are a 'natural' food. They grow wild in abundance in Finland and any manufacturer could prepare and sell a mixture of orange juice and cloudberry juice which would contain more than the legal limit of preservative without breaking the law because the benzoic acid came from a natural food! . . .

If a colour, flavour or preservative has been extracted from a food it must be tested for safety before it can be used as an additive. Yet the original food containing such substances can be freely sold because unprocessed foods are not subject to legal control. So it is true to say that processed foods can be safer than raw, natural, unprocessed foods. . . .

Organic Farming

Along with the belief that natural unprocessed foods must be harmless and, indeed, beneficial, comes the belief that organic fertilizers, i.e., animal manure or vegetable compost, are more suitable for growing plants than inorganic salts such as sulphate of ammonia, superphosphate or potash which come from the chemical factory.

The latter are often called artificial fertilizers but the titles are back to front. It is the organic material that is artificial because plants can only use inorganic salts. Manure and compost are excellent conditioners and help retain moisture in the soil, but the nutrients they contain cannot be used by the plant until they have been broken down to inorganic salts by the microorganisms in the soil. Sulphate of ammonia and other inorganic fertilizers are ready for the plant to use, so they are really the natural ones.

Claims are made that crops grown with organic fertilizers are more nutritious and tasty. There have been a few investigations into nutritional value which are relevant here. . . .

There is no evidence at all that organic fertilizers produce more nutritious food than those grown on commercial farms using various inorganic salts of potassium, phosphate and nitrogen. When used in reasonable amounts, inorganic fertilizers are in no way harmful. The only valid criticism is that when too much is used it can find its way into lakes and ponds, leading to an overgrowth of algae.

Herbicides and Insecticides

Gardeners as well as farmers use an armoury of chemicals to protect their crops from weeds, pests and plant diseases. Their use increases the yield and most modern farming would be uneconomical without them, but are they safe?

When the more modern types of herbicide and insecticide were being developed in the late 1940s, their use was not controlled and many farmers grossly overdosed their crops. Fears were expressed about their persistence in the soil, the effects on wild life and the residues left in food. There was no evidence of harm to human beings, but the possibility that substances such as DDT could accumulate in the body fat gave rise to concern. In fact, it was later shown that after a certain level was reached in the body fat, chemicals were excreted at the same rate as they were ingested. Nevertheless there was some concern arising from the unproven possibility that anyone burning up their body fat during slimming might release this into the bloodstream.

However in 1971 the World Health Organization stated that the safety record of DDT for man was 'truly remarkable'. At that time about 400,000 tons had been used and whole populations had had their clothes and themselves treated with a powder containing 10 per cent DDT to control malaria and insect infestations—without any ill-effects. It was even added to drinking water to control yellow fever.

What Are Health Foods?

There is no such thing as a health food. The term is both false and misleading—misleading because it suggests that other foods are unhealthy.

Arnold Bender, *Health or Hoax*, 1986.

Most of these problems have been solved by the development of chemicals which do not persist in the soil and by controlling their use, as well as legislating for levels of residues permitted in foods. While there is no reason to worry about harm, those chemicals left in food do not, of course, do us any good. Hence the appeal of 'health' foods that are claimed—not always correctly —to be entirely free from chemical residues. . . .

The development of more selective chemicals and the greater degree of control exercised today—together with the fact that no evidence of harm has come to light in the intervening years— means that there is little, if any, justification for claims being made for 'health' foods grown without the use of chemicals.

The Raw Food Craze

In the history of man, the discovery of fire is relatively recent, only some 40,000 years old. Primitive man was a hunter-gatherer who collected whatever he could find growing in the area as well as hunting animals. Before fire was invented he had no choice but to eat his food raw.

The modern health food addict longs to hark back to the days of the Garden of Eden where man 'must' have eaten what came naturally and 'must' have eaten his food raw. In fact, many raw foods are toxic and only become safe after they have been cooked.

Some raw foods contain substances that destroy vitamins, interfere with digestive enzymes or damage the walls of the intestine. Raw meat can be contaminated with bacteria which would be destroyed by cooking; raw fish can contain substances that interfere with vitamin B1 (anti-thiaminases). There have even been very rare cases of a deficiency of biotin (vitamin H) because raw egg white combines with this vitamin and prevents its digestion.

One example of poisoning from red kidney beans occurred in Great Britain in 1976 when a party of schoolchildren returned to camp to find that the chicken for their supper had gone bad. There were some red kidney beans soaking ready for the next day, so they ate these raw with salad. Within a few hours the teacher and eight boys were violently sick and two had to go to the hospital for treatment. The reaction was caused by natural toxins called haemagglutins, a group of chemicals which cause red blood cells to clump together (agglutinate) in a test tube. In the bloodstream they would rapidly prove fatal; when taken by mouth they cause nausea, vomiting and diarrhoea within about two hours. . . .

Processing Methods

Many suspect foods and processes were introduced long before there was any indication of potential harm and because they have been used for so long without any proof of harm we continue to eat the foods and use the processes. Novel foods and novel processes must undergo the complete range of safety testing and, if the food is likely to replace a traditional food, it must supply the nutrients in similar amounts. The types of novel foods that have been investigated (and some have reached the market) are textured vegetable protein foods made to resemble meat and foods made from yeast and moulds. Novel processes include sterilizing by irradiation, microwave cooking and a process called extrusion cooking. . . .

The degree of control of public health and safety exercised now means that strange foods—strange to us although already eaten elsewhere—would still be subjected to testing.

There is no evidence that the novel foods so widely acclaimed in health food shops—carob beans, sesame seeds, buckwheat, oil of evening primrose, extract of green-lipped mussel, garlic oil and a host of herbs—have ever been subjected to such examination. The only reason that food authorities do not demand evidence of safety is that they represent only a small part of the total food eaten—but they may be a large part of the diet of some individuals.

"By the proper intakes of vitamins and other nutrients . . . you can, I believe, extend your life and years of well-being by twenty-five or even thirty-five years."

Large Doses of Vitamins Can Improve Health

Linus Pauling

Linus Pauling is among the most well-known and most controversial figures in the battle over the usefulness of megadoses of vitamins. A Nobel laureate in chemistry and the recipient of the 1963 Nobel Peace Prize for his work toward limiting above-ground nuclear testing, Pauling's background does not seem to fit with the appellations of "quack" and "nut" that many of his critics bestow on him. But since the publication of his 1970 book, *Vitamin C and the Common Cold*, in which he argued that megadoses of vitamin C can prevent colds, he has come under widespread attack from physicians. In the following viewpoint, Pauling argues that only by taking large doses of many different vitamins can people achieve better health.

As you read, consider the following questions:

1. What does Pauling think of the conventional wisdom that all vitamins and nutrients can be obtained by eating balanced meals?
2. Does Pauling believe that taking vitamins can produce any unwanted side effects?

I believe that you can, by taking some simple and inexpensive measures, lead a longer life and extend your years of well-being. My most important recommendation is that you take vitamins every day in optimum amounts to supplement the vitamins that you receive in your food. Those optimum amounts are much larger than the minimum supplemental intake usually recommended by physicians and old-fashioned nutritionists. The intake of vitamin C they advise, for example, is not much larger than that necessary to prevent the dietary-deficiency disease scurvy. My advice that you take larger amounts of C and other vitamins is predicated upon new and better understanding of the role of these nutrients—they are not drugs—in the chemical reactions of life. The usefulness of the larger supplemental intakes indicated by this understanding has been invariably confirmed by such clinical trials as have been run and by the first pioneering studies in the new epidemiology of health.

By the proper intakes of vitamins and other nutrients and by following a few other healthful practices from youth or middle age on, you can, I believe, extend your life and years of well-being by twenty-five or even thirty-five years. A benefit of increasing the length of the period of well-being is that the fraction of one's life during which one is happy becomes greater. Youth is a time of unhappiness; young people, striving to find their places in the world, live under great stress. The deterioration in health as the result of age usually makes the period before death a time of unhappiness again. There is evidence that there is less unhappiness associated with death at an advanced age than at an early age.

For such reasons it is sensible to take the health measures that will increase the length of the period of well-being and the life span. If you are already old when you begin taking vitamin supplements in the proper amounts and following other practices that improve your health, you can expect the control of the process of aging to be less, but it may still amount to fifteen or twenty years. . . .

The Low Toxicity of Vitamins

Physicians, these days, are armed with increasingly potent drugs, which they must prescribe and administer with great care, keeping their patients under alert surveillance. In extension of this chary attitude, I think, they are cautious about vitamins. It is easy to develop an exaggerated and unjustified fear of the toxicity of vitamins. During recent years it has become the practice of writers on medical matters and on health to warn their readers that large doses of vitamins may have serious side effects. For example, in *The Book of Health, a Complete Guide to Making Health Last a Lifetime* (1981), edited by Dr. Ernst L. Wynder, president of the

American Health Foundation, it is said that "So-called mega-vitamin treatment—taking massive doses of a particular vitamin—should be avoided. Vitamins are essential nutrients, but high dosages become drugs and should only be taken to treat a specific condition. Large doses of the fat-soluble vitamins A and D have well-recognized ill effects, and this must be true of others, too. Large doses of vitamin C are mainly excreted in the urine. In the absence of certainty that 'megavitamins' are safe, they are better avoided."

The authors of this book on health are depriving their readers of the benefit of the optimum intakes of these important nutrients, the vitamins, by creating in them the fear that any intake greater than the usually Recommended Daily Allowances (RDA) may cause serious harm.

Ignorance on Vitamins

I believe that the main reason for this poor advice is that the authors are ignorant. They make the false statement that large doses of vitamin C are mainly excreted in the urine. They give no indication that they know that the RDAs of the vitamins are the intakes that probably would prevent most people in "ordinary good health" from dying of scurvy, beriberi, pellagra, or other deficiency diseases but are not the intakes that put people in the best of health. They seem not to know that there is a great span between the RDAs and the toxic amounts of those that exhibit any toxicity and that for several vitamins there is no known upper limit to the amount that can be taken. These authorities on health should show greater concern about the health of the American people. . . .

Modern Foods Inadequate

The problem with achieving adequate nutrition by eating three "balanced" meals a day is related to changes taking place in the soils of many farms, which, in turn, can change the nutritional content of our food. Soil scientists from states where truck gardens and citrus farms are located report that significant decreases in the amount of selenium, zinc, manganese, and molybdenum in the soil have occurred over the past 25 to 100 years. . . . The bottom line is that our soils have changed and the foods they grow are also changing.

Keith W. Sehnert, *Selfcare/Wellcare*, 1985.

Nobody dies of poisoning by an overdose of vitamins. I have credited the physician with caution for the patient, even though the caution is entirely misplaced. Several people have suggested another possible explanation to me. It is that the drug manufacturers and the people involved in the so-called health industry do not want the American people to learn that they can improve their health and cut down on their medical expenses simply by taking vitamins in the optimum amounts.

A Bias Against Vitamins

The bias against vitamins may be illustrated by an episode that occurred a few years ago. A small child swallowed all the vitamin-A tablets that he found in a bottle. He became nauseated and complained of a headache. His mother took him to an East Coast medical-school hospital, where he was treated and then sent home. The professors of medicine then wrote an article about this case of vitamin poisoning. The article was published in the *New England Journal of Medicine*, the same journal that had rejected a paper by Ewan Cameron and me on observations of cancer patients who received large intakes of vitamin C. The *New York Times* and many other newspapers published stories about this child and about how dangerous the vitamins are.

Some child in the United States dies of aspirin poisoning every day. These poisonings are ignored by the medical-school doctors, the medical journals, and the *New York Times*.

There are seven thousand entries in the index of the *Handbook of Poisoning* by Dr. Robert H. Dreisbach, professor of pharmacology at Stanford University School of Medicine. Only five of these seven thousand are about vitamins. These five entries refer to vitamins A, D, K, K_1 (a form of K), and the B vitamins.

You do not need to worry about vitamin K. It is the vitamin that prevents hemorrhage by promoting coagulation of the blood. It is not often put into vitamin tablets. Adults and children usually receive a proper amount, which is normally supplied by "intestinal bacteria." The physician may prescribe vitamin K to newborn infants, to women in labor, or to people with an overdose of an anticoagulant. The toxicity of vitamin K is a problem of interest to the physician who administers it to a patient.

Vitamin D and Poisoning

Vitamin D is the fat-soluble vitamin that prevents rickets. It is required, together with calcium and phosphorus, for normal bone growth. The RDA is 400 International Units (IU) per day. It is probably wise not to exceed this intake very much. Dreisbach gives 158,000 IU as the toxic dose, with many manifestations of toxicity: weakness, nausea, vomiting, diarrhea, anemia, decreased renal functions, acidosis, proteinuria, elevated blood pressure, calcium deposition, and others. . . .

Vitamin A is usually mentioned as a prime example in any discussion of the toxicity of vitamins. Thus in her 1984 *New York Times* article "Vitamin Therapy: The Toxic Side Effects of Massive

Doses," the writer about foods, Jane E. Brody, stated that "Vitamin A has been the cause of the largest number of vitamin poisoning cases." She did not mention that the patients did not die (as do many of those poisoned by aspirin and other drugs), but she did give two case histories, presumably the worst that she could find.

A 3-year-old girl was hospitalized with confusion, dehydration, hyperirritability, headache, pains in the abdomen and legs, and vomiting, the result of daily ingestion of 200,000 I.U. of vitamin A a day for three months (2,500 is the amount recommended for a child her age, theoretically to prevent respiratory infections).

A 16-year-old boy who took 50,000 I.U. daily for two and a half years to counter acne developed a stiff neck, dry skin, cracked lips, swelling of the optic nerves, and increased pressure in the skull.

These reports indicate that the long-continued daily intake of doses of vitamin A ten to eighty times the RDA may cause moderately severe effects. Dreisbach in his book on poisons says that twenty to one hundred times the RDA may in time cause painful nodular periosteal swelling, osteoporosis, itching, skin eruptions and ulcerations, anorexia, increased intracranial pressure, irritability, drowsiness, alopecia, liver enlargement (occasionally), diplopia, and papilledema. . . .

The Need To Reexamine Nutrition

I am a scientist, a chemist, physicist, crystallographer, molecular biologist, and medical researcher. Twenty years ago, I became interested in the vitamins. I discovered that the science of nutrition had stopped developing. The old professors of nutrition who had helped to develop this science fifty years ago seemed to be so well satisfied with their accomplishment that they ignored the new discoveries that were being made in biochemistry, molecular biology, and medicine, including vitamins and other nutrients. Although a new science of nutrition was being developed, these old professors of nutrition continued to teach their students the old ideas, many of them wrong, such as that no person in ordinary health needs to take supplementary vitamins and that all that you need to do for good nutrition is to eat some of each of the "four foods" each day.

Linus Pauling, *How To Live Longer and Feel Better*, 1986.

Until 1983 it was thought that none of the water-soluble vitamins had significant toxicity even at very high intakes. Then a report was made that seven persons who had been taking 2000 to 5000 mg per day (one thousand to three thousand times the RDA) of vitamin B_6 for between four months and two years had developed a loss of feeling in the toes and a tendency to stumble. This peripheral neuropathy disappeared when the high intake of the vitamin was stopped and the patients showed no damage to the central nervous system.

One Thousand Times the RDA

We may conclude that there is an upper limit, one thousand times the RDA, to the daily intake of vitamin B_6. The authors of the report were far more cautious, however; they recommended that no one take more than the RDA of this vitamin, 1.8 to 2.2 mg per day. To follow this recommendation would deprive many people of a means for improving their health by taking 50 or 100 mg or more every day. Many orthomolecular psychiatrists recommend 200 mg per day to the patients, with some patients taking 400 to 600 mg per day. Stephen Hawkins reported that "In more than 5,000 patients we have not observed a single side effect from pyridoxine administration of 200 mg of vitamin B_6 daily."

Single doses of 50,000 mg of vitamin B_6 are given without serious side effects. These large doses are given as the antidote to patients suffering from poisoning with an overdose of the antituberculosis drug isoniazid.

No fatal doses are known for folacin (folic acid), pantothenic acid, vitamin B_{12}, and biotin. These four water-soluble vitamins are described as lacking in toxicity, even at very high intakes. The values of the RDA for adult males are 400 micrograms (mg) for folacin, 7 mg for pantothenic acid, 3 mg for vitamin B_{12}, and 200 mg for biotin. . . .

Vitamin C

There is no known fatal dose of vitamin C. As much as 200 grams (g) has been taken by mouth over a period of a few hours without harmful effects. Between 100 and 150 g of sodium ascorbate has been given by intravenous infusion without harm.

There is little evidence of long-term toxicity. I know a man who has taken over 400 kilograms (kg) of this vitamin during the last nine years. He is a chemist, working in California. When he developed metastatic cancer, he found that he could control his pain by taking 130 g of vitamin C per day, and he has taken this amount, over a quarter of a pound per day, for nine years. Except that he has not succeeded in ridding himself completely of his cancer, his health is reasonably good, with no indication of harmful side effects of the vitamin. . . .

Improve Your Health

Take the optimum supplementary amount of each of the essential vitamins every day. No matter what your present age is, you can achieve significant benefits by starting the regimen now. Older people can benefit greatly, because they have special need for optimum nutrition. Steadfast adherence is essential. It is fortunate that the regimen imposes few restrictions on the diet, so that for the most part you can add to the quality of your life by eating foods that you enjoy. What is more, you can, and it is even recommended that you do, enjoy the moderate intake of alcoholic beverages. . . .

By keeping in the best of health, in particular by maintaining optimum intake of the vitamins, we can resist the entire long list of illnesses that afflict mankind. The list begins with the afflictions laid upon us by deficiencies of the vitamins, deficiencies so easily cured by restoring the functions in the biochemistry of the body; the vitamins help us to fend off infection and fortify our tissues against the self-assault of cancer and the auto-immune diseases. With the best understood vitamin, vitamin C, as our example, we have been able to envision a new kind of medicine, the orthomolecular medicine that uses substances natural to the body both to protect it from, and to cure, illness. Already, orthomolecular medicine has shown how vitamin C can prevent and cure and may yet eliminate from human experience the illness most familiar and most baffling to the old medicine, the common cold. . . .

Well-Balanced Diet Myth

The physicians and the old-fashioned professors of nutrition have for fifty years been urging that everyone adopt a diet that is described as healthful. For two or three decades we were all urged to eat a well-balanced diet, with servings of the four categories of food: meat or fish or fowl; cereals; fruits and red or yellow vegetables; and dairy products. This dietary regimen was urged on us whether or not we liked all these foods. Recently much of the enjoyment of life has been taken away from many of us by additional strong recommendations by these authorities. We are told that we should not eat a succulent steak, because of the animal fat. We are told that we should not eat eggs, because of the cholesterol they contain; instead, we are urged to eat a sort of factory product, a preparation, probably not very appealing to the taste, that is made by treating eggs with some chemical solvent to remove some of the cholesterol. We are told not to eat butter. Going to a fine restaurant then is not a pleasure, but a source of worry and a cause of a feeling of guilt.

Why are these recommendations being made to us? A part of the reason is that good health depends on a good supply of vitamins. In the past, to obtain even a passable supply of vitamins, leading to even ordinary poor health, required a moderately large intake of fruits and vegetables. In every culture in countries other than the tropical ones some special foods, such as sauerkraut and pickles, had to be eaten in order for us to survive the winter. Even with the best selection of foods the health of most people has in the past not been very good.

The revolution that is taking place now liberates us from this obsession to restrict our diet, to refrain from eating those foods that we like. The only limitations that I suggest are that you not eat large amounts of food and that you limit your intake of the sugar sucrose. This nutritional freedom has become possible because of the availability of vitamin and mineral supplements.

Moreover, it is now possible to take these important nutrients in the optimum amounts, far larger than can be obtained in foods, and in this way to achieve a sort of superhealth, far beyond what was possible in earlier times. We can be grateful to the organic chemists and biochemists of the past 140 years who laboriously solved the riddles of the nature of the compounds of carbon and the way that they interact with one another in the human body. Because of their efforts, we are now able to get greater enjoyment of life.

"The human body is simply not equipped to handle on a daily basis the amount of vitamin C equivalent to an entire carload of oranges or the vitamin A from a carload of carrots."

Large Doses of Vitamins Are Harmful

Elizabeth M. Whelan and Fredrick J. Stare

In the following viewpoint, Elizabeth M. Whelan and Fredrick J. Stare argue that the widespread public acceptance of taking large amounts of vitamins is costing people unnecessary millions of dollars and may be costing many people their health. Whelan is executive director of the American Council on Science and Health, a national organization promoting a scientific evaluation of factors affecting health, chemicals, and the environment. Stare is a professor emeritus and founder of Harvard's Department of Nutrition. He is also co-founder of the American Council on Science and Health.

As you read, consider the following questions:

1. Why do the authors compare making H_2O in the laboratory with taking too many vitamins?
2. Why are the "vitamin pushers" successful, according to Whelan and Stare?
3. How do the authors summarize their argument?

Reprinted with permission of Atheneum Publishers, an imprint of Macmillan Publishing Company from *The One-Hundred-Percent Natural, Purely Organic, Cholesterol-Free, Megavitamin, Low-Carbohydrate Nutrition Hoax* by Elizabeth M. Whelan and Fredrick J. Stare. Copyright © 1983 Elizabeth M. Whelan and Fredrick J. Stare.

Is emotional stress making your life miserable? Pop a few pills of vitamin C. Sex life growing stale? Worried about air pollution? A few hundred units of vitamin E is the remedy. So go the claims of the enthusiasts who fancy that health and happiness can be purchased in little bottles. Don't you believe it!

The Need for Nutrients

The human body is an extemely complex machine. To function efficiently, it requires the presence of some fifty different nutrients, which continually interact in an intricate series of chemical reactions. The *absence* of any single essential nutrient over a period of time will produce a deficiency disease. This does not mean that *excessive* amounts of the same nutrient will either prevent or cure disease. The body requires specific amounts; it has no use for excesses.

As an extremely simplified illustration, suppose that we are attempting to produce a small flask of water in a laboratory. Almost everyone is aware that water is composed of hydrogen and oxygen in a ratio of two to one (H_2O). If we add additional hydrogen to the chemical reaction to make water, we do not get more water unless additional oxygen is also added. And once we have enough water to fill the flask, no amount of hydrogen or oxygen will put additional water into that flask.

The same is true of the human body. "Leftover" nutrients are either excreted as waste or stored in the body, occasionally reaching dangerously high levels. No one nutrient performs a single function, and no nutrient performs *any* function without the aid of other substances that are specifically required for that function.

Vitamin A and Blindness

We have long been told, for instance, that vitamin A is "good for the eyes." It is, although it is important for other reasons as well, but by itself it cannot benefit the eyes or any other part of the body. But, confining ourselves for the moment to the eyes, vitamin A deficiency over a period of time leads to obstructed tear ducts and impaired vision in dim light (so-called "night blindness"). Severe deficiency leads to total blindness, a condition not uncommon in parts of Asia and the Middle East. Vitamin A supplements will correct a vitamin A deficiency, but they will not prevent any other types of blindness from occurring; nor will they cure blindness or other visual disorders such as nearsightedness, astigmatism, or cataracts, which are not caused by a lack of vitamin A. Similarly, because it was known that a severe deficiency of vitamin A could cause skin lesions, supplements were at one time prescribed to "cure" certain skin conditions such as acne; but there is little evidence of their effectiveness (and a great deal of evidence that high doses can prove toxic).

While it is important to understand that very large amounts (megadoses) of vitamin A are useless for anyone not suffering from vitamin A deficiency, it is *vital* to understand that these same megadoses can be exceedingly dangerous. A small serving of carrots will supply the average person with enough vitamin A for two days. What the body doesn't use, it stores in the liver. For this reason, animal liver is an excellent source of that vitamin. Eskimos learned long ago to avoid eating polar-bear liver, even though they did not know the reason that it caused death was its extremely high vitamin A content: about one million international units (IU) in three ounces, compared to a Recommended Dietary Allowance of 4,000 IU for females and 5,000 IU for males. (In other words, a small serving of polar-bear liver contains 200 to 250 times the RDA.)

The Danger of Excess Vitamins

Many substances which are harmless in small or moderate doses can be harmful in large amounts or by gradual build-up over many years. Just because a substance (such as a vitamin) is found naturally in food does not mean that it cannot be harmful. . . .

Megadoses of almost every nutrient have been demonstrated to be harmful. Too much vitamin A can cause lack of appetite, retarded growth in children, drying and cracking of the skin, enlargement of the liver and spleen, increased pressure on the brain, loss of hair, migratory joint pains, menstrual difficulty, bone pain, irritability and headache.

Victor Herbert and Stephen Barrett, *Vitamins and "Health" Foods: The Great American Hustle*, 1982.

Between 1960 and 1964, approximately twenty children in New York died from hypervitaminosis A because their mothers, marching to the "more is better" tune, doubled the recommended dosage of vitamin supplements, giving each child two capsules daily in addition to the more than adequate amounts they were already receiving from the milk, butter or margarine, and vegetables in their diet. . . .

The Modern "Medicine Men"

The public is gullible. Their fears aroused by inconclusive research studies and spurred on by slanted media stories, people are eager to try almost anything to forestall or cure cancer, arthritis, obesity, heart disease, diabetes, headache, nervousness, constipation, aging, baldness, and rundownitis. They are willing to spend billions of dollars every year for vitamins, minerals, and "wonder" substances that for the most part are virtually useless.

Nutrition misinformation and public fear have coupled to produce a new breed of quack whose slogan is, "If a little is good, a great deal must be better." The dosages recommended are usually several times—or even several hundred times—more than any one person's body could possibly use during the course of a day. If the nutrient is water soluble, most of it usually passes on through to nurture whatever forms of life may inhabit the local sewage system; if the nutrient is not soluble in water, it is stored in the body, where it may eventually accumulate to toxic levels and produce untold misery.

Although we have just used the singular form of the word nutrient, few health faddists are content to limit themselves to a mere one or two supplemental nutrients. Each one is usually purported to prevent or cure a long and diverse list of symptoms, but the most avid adherents are taking no chances! Just to be sure, they assemble an entire conglomeration of daily dietary supplements. Health-food stores even sell compartmented pill containers, but the most devout of the pill lovers find fishermen's tackleboxes more spacious for housing their supplies (à la Adelle Davis). It may sound like a joke, but it isn't.

A Lack of Education

The supplement pushers are evidently achieving considerable success. Several national surveys during the past few years reveal that approximately 75 percent of the adult population thinks that extra vitamins promote extra pep and energy, and lead to better health generally. Whether due to a lack of basic health education, or because the surge of propaganda has eventually overpowered their common sense, too few people seem to be aware of the saturation levels for vitamins or other nutrients—the point beyond which excessive amounts cannot be utilized. Further, not nearly enough people seem to understand that *all* nutrients are readily available from the food in a balanced diet. The only exceptions here are iron, which is poorly absorbed and occasionally insufficient, particularly in the diets of women of childbearing age, and flouride, unless one has access to flouridated water. Other than that, nutrient deficiencies are uncommon in most areas of the United States. In poverty areas, nutrition is often a serious problem, but what the inhabitants there need is *food*, not supplements. In affluent societies, the problem is just the opposite. Too much food is consumed, and obesity results. . . .

A danger just as serious as too few nutrients is the eventual toxic effect of too many. The human body is simply not equipped to handle on a daily basis the amount of vitamin C equivalent to an entire carload of oranges or the vitamin A from a carload of carrots. As with salt, a minimal amount is necessary to maintain life; too much can be lethal. In this country, the toxic effects of excess doses of vitamins (particularly the fat-soluble ones) are now more frequently seen by doctors than the classical vitamin deficiency diseases such as scurvy, pellagra, and beriberi. . . .

The Need for Balance

A hidden danger of megadosing is the effect that too much of a given nutrient may have on other nutrients or compounds in the body, and the body chemistry as a whole. . . .

Scientists have already spent a great many years determining what nutrients, in what quantities, people need for good health. While future research may reveal that minor adjustments are indicated, it is illogical to assume that after decades of study by countless nutritional experts, the results are meaningless.

Fragments of Fact

In the absence of hard-and-fast knowledge, the vitamin enthusiasts can take any fragment of fact known about a given vitamin and spin a wide and intricate belief about the vitamin's usefulness in, well, anything they want to use the vitamin for. It also means that the vitamin enthusiasts can be very choosy about which facts they will use to support their pet theories.

John Fried, *Vitamin Politics*, 1984.

Vitamins and minerals in proper amounts are essential for good health; beyond that they are not miracle potions. They will neither cure nor prevent anything other than a deficiency of that particular vitamin or mineral. And when we speak of deficiency, we are not alluding to a self-diagnosed deficiency. We mean a *medically* diagnosed deficiency, usually established by laboratory testing. The special danger of self-prescription is the possibility—a rather frequent one—that you may be "treating" the wrong condition. The person who prescribes for himself massive doses of vitamin C to overcome recurring symptoms of the common cold may actually be suffering from a severe sinus condition or allergic reaction; or even a lung disorder, which, left untreated, will gradually worsen.

Supplements and Prevention

Occasionally a metabolic defect will prevent the body from utilizing a nutrient, even though it is present in sufficient amounts in the diet. A classic example is pernicious anemia, an illness caused by the inability to absorb vitamin B_{12}. Here, some form of B_{12} supplementation by injection is necessary. An oral supplement of B_{12} would not correct the deficiency, because it would not be metabolized. And this does not mean, contrary to many vitamin ads, that B_{12} supplements will prevent the condition from occurring in the first place. . . .

Unneeded supplements upset the nutrient balance. Scientists know that the possibilities of adverse reactions are so far-reaching that many are yet to be uncovered. . . .

Frightening the Consumer

"How much of your vitamin C gets lost on the way to the table?" There is certainly nothing illegal in leading off an advertisement with that question. But it is surely designed to frighten the consumer into running to the store for some vitamin C tablets. True, C is one of the more fragile vitamins, and it is partially destroyed by prolonged storage and exposure to air. But even a minimum of common-sense food care allows the average person easily to obtain his RDA by consuming one serving of a vitamin C-rich food daily. . . .

No one has to look very far to encounter such vitamin hogwash as the following:

- that vitamin A will prevent some cancers, improve the skin, and cure learning disabilities;
- that vitamin B_1 (thiamine) functions as an antidepressant and reduces cravings for certain drugs;
- that vitamin B_2 (riboflavin) will overcome stress;
- that vitamin B_3 (niacin) stabilizes manic-depressive psychosis, relieves schizophrenia, and improves circulation in the elderly;
- that vitamin B_5 (pantothenic acid) restores color to gray hair (it does, in rats);
- that vitamin B_6 (pyridoxine) overcomes fatigue, anxiety, and depression, and relieves Parkinson's disease (it does not, and, paradoxically, an excess of B_6 can block the effectiveness of certain drugs like L-dopa, often used in the treatment of this disease);
- that vitamin B_{12} can relieve neuritis, neuralgia, and psoriasis, and is a hangover remedy of long standing;
- that vitamin C (ascorbic acid) prevents colds, cures cancer, relieves back pain, and lowers cholesterol (as Dr. Linus Pauling's favorite vitamin, he recommends it for almost everything);
- that vitamin D promotes general well-being;
- that vitamin E will do almost anything: overcome impotence, promote fertility, prevent aging, promote healthy skin, aid in weight reduction, prevent miscarriage, minimize birth deformities, dissolve blood clots; that it will prevent and treat high blood pressure, kidney disease, rheumatic fever, most forms of heart disease and varicose veins; that external application helps wounds and burns to heal without scars; and that taken from an early age, it will prevent senility and stroke;

221

- that biotin (a member of the B complex but also sometimes known as vitamin H, for some mysterious reason) aids scalp problems, thinning hair, and baldness;
- that folic acid (also belonging to the B complex) cures nervous disorders and prevents leukemia. . . .

From Too Little to Too Much

What the ads, booklets, flyers, and posters usually don't tell you about are the hazardous, sometimes lethal, effects of overdosing, or hypervitaminosis. The Food and Drug Administration has widely reported the story of a teenage girl who was being prepared for surgery for a brain tumor when it was discovered that her symptoms actually resulted from the massive amounts of vitamin A in her body. In other cases, vitamin A toxicity has also led to false diagnoses of meningitis.

Vitamin Fanatics

Conventional doctors, nutritionists, and biochemists have been deeply frustrated in battles against the vitamin enthusiasts. "You are dealing essentially with fanatics, and food is their religion," says Dr. Bernard T. Kaufman, chief of the Vitamin Metabolism Section at the National Institutes of Health in Bethesda, Maryland. That means, of course, that the nutrition scientist can no more convince the nutrition religionist and his would-be followers of the errors in their thinking than the evolution expert can convince a fundamentalist Baptist preacher and his congregation of the folly of the belief that man is a direct descendant of a piece of mud fashioned by a God lonely for a little companionship.

John Fried, *Vitamin Politics*, 1984.

Tragedy is not always prevented, however. A few years ago a mother in Maine alleged she had given her young daughter large doses of vitamin A after reading Adelle Davis' recommendations in *Let's Have Healthy Children*. As a result of this treatment, the infant's nervous system was damaged and her physical development dwarfed for life. After bringing suit against both author and publisher, this mother received a settlement of $150,000—small compensation for the irreparable harm that was innocently fostered by a parent's effort to keep her child "healthy.". . .

Rebound Scurvy

For example, there is the question of what is known as "rebound scurvy" among newborns. It is possible that if the infant's mother consumed megadoses of vitamin C during pregnancy, she might create in the unborn child a tolerance, and then a dependence, on these massive amounts. After birth, with vitamin C intake reduced to normal levels, the baby might present all the symptoms of scurvy; that is, vitamin C deficiency. Conceivably, excessive amounts of other nutrients could produce similar rebound results.

The complexity of nutrient interactions is not a matter for amateurs—or self-professed professionals—to tamper with. As a brief example, a deficiency of folic acid will cause anemia. However, even slightly excessive amounts taken during pernicious anemia *without a sufficient amount of vitamin B$_{12}$* can result in spinal cord degeneration. . . .

There are countless such examples. However necessary a vitamin or any other substance may be for the maintenance of life and good health, too much of anything can throw the entire system out of balance and cause it to malfunction. . . .

Like Salt for Stew

A maxim of pharmacology states that anything causing bodily changes for good can also do the opposite. This elementary principle can be applied as accurately to vitamins, minerals, and other nutrients as it is to medicinal drugs.

There is always a point of maximum effectiveness; beyond that point lies the risk of toxic effects. Further danger exists in the fact that a large dose of one nutrient sometimes blocks the body's ability to use another. Those who succumb to the vitamin-quack sales talk should realize they are taking part in a large, uncontrolled experiment.

People are often distressed to learn that the concept of a miracle potion simply doesn't stand up; they prefer to cling to their fantasies, rather than bother themselves about balanced diets and other simple and relatively inexpensive aspects of healthful living. Our contention that, in the absence of deficiency disease, almost everyone can obtain all necessary nutrients from regular, varied selections from the Basic Four Food Groups is not very spectacular. Certainly, it will not create world-shaking headlines. But it is based on sound scientific facts.

In nutrient intake, the objective is, like salt for the stew, not too little, not too much.

Recognizing Statements That Are Provable

From various sources of information we are constantly confronted with statements and generalizations about social and moral problems. In order to think clearly about these problems, it is useful if one can make a basic distinction between statements for which evidence can be found and other statements which cannot be verified or proved because evidence is not available, or the issue is so controversial that it cannot be definitely proved.

Readers should constantly be aware that magazines, newspapers, and other sources often contain statements of a controversial nature. The following activity is designed to allow experimentation with statements that are provable and those that are not.

The following statements are taken from the viewpoints in this chapter. Consider each statement carefully. *Mark P for any statement you believe is provable. Mark U for any statement you feel is unprovable because of the lack of evidence. Mark C for any statements you think are too controversial to be proved to everyone's satisfaction.*

If you are doing this activity as a member of a class or group, compare your answers with those of other class or group members. Be able to defend your answers. You may discover that others will come to different conclusions than you. Listening to the reasons others present for their answers may give you valuable insights in recognizing statements that are provable.

> P = *provable*
> U = *unprovable*
> C = *too controversial*

1. Medical schools today recognize that the majority of their graduates' future patients will suffer from a small number of chronic debilitating conditions. Nonetheless they emphasize the exotic disease.

2. All holistic practitioners recognize the fundamental interdependence between food and health.

3. The modern health food addict longs to hark back to the days of the Garden of Eden where man must have eaten what came naturally and must have eaten his food raw.

4. Vitamins in excess of what the body needs do not increase health and may actually produce disease.

5. Laws of physics govern the movement of planets, the changing of seasons, and the coming and going of tides.

6. By the proper intake of vitamins and nutrients you can extend your life by 25 or even 35 years.

7. Cooking affects the digestibility of protein; raw or lightly cooked protein is more easily digested, particularly by an individual with a healthy digestive tract.

8. In their natural state, cloudberries contain as much as 0.8 percent benzoic acid which is fifty times the legal limit.

9. If a colour has been extracted from a food it must be tested for safety before it can be used as an additive. Yet the original food containing such a substance can be freely sold because unprocessed foods are not subject to legal control.

10. It is now possible to take these important nutrients in amounts far larger than obtained in foods, and in this way achieve a sort of superhealth.

11. The healthiest, strongest, and most disease resistant cultures ever known lived on natural foods.

12. The holistic medical movement constitutes a deliberate attempt to substitute a magical for an engineering conception of the physician.

13. About four hundred children die each year of poisoning by aspirin.

14. All states of health and all diseases are psychosomatic.

15. Lower cancer rates, especially colon cancer, occur in countries with high fiber diets, as in rural areas of Africa, where native people eat mostly natural foods.

Periodical Bibliography

The following articles have been selected to supplement the diverse views presented in this chapter.

| William Evers | "Vitamin Supplements Often Wasteful," *USA Today*, February 1988. |

Susan Calvert Finn — "The Surprising Truth About 'Natural' Foods," *50 Plus*, June 1985.

Hans Fisher — "The Elusive Vitamin Requirement," *Prevention*, February 1987.

Glamour — "Vitamin and Mineral Supplements: Do You Need Them?" June 1987.

Kirk Johnson — "The Hidden Food Lobby," *East West*, January 1988.

Kathleen McAuliffe — "How Safe Is Your Food?" *U.S. News & World Report*, November 16, 1987.

Kathleen McAuliffe — "Will Your Dinner Make You Sick?" *U.S. News & World Report*, November 16, 1987.

T.M. McGuire — "Edgar Cayce's Legacy of Holistic Health," *East West*, September 1987.

Ron Rosenbaum — "Awards: The Organic Oscars," *Esquire*, May 1984.

Jeff Schein — "The Perils of Megavitamin Therapy," *Consumer's Research*, July 1987.

Utne Reader — "Are You Playing with Your Health? How To Choose What To Use," special issue, January/February 1988.

Rob Wechsler — "A New Prescription: Mind Over Malady," *Discover*, February 1987.

6 CHAPTER

How Can Health
Be Improved?

Chapter Preface

Humanity has sought to extend life, prevent sickness, and eliminate virulent diseases since organized society began. In the twentieth century, people depend on technology to come up with innovative ways to improve health. However, as life-expectancy has leveled off, and cures for diseases such as cancer continue to elude scientists, many people are questioning whether or not society has reached a plateau in improving health.

While sickness is surely a part of the human condition, people continue to ask whether or not Americans' health can be further improved. This question is debated in this chapter.

"Humanity faces the prospect of contamination overload—the high-tech holocaust."

A Cleaner Environment Would Improve Health

James Bellini

Whether industrialized nations of the world have ruined the environment and continue to harm the health of the world's population is a source of debate. In the following viewpoint, James Bellini believes the threat to world health through industrialized pollution has reached the proportions of a holocaust. He concludes by arguing that if something is not done within five years to reduce the threat, world health will sharply decline. Bellini works for the British Broadcasting Corporation where he has written and directed a number of award-winning television documentaries.

As you read, consider the following questions:

1. Why does the author believe the threat from pollution, if left unreversed, will result in a fate worse than nuclear war?
2. What does Bellini believe the example of Lake Biwa in Japan proves?

The high-tech age has given us unprecedented benefits. Without industry, and the sophisticated technologies that it has brought with it, the world would still be living in pre-modern times. There would be no supersonic aircraft, no wonder drugs, no television or video, no skyscraper cities. The popular affluence that we now take for granted in the developed countries, give or take the entrenched problem of unemployment, could never otherwise have been attained. Without industry we would be denied the many and varied benefits of abundance. And humanity would have been spared the horrors of Chernobyl, Bhopal, Thalidomide, acid rain, pesticide poisoning, the health hazards posed by contaminated and adulterated food, the insidious danger of household drinking water tainted by toxic traces, and other unwanted features of life in the late twentieth century.

Poisoned soils, poisoned bodies, a poisoned future. The price of progress is rarely assessed in full. Industrial revolution was welcomed as the catalyst of social and political change, as well as the source of prosperity for many millions. But with it came an unforeseen danger. Under the assault of a rising tide of pollution the nature of this earth was to be changed completely. Now that polluting tide threatens to upset the delicate balance of our own biochemistry. Humanity faces the prospect of contamination overload—the high-tech holocaust.

Our Worsening Habitat

The coming of industry has changed the character of our habitat for the worst. It reshaped our towns, pushed millions off the land to fill congested urban landscapes. These conurbations developed their own polluted climatic chemistry. A new breed of diseases emerged, diseases of the industrial age that were to be steadily exaggerated over the decades as industrialism transformed the ecosystem. And this Faustian pact with technology brought also the more immediate threat of sudden, unexpected disaster. From Love Canal to Minamata, from Bonnybridge to Canonsburg, from India to the Ukraine, mankind has endured a growing catalogue of toxic accidents, catastrophic explosions and invisible visitations of deathly radiation. All of them are direct threats to our bodily well-being.

Typical of the scale of the problem is the predicament created by toxic wastes from commercial processes in the chemical, petroleum and metal industries. In the United States, for instance, thousands of dump-sites clogged with toxic organic chemicals, dangerous enough to wipe out entire city populations, present the US authorities with a monumental task of disposal. For decades the problem lay dormant, hidden away from an ill-informed citizenry . . . until 1978, when heavy rains pushed leaking drums of deadly substances out of the ground at Love Canal in Niagara

Mike Konopacki. Konopacki Labor Cartoons. *People's Daily World.*

Falls, New York. Hundreds of families were driven from their homes forever. It was not to be the last such disaster in the United States: in 1983 Times Beach, Missouri was turned into a ghost town after the population was evacuated, victims of a massive spillage of toxic waste. And there will be more such cases in the future: since 1950 the US industrial complex has generated some six billion tonnes of toxic waste from chemical plants, refineries, smelters and other installations. Each year yields a further 250 million tonnes of hazardous garbage, with inadequate controls over where, and how, it is dumped.

The situation in the United States is mirrored throughout the world. In the summer of 1984, in the middle of Birmingham, the authorities uncovered a cache of illegally dumped dioxin that was sufficient to kill the entire population of the English West Midlands ten times over.

But toxic industrial waste is only one small part of the threat. The high-tech age has overtaken farming, food manufacturing, packaging, pharmaceuticals, materials, energy production and data processing. In almost every commercial sector the price of material advancement has been the creation of chemical compounds, products or processes that are toxic to man.

We have perhaps no more than five years to make a choice in favour of a cleaner, safer world. Failure to make that choice could ensure that mankind is overtaken by a fate more horrific than that of nuclear war, as the contamination of our bodies by a wide variety of toxic elements approaches lethal overload. . . .

Across the world there are thousands, even millions, of individuals who are suffering the consequences of man's decision to make a pact with a devil called industry. After the nuclear accident at Chernobyl, in the Ukraine, in the spring of 1986, we have yet another opportunity to gather circumstantial evidence about the effects of radioactivity on the human body. Only a habit of secrecy will prevent the full truth from ever being known. And not only about the tragedy at Chernobyl: a central feature of the escalating polluting threat to our health is the pattern of secrecy, complacency and lies that has prevented the flow of information to the general public, not only in the Soviet Union but in every country and in every industry where dangers exist.

That habit of secrecy and obfuscation is most apparent in the nuclear industry. But there are many other facets of that diabolical pact that have been similarly obscured from public scrutiny, ranging from chemicals in food to cancer-causing agents in plastic credit cards, from cling film to hair sprays, from pesticides to heavy metals, from acid rain to poisoned drinking water and effluent-choked river systems. But we are reaching a crossroads where the circumstantial evidence will, by its sheer weight, become incontrovertible proof that the world is facing an unsustainable toxic challenge. The high-tech holocaust will be all-embracing, all-pervasive. And time is running out. . . .

The Tally Mounts

And so the tally of biochemical dangers steadily mounts. Open any newspaper or popular science magazine; yet another concern will be identified. In January 1986, a decade after the alarm was raised over the risks from aerosol sprays, the British journal *New Scientist* carried the following news item: 'A frequent ingredient in hair spray, methylene chloride, causes cancer in mice and may soon be banned by the US government. But the chemical will remain in decaffeinated coffee.' Another publication contained details of a study from the United States that suggests that the modern American male produces less than half the sperm produced by the average male fifty years ago. One possible cause, says Dr Ralph Dougherty of Florida State University, is the presence of a flame retardant, Fyrol FR2, used to cut down fire risks in foam furniture. Other scientists around the world have discovered high concentrations of PCBs—the same chemical leaking from millions of failed fluorescent tubes—in semen samples. Other chemicals known to have adverse effects on male fertility include dibromochloropropane, a soil fumigant, and chlordecone, a pesticide for long ranked second only to dioxin as the most toxic of toxins.

Pushing Back the Future

There are signs, of course, that humanity is fighting back. But the prospects of reversing the welling tide of toxic danger this side of the year 2000 are slender. To begin with, it now seems clear that self-regulating, self-cleansing mechanisms of the earth's ecosystem are losing their capacity to cope. The drift towards contamination overload seems inexorable, even in the face of ambitious efforts to slow its momentum.

The example of Lake Biwa in Japan is a telling one. In the early 1970s Japan was being engulfed by industrial contamination. In those days, warnings of photochemical smog were sent out on three hundred days of the year in Tokyo; five thousand victims of atmospheric pollution were being recorded each year in the Japanese capital alone. Through official and corporate endeavour, at immense cost to industry and the community, air pollution was cut dramatically; smog alerts were reduced by nearly two-thirds. But today, at Lake Biwa, the signs point to another sad chapter in the breakdown of environmental purity.

Danger: Toxic Air Contamination

A warning sign could be hung somewhere in every city: *Danger, Toxic Air Contamination.*

This time there will be no evacuation. This time there is nowhere to hide.

The poisons once thought to be a serious concern only near a place such as Love Canal are known now to be everywhere. They appear in the air of an Alpine forest, or over a Pacific island. They are also in the cabinet under the kitchen sink.

Solvents, refrigerants, methane, and oxides—all are among the pollutants that are increasingly gathering in the atmosphere. There they may be dangerously altering the natural ozone layer that protects us against harmful radiation from space, or are causing the "greenhouse" effect, blocking the escape of heat from the earth's surface and, in so doing, threatening to raise the planet's temperature to the point where lush farmland would turn to dust bowls, and polar ice would melt.

Michael H. Brown, *The Toxic Cloud*, 1987.

Japan's largest lake, some 674 square kilometres in area, is being killed by pollution as the population moves into new satellite towns in the region, from Osaka and Kyoto. The tragic consequences are summed up in a recent narrative on the fate of Lake Biwa: 'The resulting effluent pouring into the lake, coupled with acid rain from the huge industrial areas nearby, is now rapidly turning it into a graveyard. Attempts to cut the input of phosphates, by banning the sale and use of phosphate detergents, began in 1980 but came too late; it is unlikely that the lake water will show major improvement this century.' Similar problems now beset other watercourses in the country. Surveys of water in various wells show that some sources are tainted by cancer-causing chemical compounds at up to six hundred times the level regarded as safe by the World Health Organisation. About one-third of Japan's drinking water comes from underground sources. And Japan is not alone.

Current Actions Not Enough

This losing battle is not for lack of official recognition of the seriousness of Planet Earth's precarious condition. A stream of books, international conferences and action programmes testifies to a growing awareness. From as long ago as 1962, with the publication of Rachel Carson's book *Silent Spring*, there has been no shortage of evidence of the deteriorating situation of the countryside, and the wildlife it once supported, because of the chemical warfare now waged by farmers in the interest of better yields. The United Nations Conference on the Human Environment, in Stockholm in 1972, represented a landmark in international acceptance of the growing threat. In 1973 the nations of the European Economic Community adopted their First Action Programme, with the aim of taking radical steps to avert environmental collapse. In the United States the work of the Environmental Protection Agency and other bodies has raised public knowledge of the hazards that surround them, and has thereby helped strike out in a new direction.

But such actions are not enough. Governments alone cannot change the habits of industry, nor replace public apathy with informed interest, criticism and vigilance. As much was admitted by the EEC eleven years after that First Action Programme, when it reviewed progress towards a cleaner, safer Europe: 'What has been done—substantial though it is—is clearly not enough. . . . We have not so far even begun to tackle the much more fundamental question of whether—and for how long—human beings and ecosystems can continue to accept the total pressure placed upon them by the increasing use of chemicals.'

The cause of that ever-mounting pressure is man's insatiable desire to manufacture, to innovate and to enjoy the fruits of industrial growth. The key to that growth is technology in all its forms—in energy, materials, chemical compounds, packaging and processing methods, information handling, genetic engineering.

These technologies produce waste and by-products, as does humanity itself. Together they comprise the equation of toxic hazard that is the causal foundation of the high-tech holocaust. Only by controlling and changing that equation can eventual disaster be avoided. And this will demand a new understanding amongst wealth-makers, waste-makers and consumers. . . .

What is certain is that if the scale of the assault on our bodily well-being is not reduced, but instead continues to accelerate at the speed witnessed over the past quarter-century, then humanity will itself become the species facing a slow, but inexorable, journey to extinction. We have, perhaps, five years to make the choice.

"Many people become profoundly concerned with news of trace contamination of food, water, or air. . . . There is no scientific evidence that justifies such concerns."

A Cleaner Environment Would Not Improve Health

Leonard A. Sagan

In the following viewpoint, Leonard A. Sagan contends that environmental pollution has not had a significant impact on public health. Instead, he argues that mental health, social class, and the cohesiveness of family and community are far more influential sources of good or bad health. Sagan is a physician and epidemiologist based in Palo Alto, California. He has written extensively on the health effects of radiation.

As you read, consider the following questions:

1. Why does the author argue that animal experimentation to substantiate the effects of environmental pollution is largely irrelevant to humans?
2. What percentage of ill health does Sagan believe is caused by environmental factors? How does this view contradict James Bellini's, the author of the opposing viewpoint?

Although we Americans appear to be in the midst of rapidly increasing concern for health, the concept of health that arises from [my] analysis differs considerably from that which is being sold in "health food" stores, sun-tan parlors, and exercise studios. Those trendy activities implicitly define health as physical fitness, in contrast with a more global concept of health, which I view as largely cognitive and emotional. It is the brain that is the true health provider. I am not opposed to physical fitness; a sense of subjective well-being is often associated with improvements in fitness. But I am concerned that physical fitness is being equated with health to the neglect of mental health. Similarly, our overwhelming concern with environmental conditions, directed toward the physical-chemical environment, ignores the importance to health of family and other interpersonal relationships, i.e., the social environment. . . .

Revisiting the Biomedical Model

I suggest that the medical model on which health policy is based is a set of arguable assumptions. One of these assumptions is the primary role of disease in determining health: we are assumed to be healthy until proven to be diseased. Another major assumption is that those diseases largely have their origin in the environment. Just as in the nineteenth century bacterial germs were accepted as the cause of disease, today we assume that chemical "germs" are a major cause of disease and death.

Still another assumption is that cultural and behavioral factors are relatively unimportant as determinants of health and disease. In this view diseases are largely explainable on the basis of chance encounters with environmental contaminants; the individual's predisposing characteristics are unimportant. Mental health is seen as important in determining the quality of life but not in determining the onset or outcome of the major causes of death.

Throughout history, prevailing attitudes toward individual responsibility for health maintenance have moved between extremes. Hippocrates and Galen believed that diet, exercise, and characteristics of good mental health were the primary determinants of physical health. Individuals were considered responsible for their own health. Throughout European history the human body was considered to be the seat of the soul. As the gift of God, it was the responsibility—a religious duty—of the individual to maintain health. American rugged individualism encouraged people to be responsible for their own medical care. Every family had its own self-help medical encyclopedia and homemade remedies—a collection of tonics, cathartics, and herbs.

With the recognition of the influence of environmental factors in disease at the end of the nineteenth century, there was a shift of responsibility for health from the individual to the physician and to public health authorities. At this time government was also assigned an important role in health protection. Since that time individuals' role as their own "health care provider" has contracted, and the government's responsibility to protect us against environmental sources of disease has expanded.

If, as I have proposed, health and life expectancy are as much, or more, a matter of psychosocial factors than of sanitation and medical care, then some important policy implications exist for us as individuals and for several of our institutions responsible for health. What, then, should be the new directions for individual and institutional reform? . . .

The Danger of Pessimism

There is a real danger in the unfounded pessimism fueled by two intertwined phenomena: a cadre of journalists, politicians, and those claiming to represent the public interest that seems to relish bad news, apparently committed to the philosophy that the public craves negative assessments about the quality of life in America; and a tongue-tied medical/scientific community that for some reason has remained mute during the onslaught of reports of America's deteriorating health.

The result of this combination is a twofold risk. First, as noted by scientist and author Lewis Thomas, Americans are quickly becoming "a nation of healthy hypochondriacs, living gingerly and worrying themselves half to death." Second, the pervasive anxiety about ill health and the associated antipathy toward technology continues to generate a maze of "health" -oriented environmental legislation aimed at fixing a bicycle that isn't broken, thus threatening to dismantle the very system that brought us to the heights of health and offers us hopes of soaring even higher.

Elizabeth M. Whelan, *USA Today*, May 1987.

As a nation, we appear to be obsessed with stress and its consequences. I believe that the dangers of stress, while real, must be carefully distinguished from the benefits of confronting challenge. It is as important to strengthen our coping skills as it is to reduce our exposure to excessive and unnecessary stressors. We should not allow our concern with stress to deter us from attempting to achieve excellence. The difference is a subtle one; while those with a low threshold for stress are likely to be impaired by stressful situations, those who possess robust coping mechanisms can tolerate and benefit from challenging experiences.

We also are obsessed with diet, vitamins, cholesterol and salt content, or whatever is the current trendy faddism in foods. Somehow little credit is given to good common sense in dietary choices. Beyond the necessity of maintaining reasonable body weight, there is little persuasive evidence that differences in diet are important to health, given a reasonably balanced diet. Furthermore, it must be recognized and remembered that eating should provide pleasure and be joyful, and not medicalized or viewed only as a means of beautifying the body. Recently, I overheard teenagers discussing whether or not to eat ice-cream cones. They decided against it because of their concern with dieting and obesity although they were not obese. . . .

Finally, we must not permit fear to dominate our concern with health. Many people become profoundly concerned with news of trace contamination of food, water, or air, particularly with industrial chemicals. There is no scientific evidence that justifies such concerns. . . .

Implications for Public Health Policy

Public health policy in the United States is based on a biomedical model that assumes that disease, both acute and chronic, results largely from environmental agents and that, just as infectious disease was "conquered" during the past century through improvements in sanitation, the future of disease eradication in this century and the next will also result from improvements in the environment rather than changes in human behavior. We annually spend tens of billions of dollars on environmental improvement based largely on the hope that through such means we shall reduce cancer and other chronic diseases thought to result from contamination of the environment. Such a strategy ignores the fact that life expectancy rose in the United States most rapidly during the early decades of this century, when environmental contamination was most intense. In fact, just as with the medical care system, the enormously expensive environmental movement of the past few decades was initiated largely after the major improvement in American health had begun to plateau.

The evidence of hazard from these exposures derives from observations in highly susceptible laboratory animals exposed to unrealistically high doses throughout their lives. Rarely are estimates of health hazards based on observations of human populations and when they are, they are experiences with accidental or prolonged occupational exposures to very high concentrations. Nevertheless, because of those associations, it is assumed that even the briefest exposure to even very small concentrations is hazardous.

When estimates of risk are based on "hard" evidence—on reliable observations in human populations—then only a very small percentage—less than 1 percent—of all mortality can be traced to such exposures. Consider as examples the cases of diethylstillbestrol (DES), vinyl chloride, and ionizing radiation, three of the small group of agents known to be carcinogenic to humans.

During the 1950s, DES was routinely prescribed to women early in their pregnancy when there was a history of habitual abortion. Although the drug was effective in preventing abortion, it was later found that female children who had been exposed to the drug as a fetus were at increased risk of vaginal cancer. Millions of women had thus been exposed, yet the total number of such cancers worldwide is less than five hundred. Even this number is tragic, but the point is that even with the very high doses of DES that were used, only rarely did the woman's offspring develop cancer. One estimate is that one cancer resulted in the daughter of each thousand women for whom the drug was prescribed.

Gloom and Doom Environmentalists

Many of the often-quoted "environmentalists" and "consumer advocates" are in the business of keeping themselves in business.

Whether you are an optimist or pessimist, this is something that all readers and viewers should keep in mind when coming across stories of deadly chemicals that have caused no discernible harm to anyone. If the public comes to understand that there is no "conspiracy" to poison America, no "man-made epidemic," and no massive cancer increase caused by minute traces of this, that, or the other chemical-of-the-month, then where will the gloom-and-doom environmentalists and consumer advocates turn for money? They may have to go find an honest job, while the rest of us relax and savor the good fortune that we have to live in a wealthy and healthy country.

Elizabeth M. Whelan, *USA Today*, May 1987.

Vinyl chloride is the basic material from which one of the commonest of all plastic materials, poly vinyl chloride, is made. Vinyl chloride is now known to produce an unusual cancer of the liver, hemangioendothelioma. In spite of the extensive industrial use of this plastic, less than one hundred cases of this disease are cited in the world literature.

Ionizing radiation is established as a carcinogenic agent, yet, like the other agents just described, its effects are not terribly potent. For example, among the 285,000 persons who survived the atomic bombings in Japan, there have now been 67,660 deaths. Of these, it is estimated that 526 were from cancers that were the result of weapons-produced radiation. This represents an increase of about 5 percent in cancer risk in a population that was exposed to massive radiation.

The exception to the observation that human populations are generally highly resistant to the toxic effects of harmful agents is cigarette smoking; the combustion products of tobacco are powerful carcinogens, but several daily inhalations directly into the lungs over many years in high concentration are required to produce cancer or other health hazards.

All of these examples relate to cancer. Although we do know something of the ability of certain agents to increase the incidence of particular cancers, our knowledge is fragmentary. We often assume that contamination with traces of these agents are harmful; yet, we still know precious little about the processes through which a cancer is initiated or promoted. We do know that many, if not most, of the natural plant substances found in our diet, as well as many of the hormones in our bodies, can be carcinogenic under certain conditions. Almost certainly, the role the exogenous agents in the origin of human cancer has been exaggerated.

An Exaggerated View

Other than for cancer, we have little evidence that other diseases are related to exposure to environmental agents (except microorganisms). Why is it, then, that the public holds such an exaggerated view of the influence of environmental agents on health and has so little concern about personal or psychosocial factors as determinants of disease? Why is it that we divert enormous resources to study and/or remove unproven sources of disease in the environment while ignoring obvious human problems of neglect, brutality, loneliness, and ignorance? Certainly the explanations are complex, but at least part of the blame lies in our faith in our theoretical model of the origins of disease and our ignorance of health. While I endorse a thoughtful environmental improvement, I also feel that the promise that such improvement will alone contribute to health in an important way is badly misguided. If the intent is to improve health, there are clearly better ways to expend those funds. I have identified a number of social problems for which investment of resources is much more likely to contribute to improved health. The homeless could be housed, more attractive conditions could be created for the elderly and the disabled, and the illiterate could be rehabilitated. Recognizing the devastating effects to health that follow psychologically traumatizing events such as rape, we must create the social support mechanisms necessary to support victims and mitigate the health consequences. Rape, for example, is extremely common and growing rapidly. Rape is said to be the fastest growing of the violent crimes. It is estimated that one in six women will be raped during her lifetime. We must recognize these events as being just as much public health problems as are smallpox epidemics.

"You have primary responsibility for your health."

A Positive Mental Attitude Can Overcome Disease

Peter Ways

One of the precepts of holistic medicine is that people must be responsible for their own health by adopting healthy behaviors and attitudes, rather than relying on physicians to make medical decisions for them. Followers of holistic medicine, then, believe that physical disease has a psychological and behavioral meaning for the ill person. In the following viewpoint, Peter Ways endorses this view and argues that instead of seeing illness as a failure of the body, everyone should work to improve their attitude to overcome illness. Ways is a medical doctor and the author of *Take Charge of Your Health*, excerpted in this viewpoint.

As you read, consider the following questions:

1. What underlying attitudes does the author cite as examples of unhealthy thinking?
2. What does Ways mean when he says that human beings are "holistic"?
3. What role does the author see cancer victims playing in their disease?

Your health is closely related to your long-term habits and behaviors. Underlying those behaviors are your beliefs about health and medical care, e.g., "If I'm sick it's up to doc to fix me," or "It's just a matter of bad luck (fate) when I get sick." Health beliefs are an essential factor in the initiation and persistence of habits like smoking. They also affect how you behave with your physician and how you *feel* about and define health and illness. Most important, they determine the extent to which you *participate* in your own healing and prevent or minimize disease and medical problems in your future.

The essential foundation for a program of personal health competence is a congruent system of health beliefs. From them a person's PHC derives its vitality and maintains momentum.

People are programmed with respect to health beliefs. Certain stimulae give predictable responses. Often we are not aware of the extent to which our beliefs determine our everyday behavior. Most programs make it difficult to clearly see alternatives. People who are "on" their programs are not making choices; they are responding automatically. That's the bad news. The good news is that we can change our programs. The biggest part of that task is to acknowledge how powerfully they influence our behavior. Once this is done, we realize that *we have choices.* . . .

Six Health Beliefs

Here are six health beliefs of personal health competence. All of them are fundamental.

1. You have primary responsibility for your health.

2. We human beings are holistic; body, intellect, and affect-spirit strive to function as a single unit.

3. Health is more than just the absence of disease, injury, or other problems.

4. There are valuable alternatives to contemporary western medicine with its pills, surgery, and sophisticated technology.

5. Learning and change vis-a-vis health is a process of disciplined attention to the tasks at hand, not a series of isolated instructional episodes.

6. When they occur, we can learn and grow as a result of illness, emotional problems, or other adversities.

You have primary responsibility for your health

To a highly significant degree, it is possible for you to practice self-determination and to be involved in virtually all aspects of your health and medical care. This is desirable and essential if you are to grow in health competence.

Consider the following question: "If you get sick, do you believe it is *primarily a matter of fate* (destiny, God's will) or that *you have a great deal to do with it?*" Many people reflect the attitude that their illnesses are primarily a matter of fate, but adherence to this belief means you do not accept responsibility for your health or sickness: that you concur with the idea you have little to do with whether you get ill or not in the first place, and that you have little involvement in the decisions made in the course of diagnosing and treating sickness or injury. Your will to recover from illness may be weakened.

Responsibility and Power

In contrast, the belief that you *are* responsible for your health has great power. Operating from this belief is more likely to lead you to healthy habits, avoiding unhealthy ones, and increasing your well-being. Further, you will be empowered with appreciable influence on the course and severity of illness when it does occur. This happens in two ways: first, by being actively involved in the decisions which must be made in diagnosis and treatment; second, by acknowledging what you can do to care for yourself— both in terms of concrete activities (like changing diet or doing exercises to strengthen an injured leg) and as the channel for that intangible spiritual energy which hastens and enriches the healing process.

Disease Is Dictated by Personality

Research over the past 20 years has been revealing that some of the scientific theories upon which modern medicine has been built are quite simply fallacious. Disease is *not* only an organic process; germs, viruses and toxins do play a part, but it is, however, a relatively minor one. . . .

Research is beginning to show that some personality types are more susceptible than others and that people are most at risk when exposed to certain kinds of stress—retirement, being laid off, bereavement and so on. It is as if our personalities dictate the type of disorders we are most likely to suffer from (heart disease or cancer for example); our lifestyles decide the level of risk (our vulnerability); and stress precipitates the outcome—the disease.

As recently as 10 years ago, this interpretation would have been rejected outright by the medical profession. Now, it is surprising how many doctors are willing to admit the importance of a patient's lifestyle, personality, diet and so on, in the maintenance of health.

Brian Inglis and Ruth West, *The Alternative Health Guide*, 1983.

This *acceptance* of your responsibility and impact is called *owning* your health. Such ownership is a basic "requirement" for attaining health competence. It does *not* mean that other factors are not at work, that you are always entirely responsible for whatever the problem is. It does *not* mean that you can't get support in resolving your illness or increasing your well-being. It *does* mean that your body-mind played a significant role in the genesis of the illness, the unhealthy habituation, or the failure to exercise, *and* that you must make the change if change is to be made.

Checking Out Psychologically

People who do not accept responsibility for their health and medical care often put themselves psychologically in the hands of the physician. "Physicians are all powerful." "The doctor should have sole responsibility for medical decisions." "I'll do whatever doc suggests." These attitudes have major implications.

One implication is that people give up significant participation and decision making in their own health and healing. Their welfare *is* in the hands of their physician. They are vulnerable to poor care and automatic decision making. They also become vulnerable to any doctor who is not healthy himself, who smokes, drinks, doesn't exercise, or is overweight. More likely than not, this physician gives neither time nor investment in his practice to health maintenance and prevention. He may give very good advice while obviously not living the same game. This is not very persuasive.

In contrast, you may believe . . . that your physician is merely an expert whose job is to help you make decisions. If so, you are asserting your own primacy, control and power vis-a-vis your medical and health affairs. You are in a position of effectiveness and strength! You have accepted your responsibility.

The fact that self-responsibility is a cornerstone of health competence should not be used to "blame the victim." To accept responsibility for self requires relative freedom to choose. For example, a 17-year-old woman with two parents and close friends who smoke cannot always perceive the choice not to smoke. The black ghetto youngster whose environment is steeped in poverty and crime may not perceive *not* stealing as a good choice.

Part of the process of helping people move to well-being is helping them become freer to make choices—to own their choices. This may be very difficult. People must not be blamed for their own situation if they have never had the opportunity to see a way out.

Humans Are Holistic

We human beings are holistic; body, intellect, and affect-spirit strive to function as a single unit

This belief is fundamental to health competence. A healthy view of the person demands not only that we stop talking about a diseased liver or a pain in the belly (and instead talk about the person in whom the trouble occurs) but also that we never forget the profound connections between intellect, body, and affect-spirit. One of the reasons that good food, exercise, meditation, and yoga are all health-giving activities that increase our well-being is that they impact both our bodies and our minds.

This body-mind connection, as I call it, prefers unified function. Thus, there is no such thing as a purely physical act or disease, and there are few, if any, emotions or spiritual activities, stresses, or crises which do not have their reflections in our bodies.

Health is more than just the absence of disease, injury, or other problems

What is that "more"? It goes by many names: health promotion, health maintenance, prevention, wellness medicine, wellness and well-being. For me it makes most sense to talk about *health maintenance* and *well-being*. Together they are the "what's more."

The Responsibility for One's Own Health

Self-care and responsibility are difficult to adjust to in a society where people are used to putting themselves and their medical problems in the hands of a doctor. People want immediate results. We live in an era when quick and exact answers are expected, rather than abstract concepts. Self-care and holistic medical approaches are much more abstract than high-technology science and, as such, are harder for many people to accept. . . .

Medical problems cannot be fully examined without examining life and lifestyle as well. Too often, these areas are left unexamined. Doctors resist the time this takes, and patients resist the effort it takes to implement changes in their lifestyle and health habits.

D. Walters Conlin, *The Futurist*, May/June 1988.

Health maintenance involves standard immunizations and the appropriate kinds of periodic health checks by your doctor. It also includes things done by the community which we all take for granted (pure water, sewage disposal, licensing of restaurants, to name some). Beyond these things, however, it includes the behaviors we adopt to prevent disease which we know we are susceptible to. Fastening your seat belt is also an act of health maintenance, as is restricting fat in your diet to help prevent heart disease and probably breast cancer. Health maintenance is whatever you do that will help decrease the likelihood that you will develop an illness or problem in the future. . . .

Learning and change vis-a-vis health is a process of disciplined attention to the task(s) at hand, not a series of isolated instructional episodes

The "process" involves a repetitive cycle of personal assessment, stating values and goals, the clarification of alternatives, making choices, carrying through on them, and monitoring and evaluating progress and outcomes.

The emphasis is not on what you *know*, but on what you *do* with what you know and *how* you do it. This includes the ability to see when you need further information and how to acquire it. It means that the approach or way you go about doing things is more important than the exact amount of information you have and can recall when asked. . . .

Beliefs and Illness

We have already seen that your health beliefs play a significant role in generating the habits and behaviors that determine your risk for heart disease, many cancers, and other problems. These health beliefs are intimately related to your emotional-spiritual health and background, so there may be no such thing as a purely physical or purely emotional-spiritual problem. The workings of body and mind are intricately interwoven. Few days pass that this is not demonstrated clearly for each of us. *Physical and emotional sickness do not exist separately.* . . .

Cancer and the Mind

There is probably no disorder more widely feared than cancer. Most people think and talk of cancer as a mystery over which an individual has no control. Nowhere in medicine is the "victim" mentality more pronounced, i.e., "poor John, he has cancer." However, recent evidence suggests that such attitudes may not be entirely justified. In fact, they may be counterproductive in terms of cancer prevention and treatment.

Carl and Stephanie Simonton speak of a psychological process which frequently precedes cancer. It distinguishes those who do from those who don't get cancer; the following elements may or may not all be evident in the same person:

1. Childhood experiences lead to decisions to be a certain kind of person, e.g., since my father hits my mother I will always be gentle and not "get angry." "Or some children make an early decision that they are responsible for the feelings of other people, and whenever other people are unhappy or sad . . . it's their responsibility to help them feel better."

2. A "cluster" of stressful life events occur in the ten-year period before the cancer appears. They threaten personal identity: e.g., a student graduates from college, leaves the student role, and must earn his own living; a homemaker who has "existed" to support her husband's career and raise their children finds the children gone from home and her husband suddenly dead from a heart attack.

3. One or more of these events create a problem difficult or impossible for the person to deal with because of the rules he/she has set up in early life. For example, the woman cited above may have decided in early life that she would be passive and meek like her mother, since she herself had suffered from her father's aggression. Now that her husband is dead and children gone, she

247

finds it difficult to become aggressive enough to successfully find a good job.

4. As a result, the individual now sees no way to change the rules about how he must act and consequently feels trapped and helpless—the victim mentality of "Life is acting upon me" (not they upon their lives).

5. The individual becomes static, unchanging, and rigid. Although externally the individual may seem to be coping well, internally life holds no meaning. Serious illness then represents a solution or postponement to the problem.

Not only have the Simontons identified this mind-body process leading up to the development of cancer, they have also had success in slowing the progress of terminal cancer by helping people reverse these "hangups" and attitudes and by having them actively and repetitively visualize their cellular defense mechanisms against cancer as becoming more active and aggressive. Through such guided visualizations, psychotherapy, strategies designed to overcome communication blocks, and awakening spirituality, they have obtained remarkable improvement in the length and quality of life for many of their cancer patients. "They are victims no longer.". . .

A Nation of Sissies

We are becoming a nation of sissies and hypochondriacs, a self-medicating society easily intimidated by pain and prone to panic. We understand almost nothing about the essential robustness of the human body or its ability to meet the challenge of illness. . . .

The American people have yet to learn that at least one-third of all medications carry specific risks and that most of the time the human body writes its own prescriptions for most illnesses. Public health education should give us greater knowledge about our own resources and help to offset the hypochondria that is rapidly becoming an American characteristic. It should encourage people to know that the human body is beautifully equipped, given reasonable care, to meet most of its needs.

Norman Cousins, *Los Angeles Times*, February 1, 1988.

In summary, the body and mind essentially work as one. A physical problem does not exist without emotional-spiritual impact. Emotional illness often has associated physical symptoms (e.g., sleeping poorly when depressed). Healing either the illnesses we call emotional or those we call physical is greatly facilitated by belief in our own power to heal ourselves and faith in other therapies that are used. People who are healthy in the emotional-spiritual realm have a head start on health and health competence.

"Belief in disease as a direct reflection of mental state is largely folklore."

Mind Over Disease Is a Myth

Marcia Angell

In 1979, Norman Cousins published *Anatomy of an Illness*. In it, Cousins describes how he cured himself of a debilitating disease by taking Vitamin C and keeping a positive mental attitude by watching comedy films. Since Cousins's account, more literature has been devoted to the idea that people can control their immune systems with their minds. In the following viewpoint, Marcia Angell, a medical doctor, takes issue with Cousins and others who advocate this view. Angell argues that there is no proof that people can slow a disease's progress. Suggesting that they can, she argues, is blaming the victim.

As you read, consider the following questions:

1. Why does the author compare tuberculosis in the nineteenth century with cancer today?
2. How does telling patients they can change the course of their diseases harm them, according to Angell?

Marcia Angell, "Disease as a Reflection of the Psyche," *The New England Journal of Medicine*, vol. 312, pages 1570-1572, 1985. Copyright © 1985 by the Massachusetts Medical Society. Reprinted with permission.

Is cancer more likely in unhappy people? Can people who have cancer improve their chances of survival by learning to enjoy life and to think optimistically? What about heart attacks, peptic ulcers, asthma, rheumatoid arthritis, and inflammatory bowel disease? Are they caused by stress in certain personality types, and will changing the personality change the course of the disease? A stranger in this country would not have to be here very long to guess that most Americans think the answer to these questions is yes.

The popular media, stirred by occasional reports in the medical literature, remind us incessantly of the hazards of certain personality types. We are told that Type A people are vulnerable to heart attacks, repressed people (especially those who have suffered losses) are at risk of cancer, worry causes peptic ulcers, and so on. The connection between mental state and disease would seem to be direct and overriding. The hard-driving executive has a heart attack *because* he is pushing for promotion; the middle-aged housewife gets breast cancer *because* she is brooding about her empty nest.

Furthermore, we are told that just as mental state causes disease, so can changes in our outlook and approach to life restore health. Books, magazines, and talk shows abound in highly specific advice about achieving the necessary changes, as well as in explanations about how they work. Norman Cousins, for example, tells us how he managed to achieve a remission of his ankylosing spondylitis by means of laughter and vitamin C—the former, he assumes, operating through reversal of "adrenal exhaustion." Carl and Stephanie Simonton prescribe certain techniques of relaxation and imagery as an adjunct to the conventional treatment of cancer. The imagery includes picturing white cells (strong and purposeful) destroying cancer cells (weak and confused).

Defeating Disease

Clearly, this sort of postulated connection between mental state and disease is not limited to the effect of mood on our sense of physical well-being. Nor are we talking about relaxation as a worthy goal of itself. Cousins, the Simontons, and others of their persuasion advocate a way of thinking not as an end, but rather as a means for defeating disease. The assumption is that mental state is a major factor in causing and curing specific diseases. Is it, and what is the effect of believing that it is?

The notion that certain mental states bring on certain diseases is not new. In her book, *Illness as Metaphor*, Susan Sontag describes the myths surrounding two mysterious and terrifying diseases—tuberculosis in the 19th century and cancer in the 20th. Tuberculosis was thought to be a disease of excessive feeling. Overly passionate artists "consumed" themselves, both emotionally and through the disease. In contrast, cancer is seen today as a disease of depletion. Emotionally spent people no longer have the energy to battle renegade cells. As Sontag points out, myths like these arise when a disease of unknown cause is particularly dreaded. The myth serves as a form of mastery—we can predict where the disease will strike and we can perhaps ward it off by modifying our inner life. Interestingly, when the cause of such a disease is discovered, it is usually relatively simple and does not involve psychological factors. For example, the elaborate construct of a tuberculosis-prone personality evaporated when tuberculosis was found to be caused by the tubercle bacillus.

Only Some Behaviors Can Be Controlled

Whether or not all of our actions are determined by genes and environment, it is indisputable that our behavior is malleable. New information, new urgings and advice, new ways of looking at things become determinants themselves, causing us to change our ways. Biofeedback, if it works, is better suited to a deterministic universe. So is health education. What matters is not whether our actions are caused, but what the causes are.

The difficulty holists must face is not that all choices are determined but that some are. Or, rather, that some changes seem to be beyond the ability of some individuals, however well-motivated. Holists provide constant reassurance that individuals can do whatever they want, make any decisions that might benefit them, regardless of heritage or environment. . . .

It is difficult to know how to evaluate these claims. What would count as evidence against them? Could it be the failure of countless highly-motivated individuals to make the changes that the holists insist can be made simply by deciding to do so? Apparently not. The holistic insistence on the reality (or at least possibility) of positive autonomy in all circumstances must, then, be either mystical or false.

Daniel Wikler, *Examining Holistic Medicine*, 1985.

The evidence for mental state as a cause and cure of today's scourges is not much better than it was for the afflictions of earlier centuries. Most reports of such a connection are anecdotal. They usually deal with patients whose disease remitted after some form of positive thinking, and there is no attempt to determine the frequency of this occurrence and compare it with the frequency of remission without positive thinking. Other, more ambitious studies suffer from such serious flaws in design or analysis that bias is nearly inevitable. In some instances, the bias lies in the interpretation. One frequently cited study, for example, reports that the death rate among people who have recently lost their spouses is higher than that among married people. Although the authors were cautious in their interpretation, others have been quick to ascribe the finding to grief rather than to, say a change in diet or other habits. Similarly, the known physiologic effects of stress on the adrenal glands are often over-interpreted so that it is a short leap to a view of stress as a cause of one disease or another. In short, the literature contains very few scientifically sound studies of the relation, if there is one, between mental state and disease.

B.R. Cassileth et al. report the results of a careful prospective study of 359 cancer patients, showing no correlation between a number of psychosocial factors and progression of the disease. In an earlier prospective study of another disease, R.B. Case et al. found no correlation between Type A personality and recurrence of acute myocardial infarction. The fact that these well-designed studies were negative raises the possibility that we have been too ready to accept the venerable belief that mental state is an important factor in the cause and cure of disease.

Is there any harm in this belief, apart from its lack of scientific substantiation? It might be argued that it is not only harmless but beneficial, in that it allows patients some sense of control over their disease. If, for example, patients believe that imagery can help arrest cancer, then they feel less helpless; there is something they can do.

Patient at Fault for Disease

On the other hand, if cancer spreads, despite every attempt to think positively, is the patient at fault? It might seem so. According to Robert Mack, a surgeon who has cancer and is an adherent of the methods of the Simontons, "The patients who survive with cancer or with another catastrophic illness, perhaps even in the face of almost insurmountable odds, seem to be those who have developed a very strong will to live and who value each day, one at a time." What about the patients who *don't* survive? Are they lacking the will to live, or perhaps self-discipline or some other personal attribute necessary to hold cancer at bay? After all, a view that attaches credit to patients for controlling their disease also implies blame for the progression of the disease. Katherine Mansfield described the resulting sense of personal inadequacy in an entry in her journal a year before her death from tuberculosis: "A bad day . . . horrible pains and so on, and weakness. I could do nothing. The weakness was not only physical. I must *heal my Self* before I will be well. . . . This must be done alone and at once. It is at the root of my not getting better. My mind is not *controlled*." In addition to the anguish of personal failure, a further harm to such patients is that they may come to see medical care as largely irrelevant, as Cassileth et al. point out, and give themselves over completely to some method of thought control.

The medical profession also participates in the tendency to hold the patient responsible for his progress. In our desire to pay tribute to gallantry and grace in the face of hardship, we sometimes credit these qualities with cures, not realizing that we may also be implying blame when there are reverses. William Schroeder, celebrated by the media and his doctors as though he were responsible for his own renascence after implantation of an artificial heart, was later gently scolded for slackening. Dr. Allan Lansing of Humana Heart Institute worried aloud about Schroeder's "ostrich-like" behavior after a stroke and emphasized the importance of "inner strength and determination."

Responsibility as Liability

In the context of holistic medicine, the notion of personal responsibility for health will be understood as grounds for blaming the victim, exonerating the environmental factors that made him sick, and excusing medical intervention that failed to restore health.

Daniel Wikler, *Examining Holistic Medicine*, 1985.

I do not wish to argue that people have no responsibility for their health. On the contrary, there is overwhelming evidence that certain personal habits, such as smoking cigarettes, drinking alcohol, and eating a diet rich in cholesterol and saturated fats, can have great impact on health, and changing our thinking affects these habits. However, it is time to acknowledge that our belief in disease as a direct reflection of mental state is largely folklore. Furthermore, the corollary view of sickness and death as a personal failure is a particularly unfortunate form of blaming the victim. At at time when patients are already burdened by disease, they should not be further burdened by having to accept responsibility for the outcome.

"It makes more sense to prevent a disease than to put the emphasis on treatment."

An Emphasis on Preventing Disease Will Improve Health

Albert L. Huebner

Over the last decade, both medical professionals and interested laypeople have placed an emphasis on prevention as a way to improve health. In the following viewpoint, Albert L. Huebner, a writer for *East West Journal*, writes that prevention could largely inhibit and perhaps even substantially decrease the incidence of disease. Huebner argues that an emphasis on treatment, rather than prevention, is responsible for increasing cancer rates.

As you read, consider the following questions:

1. Why does the author claim that smoking is not a "voluntary" activity?
2. How does diet contribute to cancer, according to Huebner?
3. How does the author believe people can prevent cancer?

Albert L. Huebner, "The No-Win War on Cancer," *EastWest*, December 1987. Reprinted with permission of the author.

A fundamental principle of any rational approach to health is that it makes more sense to prevent a disease than to put the emphasis on treatment. This is especially important with cancer, for which strategies of prevention show enormous promise while the treatment hasn't gained much ground against major forms of the disease. Yet since passage of the National Cancer Act in 1971, repeated attempts to improve priorities in the "war on cancer" that was launched by this legislation have had little success.

During the mid-1970s, dispute raged over the small percentage of its budget the National Cancer Institute (NCI) allotted for prevention. It had been generally accepted by then that about 70 to 90 percent of human cancers have "environmental" causes, where environmental is used in a broad sense that includes food and tobacco smoke ("lifestyle" factors) as well as occupational chemicals and a wide range of industrial pollutants. The clear implication was that many of these cancers were preventable, yet the cancer establishment continued to concentrate its efforts on treatment. Criticism of priorities in the cancer war has continued, although frequently deflected by claims of remarkable new cures and rising survival rates.

New Research

Recently, however, cancer researchers John Bailar and Elaine Smith created new tremors with their well-documented claim, published in a May 1986 issue of the *New England Journal of Medicine*, that the war on cancer is being lost. They cited data from the National Center for Health Statistics indicating that, from 1962 to 1982, deaths from cancer, after adjustment for the increasing size and age of the population, increased by 8.7 percent. Perhaps equally important when focusing on causation, from 1973 to 1981 the age-adjusted *incidence* rate of the disease increased by 8.5 percent.

Bailar and Smith don't deny that there has been remarkable progress in treating some cancers. Childhood cancer and Hodgkin's disease, for example, provide remarkable success stories. But these forms of the disease are such a small proportion of the total that they are almost lost in the statistics. Vincent DeVita, director of NCI, acknowledges that "50 percent of all cures through chemotherapy occur in 10 percent of all cancer patients." That 10 percent consists mostly of children and patients with Hodgkin's disease.

It's the other 90 percent of patients that worry thoughtful analysts like Bailar, who insists that "the overall picture is pretty grim." His colleague at the Harvard School of Public Health, cancer expert John Cairns, put it more forcefully. In *Science* magazine, the publication of the American Association for the Advancement of Science, Cairns said that "there have been no significant gains in survival from any of the major cancers since the 1950s" and that "the cancer data are so discouraging that it is difficult to discuss them in public." Lung cancer in particular, which has a major impact on cancer statistics, still has an extremely poor prognosis.

Cancer Treatments Have Failed

Given these trends, Bailar and Smith write, "The major conclusion we draw is that some thirty-five years of intense effort focused largely on improving treatments must be judged a qualified failure." And they renew a call for a "shift in emphasis, from research on treatment to research on prevention," essential "if substantial progress against cancer is to be forthcoming."

Rip-Roaring Health

Americans spend vast sums of money for the treatment of diseases that could have been prevented free. They undergo god-awful suffering and give up years of life because health and well-being seem too much trouble to think about—until it is too late. The most crippling iatrogenesis (doctor-caused illness) inflicted by the medical establishment is benign in relation to the illness which individuals foist upon themselves through destructive lifestyles.

But you can join the ranks of thousands who have started to look to themselves for health—and who use modern medicine (and what is misleadingly called the health system) only when they have already done what they can for themselves. What you can do for yourself is a great deal; what medicine can do for you is rather limited. My emphasis is on what is within *your* power and my concern centers around self-responsibility for rip-roaring good health and well-being. This approach is known as high level wellness. I call it an alternative to doctors, drugs, and disease because a lifestyle that's consistent with wellness principles and that integrates wellness dimensions will help you avoid disease and need doctors and drugs far less than you probably do right now.

Donald B. Ardell, *High Level Wellness*, 1986.

This recommendation is unlikely to find more tangible support now than it has in the past, however. A spokesperson for the NCI responded that, under the present program, steady progress is being made against the disease. He insisted that the institute's goal of cutting mortality in half by the year 2000 is realistic, although it isn't at all clear what might produce this dramatic drop in the cancer death rate in the next thirteen years.

The NCI's response to the article by Bailar and Smith, like its response to earlier calls for greater emphasis on prevention, illustrates why the cancer war isn't being won. Soon after the Bailar and Smith study created a stir, the NCI announced, with great fanfare, that the cancer fatality rate decreased [in 1986] among Americans under age fifty-five. DeVita called this "one of the most encouraging cancer statistics we see," and attributed the decline to advances in treatment.

The realities are that the cancer death rate for people fifty-five and over, who account for more than three-fourths of all cancers, rose, so that the *total* death rate from cancer actually increased. The incidence rate for people under fifty-five also rose. And although NCI was elated over changes in the lung cancer rate among women, that rate didn't fall, it merely rose less rapidly than previously.

Bailar observed, "NCI is very selective in what figures it gives prominence," and he added, "I think it's unfair to the public and unfair to the news media and Congress to try to cover up the general failure [in the war on cancer] . . . by emphasizing the bright spots."

In the past, the NCI has acknowledged that a great deal is known about how to prevent cancer. When critics have voiced complaints about the low priority given to prevention, the NCI has drawn a distinction between trying to change lifestyle factors to curtail cancer, and trying to control industrial carcinogens. The NCI has argued in effect that smoking, diet, and other lifestyle factors, which account for about two-thirds of environmental cancers, are "voluntary" factors best left to the individuals for action. Only 10 to 15 percent of environmental cancers result from industrial pollution, so the institute claimed justification in directing roughly 10 percent of its budget to all environmental carcinogens, including those attributed to lifestyle. Even if NCI and other agencies had sharply reduced the threat from chemical pollutants—which they didn't—in ignoring most of the causes of cancer the institute was guaranteeing that cancer mortality would remain far higher than need be.

Personal Habits Are Involuntary

The NCI was also ignoring the problem inherent in viewing personal habits as completely voluntary, which suggests that the individual could easily eliminate these habits, and the cancer they cause, if he or she wanted to. This argument is the basis for the opinion that lung cancer, chiefly caused by cigarette smoking, shouldn't be included in cancer mortality statistics. And when proponents of this lifestyle doctrine push it to extremes, the implication is strong that if you get certain kinds of cancer, it's probably your own fault.

It can be argued, however, that this division into voluntary and involuntary exposures to cancer-causing substances is artificial, in view of the enormous advertising budgets used to push tobacco and processed food, and the influence advertising holds over the consuming public. Success against cancer will entail dealing broadly with these factors, as well as the toxic substances involved in many industrial and occupational cancers. The evidence indicates that the cancer establishment is marking time or in many cases moving backwards, in confronting these issues. . . .

Despite [a] formidable combination of the addictive properties of tobacco and the youth-directed advertising, antismoking campaigns are not futile. On the contrary, they've been extremely successful on those rare occasions when they've been promoted seriously.

A program begun in 1967 provides a striking illustration both of the path toward conquest of cancer, and of the too-frequent turns away from that path. That year the Federal Communications Commission, in response to a petition from a young attorney, obligated radio and television broadcasters to give a "substantial" amount of time—although not equal time—to the "other side" of the cigarette controversy. For more than three years, creative ads urged smokers to quit and nonsmokers not to start. During that period, an unprecedented 10 million Americans quit smoking and, after years of virtually uninterrupted growth, per capita consumption of cigarettes plummeted.

Cancer Is Preventable

Cancer is *not* an inevitable, unavoidable consequence of aging. Cancer, like heart disease, is preventable. The realization that we are not at the mercy of our own bodies, that life and health are not a giant lottery, comes as a happy shock and a gratifying surprise, after my years as a practicing physician.

Robert G. Schneider, *Cancer Prevention Made Easy*, 1984.

The antismoking campaign was torpedoed when Congress passed legislation, privately supported by the manufacturers, that banned radio and television cigarette ads. The industry merely shifted its radio and television advertising to other media. But the ban on cigarette advertising over the electronic media eliminated the "Fairness Doctrine" obligation of stations that was at the heart of the effective antismoking campaign. Predictably, the sharp decline in cigarette consumption was reversed in 1971, the year the advertising ban went into effect.

This successful experiment in health education received scant financial support from the federal agencies publicly funded to conduct the war against cancer—never more than $1 million per year. Nearly twenty years later, a bill before Congress would appropriate that same amount of money (actually much less when inflation is accounted for) to run some public service announcements informing women of tobacco's risks. Even during the highly publicized anticigarette campaign of former Health, Education, and Welfare Secretary Joseph Califano, however, total funding for this purpose was never more than a small fraction of what the government spends in *support* of tobacco use: federal price supports, tobacco agricultural research, market research, and most cynically, export to needy countries under the "Food for Peace" program.

Cancer and Diet

A second major lifestyle factor affecting cancer is diet, which differs from smoking in that it plays both a positive and a negative role in influencing the disease. But as with smoking, the NCI has been ineffective in exploiting this opportunity to make progress against cancer.

As early as 1944 it was observed that the incidence of certain cancers changed dramatically when people moved from one country to another and adopted new eating habits. American blacks have much lower rates of liver cancer, but much higher rates of colon cancer, than African blacks. Similarly, there is a higher incidence of stomach cancer and a lower incidence of colon cancer in Japan compared with the U.S. But when Japanese migrate to the U.S. and adopt the diet of their new home, they acquire the U.S. stomach and colon cancer rates as well.

The implications that many cancer researchers drew from these epidemiological studies, and other early observations, is that compared to the current average American diet, a prudent anti-cancer diet would be lower in calories, lower in fat and higher in fiber, with more fruit, vegetables, and whole grains and less red meat, eggs, and fat-rich dairy products. Another implication is that additives such as nitrates and nitrites should be avoided, and intake of protective vitamins, notably A, C, and E, should be judiciously increased.

It's true that exactly *how* these dietary components prevent or promote cancer wasn't known when the cancer war was launched, and many of the details still aren't fully understood. A reasonable course for NCI would have been to vigorously publicize the prudent data (a healthful diet for reasons that go beyond cancer prevention) until every American got the message, while doing the research needed for a more precise understanding.

But despite its burgeoning budget, NCI did little. During the late 1970s, the agency was repeatedly chided by prominent members of Congress, in particular Senators Robert Dole and George McGovern, for neglecting the nutrition connection to cancer. It wasn't until quite recently that NCI finally took a firm stand on the low-fat, high-fiber diet, and the American Cancer Society, which does much of NCI's public relations, began promoting a few elements of the prudent diet in ad campaigns.

If advocacy of an anticancer diet has been at best lukewarm, research has also lagged behind. Dr. Ruth Shearer, an NCI-funded researcher with a passionate dedication to defeating cancer and an admirably independent mind, has pointed out that as late as 1977 only $3 million a year was going into nutritional research on cancer, while $57 million was being spent for the virus program. "There's more prestige in the virus theory," she has said, adding wryly, "Nutritional research conjures up the picture of a school lunch program."

Physicians Should Emphasize Prevention

Until such time as we have specific and effective cures or preventions for the major killer diseases of today, there is much more that we can do as a profession, through advocacy and involvement, to promote preventive medical practices. We wait in our offices until patients come to us with illnesses. We have been very busy and ingenious in our efforts to cure them. This has contributed, in our imperfect state of understanding, to ever-escalating costs. We physicians have contributed to the attitude of members of our society that they can indulge any manner of life style, and when it is time to pay the consequences with illnesses the medical profession will be there with a medicine or an operation to cure them. We have been reimbursed handsomely for this role, and there has been little incentive for us to do otherwise.

Alexander Leaf, *The New England Journal of Medicine*, March 15, 1984.

If smoking and diet, however important as causes of cancer, are too humdrum to generate much enthusiasm among researchers, the toxicity of chemicals in the workplace and the environment ought to be more stimulating. Yet this aspect of cancer control has had no greater success.

In 1976, Congress passed the Toxic Substance Control Act (TSCA). Its stated goal was to provide a testing ground, other than "the nation's population and environment," for the potentially dangerous chemicals that pour into commerce in massive amounts each year. After several years of inaction by the Environmental Protection Agency (EPA), which administers TSCA, complaint was brought to federal court by an environmental group, the Natural Resource Defense Council (NRDC), along with the AFL-CIO. Significantly, the EPA was joined in defending itself by the Chemical Manufacturers Association and the American Petroleum Institute.

Ruling on the case in 1984, a U.S. District Court judge found that "in the more than seven years since TSCA's enactment, though seventy-three chemicals have been designated by government scientists for priority rule-making consideration"—that is, formal testing procedures—"EPA has yet to finalize a single test rule. Congress could not have intended (or envisioned) this result."

Congress really had no right to expect much from the EPA, given its own performance. While a series of national scares took place around toxic substances ranging from DDT to vinyl chloride and from polychlorinated biphenyls to Tris, Congress delayed passage of TSCA. It was one thing to declare war on cancer, but quite another to crack down on the manufacturers of cancer-causing substances. Finally, after five years of debate, the bill passed was a thoroughly watered-down version of the original.

For obvious reasons, an especially critical group of environmental carcinogens are chemicals in food. In this case, rather than mere foot-dragging, the steps taken have been *backward*.

The Delaney clause, passed by Congress in 1958, bans the use of any substances that cause cancer in animals as additives to food, cosmetics, and drugs. The clause has been under increasing attack for more than a decade. In 1981, Secretary of Health and Human Services (HHS) Richard Schweiker officially took the position that it should be scrapped. He insisted, "We have to redefine the clause in terms of a risk-benefit ratio."

That redefinition has been eroding the clause ever since. For example, risk-benefit considerations were cited for the Food and Drug Administration in approving use of two drugs and cosmetic dyes recently, despite the language of the clause, which clearly imposes an absolute ban on cancer-causing additives. The FDA commissioner argued, "It makes no sense at all to brand as illegal, and by doing so to disrupt the marketing of a considerable number of products, additives that present a risk that is barely more than theoretical. . . ."

As a general principle, the risk-benefit approach might have some justification if the group taking the risk and the group reaping the benefits were the same, but usually they aren't. In the specific case of the dyes, the commissioner's own scientific staff argued against approval on grounds that the risk estimates used, based on industry calculations, may have significantly underestimated the true risk. . . .

Ineffective Programs

It's clear that many components of what should be a coherent anti-cancer program are operating ineffectively. Individual agencies rarely pursue the war against cancer with the tactics and intensity required. The number of different agencies involved—NCI, EPA, FDA, OSHA [Occupational Safety and Health Administration], among others—has led to confusion about the causes of cancer, and how to prevent it. Commercial pressures add to the confusion.

The consequences of this fragmentation are illustrated by standard tabulations of the causes of cancer, where the numbers are made to add up to 100 percent. In a more realistic tabulation the totals would be greater than 100 percent, reflecting multiple, interactive causes.

The prevailing artificial tabulation obscures important preventative measures that need attention. For example, cancer epidemiologist Samuel Epstein believes that smoking, although certainly the most important single cause of lung cancer, nonetheless has been overestimated as a cause, and occupational carcinogens underestimated, because in many studies lung-cancer deaths of smoking workers were routinely attributed to smoking and not occupation. This underestimation of occupational cancers weakens attempts to regulate carcinogens in the workplace.

Similarly, Epstein and other prominent researchers think that one of the ways in which fat consumption increases cancer may be its ability to bring fat-soluble pesticides and industrial chemicals into the body. If so, then some cancers attributed to a high-fat diet should also be charged against pollution or occupational causes.

Insight into the artificiality in tabulating cancer causes, and of dividing cancer control among an alphabet soup of government agencies, reveals another artificiality: the division between regulating industrial and agricultural carcinogens to control cancer, and changing lifestyles to control cancer. As one researcher has observed, occupational hazards and toxic waste dumps are the production side of the cancer problem, while smoking, alcohol, improper diet, and polluting automobiles are the consumption side.

The Need for More Research

This holistic view shows clearly that cancer will not be stopped by government agencies alone, or by individuals acting alone. True, roads not taken by agencies are not necessarily barred to individuals, who can improve their odds by eating an anti-cancer diet, not smoking, and avoiding carcinogens as much as possible. But individuals need help that the agencies are well-qualified to supply, if their priorities are set straight. This reordering would free them to do needed research, to issue and enforce effective regulations against discharge of carcinogens into the environment, and to disseminate essential information to the public.

Needed, in short, are the responsible and harmonious efforts of both individuals and agencies, directed at the primary goal—prevention.

"Even the most scrupulous observance of health warnings is clearly no guarantee of safety."

Prevention Is Misused and Exaggerated

Lenn E. Goodman and Madeleine J. Goodman

The idea that one can prevent debilitating disease by controlling dietary and environmental factors rages through the popular media from health journals to women's magazines. How accurate is this claim? In the following viewpoint, Lenn E. Goodman and Madeleine J. Goodman argue that well-publicized preventive campaigns are often based on scanty proof. They conclude that the ability to prevent diseases, especially cancer, is limited. Lenn Goodman is a professor of philosophy at the University of Hawaii. Madeleine Goodman is assistant vice-president for academic affairs and professor of general science and women's studies at the University of Hawaii.

As you read, consider the following questions:

1. What is the authors' opinion of diet as a contributing factor to cancer?
2. What evidence do the authors give that preventive efforts are largely the result of media campaigns?
3. While the Goodmans believe preventive medicine is a good concept, why do they argue that it is misused?

Lenn E. Goodman and Madeleine J. Goodman, "Prevention—How Misuse of a Concept Undercuts Its Worth," *The Hastings Center Report*, April 1986. Reprinted with permission.

Today the mounting costs of acute health care place an economic premium on preventive measures. The classic model is the mass vaccination campaign, but beyond that model lie notions and practices grafted to the image of prevention, sharing in its magic but lacking a sound conceptual basis for their claims. Misuse of the idea of prevention can occur in a variety of ways. The examples we have selected are not isolated incidents, nor are they limited to peripheral health promotion efforts. . . .

In recent years claims that a specific dietary mode will decrease cancer risk have become more frequent and insistent. The Office of Technology Assessment, which undertook a study of cancer risk for the 97th Congress, concluded that the "overall association of cancer with diet exists, but there is no reliable indication of exactly what dietary changes would be of major importance in reducing cancer incidence and mortality." Nevertheless, in testimony before the Senate Subcommittee on Nutrition in October 1979, Arthur Upton, then director of the National Cancer Institute (NCI), forcefully laid a basis in policy for claims about the impact of diet on cancer risk: "Despite the . . . inability to pinpoint specific dietary carcinogens, scientists generally agree that factors in diet and nutrition—including drinking water contaminants—appear to be related to a large number of human cancers, perhaps 50 percent."

Reviewing a great body of pertinent studies, Richard Doll and Richard Peto wrote in the *Journal of the National Cancer Institute*, "It may be possible to reduce U.S. cancer death rates by practicable dietary means by as much 35% ('guestimated' as stomach and large bowel 90%; endometrium, gallbladder, pancreas, and breast 50%; lung, larynx, bladder, cervix, mouth, pharynx, and esophagus 20%; other types of cancer 10%)." The figures are impressive, and Doll and Peto explain in detail how they are derived; nations where meat and fat consumption are high are found to have high incidences and mortality rates of cancer.

Cancer and Diet Problematic

But the inference that an altered diet can produce a corresponding change in incidence is problematic. Mary Enig and colleagues have observed that in Greece the incidence of breast cancer is less than one-fourth that in Israel, but total dietary fat intake is essentially the same. Breast cancer mortality is three times higher in France and Italy than in Spain, although the total dietary fat intake is slightly higher in Spain. Puerto Rico has only 30 to 40 percent of the U.S. incidence of breast and colon cancers, despite substantially higher reliance on animal fat. Breast and colon cancer are twice as frequent in the Netherlands as in Finland, but animal fat consumption is estimated to be identical. Indians of the American Southwest have high intakes of animal fat but low breast cancer rates. Enig argues that it is fallacious to attribute increased cancer rates in the United States to increased consumption of animal fat, since daily per capita consumption of animal fat decreased from 104 grams in 1909 to 97 grams in 1972.

A nineteen-year study of cancer in men suggests that milk, fatty fish, eggs, and butter—foods high in vitamin D but usually restricted in "anticancer" diets—may have a protective effect against colorectal cancer. The low rate of colon cancer found in Seventh Day Adventists is often attributed to vegetarianism, but Mormons have a similarly low rate. Their faith, like that of the Adventists, proscribes smoking, drinking, coffee, and stimulants. But they are not generally vegetarians. In a major international epidemiological study by B. Armstrong and Doll, GNP [Gross National Product] was as potent a correlate with cancer as any dietary factor.

The Costs and Risks of Prevention

The beneficial effects of prevention on health are increasingly well known, but its costs and risks are not as clear. These dimensions, too, need to be assessed. Making good choices in health, as in other fields, requires consideration of the full range of outcomes—health benefits, health risks, and resource costs. In an era when containing medical costs has become a serious concern, it is particularly important to choose wisely in order to gain the most health from our limited resources. We need better evaluations of prevention to ensure that it receives a reasonable share of resources and that those resources are allocated to the most effective preventive programs.

Bruce K. MacLaury, *Is Prevention Better Than Cure?*, 1986.

Individual diets vary within nations geographically, culturally, ethnically, and with age, sex, and socioeconomic status. Familial and individual differences in food preparation, waste (for example, are cooking fats reused?), alcohol consumption, and other factors affect the impact of diet. Women of Japanese ancestry in the United States have a breast cancer rate closer to that of American women than to that of Japanese women living in Japan. But the changes in incidence have not been directly tied to diet. They are observed among the granddaughters of immigrants. There has not yet been a controlled study of the effects of diet over the lifespan of individuals. . . .

Health Foodists

George Kerr of the Human Nutrition Center at the University of Texas School of Public Health cites the extremity of some recommendations as one factor justifying the promulgation of a cancer prevention diet before any dietary hypothesis is confirmed. The public, Kerr argues, demands information and will turn to the ill-founded, often dangerous diets of quacks and "health foodists" if reputable nutritionists do not provide responsible cancer preventive dietary guidelines. Recognizing that the causation of cancer must be multifactorial, Kerr does not simplistically equate reduction of a risk factor with reduction of risk: "Stating that diet is involved in the causation of 50% of cancers should not be interpreted to mean that dietary modification can prevent 50% of cancers," he points out. This important insight is lost sight of in the voluminous pages of Doll and Peto and in the NRC [National Research Council] report. But Kerr himself does not believe that such reservations should inhibit efforts at dietary reform.

Kerr advocates dietary guidelines that are more moderate than those he seeks to preempt but they suffer nonetheless from some of the same weaknesses: the cancer prevention claims remain unproven, and the reasoning seems to be similar to that of the food culturists. The NRC acknowledges that the contribution of diet to reducing cancer risk cannot be quantified presently; it even concedes that the crucial effects of diet may occur in childhood or adolescence and that dietary modifications later in life may have a negligible or negative effect. But proponents of the cancer prevention dietary guidelines argue that the recommended diet is a healthful one on general principles, even if it does not succeed in reducing cancer incidence and mortality.

Overselling: The Ethos of Prospero

A preventive health campaign is a marketing effort, subject to all the risks of motivational marketing—hyperbole, demagoguery, or playing upon fears and prejudices. Here ignorance is not the excuse for oversimplification: relevant data deemed contrary to the desired outcome, or not sufficiently productive of that outcome, are overlooked or understated. But an oversold campaign can undercut its own authority, causing the audience to tune out or even respond adversely. . . .

In the case of swine flu, the use of a hard sell almost from the inception of contingency planning gave the program a momentum that inhibited deliberation. When swine flu was detected in February 1976 among recruits at Fort Dix, officials of the Centers for Disease Control in Atlanta rapidly recognized that the strain might represent a recurrence of the pandemic influenza of 1918, endangering perhaps a million American lives. Health planners proposed a voluntary immunization over three months of some 200 million Americans at a cost of $134 million.

The decision-making process throughout was characterized by concern about blame, eagerness to showcase preventive medicine, and a crisis mentality, all of which tended to eclipse clinical and epidemiological evidence. The rhetoric deployed at each level effectively forced the hand of those who would carry the decision to the next. External factors such as the attitude of the insurance industry, the outbreak of Legionnaires' disease, and the status of President Ford's anti-inflation campaign proved more decisive than the early production problems and the evidence from field trials concerning the difficulties of producing a vaccine both safe and effective for children between the ages of three and ten. . . .

Transference of Responsibility

A woman diagnosed at twenty-two with spina bifida reports, "My mother still to this day is asking herself what she ate or drank to cause this." The mother of a seven-year-old victim asks, "I'd like to know why it happened. I never drank, I never smoked, I never took drugs. . . ." When tragic accidents of birth or development occur, it is natural to seek a meaning, and in all human societies the terms of reference for that meaning may be moral. Something was wrongly done or left undone. Moralizing health concerns by treating them as foci of discipline and surrounding them with prudential counsels generates a context of expectations in which any tragic outcome may seem incomprehensible unless it can be ascribed to infraction of some hygienic rule. Adelle Davis

---

Taking Advantage of Fear

It seems that people will do almost anything to avoid the possibility of cancer—as long as it doesn't require too much effort. A large segment of the population finds it far easier to stamp its feet and fuss about a purely hypothetical risk like food additives (which have never been shown to cause cancer in the amounts used in the human diet) than to give up cigarette smoking, which is a proven contributor to lung cancer. This witless displacement of concern simply does not jibe with scientific data.

Elizabeth M. Whelan and Fredrick J. Stare, *The One-Hundred-Percent Natural, Purely Organic, Cholesterol-Free, Megavitamin, Low-Carbohydrate Nutrition Hoax*, 1983.

---

blamed her fatal stomach cancer on her failure to adopt a health-preserving diet early enough in life. Followers of Jimm Fixx blamed his fatal heart attack at fifty-two on his late initiation into the running regimen. When disease strikes, solace and exoneration are found in assigning blame to doctors, patients, parents, genes. Explanation becomes a tug-of-war—your side of the family or mine, heredity or environment, society, economic conditions—in which something, preferably someone, must bear the blame. Doctors are professionals in this contest, having used the reproof "if only you had come sooner, something might have been done" at least since the days of Imperial China.

The obverse of blaming the victim is imparting a false sense of security. Even the most scrupulous observance of health warnings is clearly no guarantee of safety when the warnings themselves are derived from statistical trends. Studying the records of breast-cancer patients in Iowa (1980-81), Elaine Smith and Trudy Burns found no significant difference in tumor size, stage, or lymph node involvement between women who practiced breast self-examination monthly or more often and those who did not, and they found no evidence as yet of a decline in breast-cancer mortality to correspond with increased reliance on breast self-examination. Cancers detected by breast self-examination tend to be larger and more advanced tumors than those discovered by means such as mammography. Even massive educational programs on breast self-examination do not reduce tumor size or lymph-node involvement at detection, as the experience of the 1977-80 San Diego County Medical Society Breast Cancer Education Program has clearly shown. Mammographic screening does lead to earlier detection of tumors, but whether the lead time gained can be translated into a reduction in cancer mortality or whether it means only a prolongation of the interval between diagnosis and death remains to be determined.

Significant Effects

The effects of shifting responsibility from the health care sector to the individual can be significant. Thomas Cole has shown skillfully how health reformers of the mid-nineteenth century preached a secular gospel: discipline and prophylaxis would preserve health and self-sufficiency to a vigorous old age. Hygiene and optimism were the works and faith of modern valetudinary salvation:

> Only the shiftless, faithless, and promiscuous were doomed to a premature death and old age. . . . As late as 1901, Frederick L. Hoffman of Prudential Life Insurance, for whom the relationship between longevity and dividends was more than a metaphor, reiterated the increasingly unrealistic argument that temperance, frugality, and industry were the sole requirements for a comfortable, healthy old age.

Not surprisingly Hoffman became an ardent opponent of state pensions for elderly workers.

Today the attitude that individuals hold the power to preserve life and good health in relative unconcern for genetic frailties and environmental hazards might seem out of date and out of place. Yet in July 1979, at the climax of Jimmy Carter's administration, a Surgeon General's report titled *Healthy People* concluded that the foremost causes of illness lie in individual behavior and are to be met most effectively and economically through extensive changes in the lifestyles of almost everyone. The report was hailed as the manifesto of "a second public health revolution." Deane Neubauer and Richard Pratt have explained that assignment to the individual of the major responsibility for preventive health shifts the onus away from social agencies. Similarly, advocates of preventive health programs often present such programs as vehicles of social engineering, using the rhetoric and concern of prevention to redirect public attention and resources—a political act masquerading as a hygienic one.

An optimum mix of personal, familial, private, communal, social, and governmental responsibilities is probably best worked out in specific contexts. To address preventive health in moralistic terms—your diet, my exercise—diffuses the issue and directs attention away from the large and known area of world health needs such as pollution control, vector control, and vaccination to more nebulous areas like fiber in the diet. Rather than facing questions about social responsibility, it finesses them. Recognizing the effectiveness and relevance of individual human efforts and choices is a great step for professions that often see causation as completely divided between genetic and environmental "determinants." But recognizing the role of individual choice and discipline is no substitute for health insurance, research, therapy, or exercising responsibility for the environment.

"Health-Food" Treatments

For a long time now the health-food industry has been busily cashing in on the almost universal fear of cancer. The array of cures and preventatives outnumber even the many forms of cancer; yet each is usually dubbed a cure-all. In some cases we must assume the intentions are honorable, but the same fallacy occurs over and over: A shred of inconclusive information is used to build a theory, but there is no solid foundation to support it.

Elizabeth M. Whelan and Fredrick J. Stare, *The One-Hundred-Percent Natural, Purely Organic, Cholesterol-Free, Megavitamin, Low-Carbohydrate Nutrition Hoax*, 1983.

In every society people project hopes and fears, using their own language and symbols. The amulets and incantations of shamans may seem primitive if they use alien language and exotic dyes and feathers. But the idea is universal that the wise, who know the workings of the cosmos, have the power to cure, prevent, or even cause disease. Only the symbols by which wisdom seeks outward recognition vary widely.

Since magic operates by the logic of association, its presence is readily identified. A practice, for example, may be deemed healthful because healthy people do it. (The commonplace confusion of the words *healthy* and *healthful* is indicative of the direction wishes take.) Running is perhaps the salient symbol of health in our society at the moment. The association is not arbitrary. Habitual exercise is associated empirically with reduction in the risk factors of cardiovascular disease. Enhanced energy and stress reduction are also associated with regular exercise. But the terms are difficult to define and quantify objectively. Many runners believe that exercise helps prevent colds and flu. Harvey Simon reviewed ten studies of 132 healthy volunteers ranging from the sedentary to marathoners; he found no evidence of such a relationship. Further studies may yet find one, perhaps masked by the contrary effects of overexertion. Orthopedic surgeons are growing increasingly alarmed at the bone damage associated with running, and a Rhode Island study estimates an annual fatality rate from running of one per 8,000 runners. But the belief among runners in the protective effects of exercise did not arise from scientific studies and will not disappear merely as a result of scientific counterevidence. The belief is partly a matter of projection and speaks more to the symbolic significance of exercise—and to the power of marketing—than to physiology.

Henry Solomon of Cornell Medical College, a cardiologist, points out that lack of exercise is among the least significant of the secondary risk factors for coronary artery disease. The primary factors are hypertension, high blood cholesterol, and cigarette smoking. The secondary include diabetes, socioeconomic status, stress, and abnormal EKGs. "Whatever benefits the human body derives from exertion are yours whenever you take a good brisk walk or enjoy yourself—without pushing yourself—at some other sport you enjoy," Solomon argues. Excessive exercise is a folly and a danger, a fad on which excessive hopes are lavished. The power of this fad derives in part from hope and fear, in part from the association of heroic exertion with virtue and of virtue with reward.

Questions the Disease Asks

In the film *Fighting Back Cancer*, broadcast on BBC4's Broadside series in 1983, the Bristol Cancer Health Center is presented as a source of hope for cancer patients, especially those who reject or resent anticancer drugs. Controversial new research, we learn, suggests that a patient's determination and fighting spirit can be critical in facing cancer. A cancer patient must take charge of her own life, rather than "doctors having their will with me." The Bristol Center offers diet, counsel, and meditation. Absolutely pure raw foods containing "no chemicals" complement the spiritual purification, which "runs through your personality to find out what your defects are." The regimen is "enormously difficult." Some patients have trouble giving up meat. The vegetarian melange presented to the camera seems designed to appear unappetizing. But self-denial is the substance of catharsis: "We don't offer people a cure— [we say if you make certain changes in your lifestyle, you'll be] answering the questions the disease is asking."

While no medical claims are made about a cure, a patient can report "deep relaxation . . . visualizing my immune system getting rid of these malignant cells . . . a wildly exhilarating experience. . . . I just knew that I was actually getting rid of the cancer." As the film closes, a woman offers testimony that counseling "has prevented the disease."

Clearly morale affects the course of many diseases, but we lack evidence to sustain the suggestion that imagination, even aided by diet, has the power to "fight back" or exclude cancerous growths. Indeed Barrie Cassileth has found evidence that attitudinal factors among patients with advanced or inoperable cancers do not influence remission or survival. Marcia Angell argues that medically encouraged "folklore" about the relation between cancer and mental outlook has led some patients to believe that they were to blame for their illnesses. Guilt, of course, along with fear, regret, and others of the emotions that Spinoza called passive are important factors in the pathology of superstition.

The purity of the Bristol diet and others like it is not merely hygienic but symbolic. "Chemicals" are a category only for the imagination. Meat is a symbolic issue in every culture, since animals' lives are involved. It has become even more a moral issue in recent years, through claims that eating meat appropriates an unfair share of the world's grain. But the idea that moral guilt can be expiated by vegetarianism or that moral guilt or innocence (however imputed) can be relevant to the incidence or course of cancer is a classic structural interchange: my guilt (symbolized through food) brings on my cancer; my purgation (through ascesis, symbolic rejection of sin) is my protection.

The dynamics of such symbolic exchanges are varied and complex. It is not a coincidence or even a paradox, we suspect, that a kind of moralistic vegetarianism, often linked with a narcissistic or excessive interest in exercise as fitness, should come into vogue simultaneously with the "sexual revolution" and, for that matter, with increased reliance on drugs for both mental and physical effects and the heightened prominence of new cults and old credos.

Chastity and Pap Smears

Our final point regarding magic has to do with the taboos of priestly language. The point can be made briefly, because the usages are familiar. Pap smears prevent cervical cancer deaths, but so does chastity. . . .

If multiple sexual partners are a risk factor for cervical cancer, why is little said about this in the popular literature of disease prevention, or even in the massive output of sex education/birth control information? The answer, we suspect, is that the authors of such materials fear to weaken their authority and muddy their message by appearing in the eyes of their constituents to have taken open issue with the notion that sex as such and in all forms, with very rare and unmentionable exceptions, is (like "fitness" and unlike "stress") a Good Thing.

The appeal of the idea of prevention rests on a real but limited achievement. There is no great conspiracy to misuse the idea of prevention. But the fashionable tendency to rely too heavily on prevention is not confined to faddists or propagandists; it extends to the most respected and responsible health leaders and researchers. Most of the problems we have described arise in the overenthusiastic promotional activities of well-meaning health practitioners. Yet taken together they constitute an abuse of the concept of prevention. Enthusiasts adulterate the value of this concept by conflating it with other ideas, hoping that its repute will carry over into projects of their own. But, like ancient alchemists, they are more likely to debase their own coinage than to transmute base metal into gold.

Recognizing Deceptive Arguments

People who feel strongly about an issue use many techniques to persuade others to agree with them. Some of these techniques appeal to the intellect, some to the emotions. Many of them distract the reader or listener from the real issues.

Below are listed a few common examples of argumentation tactics. Most of them can be used either to advance an argument in an honest, reasonable way or to deceive or distract from the real issues. It is important for a critical reader to recognize these tactics in order to evaluate rationally an author's ideas.

a. *scare tactics*—the threat that if you don't do or don't believe this, something terrible will happen

b. *strawperson*—distorting or exaggerating an opponent's arguments to make one's own seem stronger

c. *testimonial*—quoting or paraphrasing an authority to support one's own viewpoint

d. *slanters*—trying to persuade through inflammatory and exaggerated language instead of through reason

e. *generalizations*—using statistics or facts to generalize about a population, place, or thing

f. *deductive reasoning*—claiming that since a and b are true, c is also true, although there may not be a connection between a and c

The following activity will allow you to sharpen your skills in recognizing deceptive reasoning. Some of the statements on the next page are taken from the viewpoints in this chapter. *Beside each one, mark the letter of the type of deceptive appeal being used. More than one type of tactic may be applicable. If you believe the statement is not any of the listed appeals, write N.*

1. The polluting tide threatens to upset the delicate balance of our own biochemistry. Humanity faces the prospect of contamination overload—the high tech holocaust.

2. Physical and emotional sickness do not exist separately. Our emotional-spiritual self affects our body with a peptic ulcer and our body affects our mind, as when a heart attack causes depression.

3. Everyone's health is affected by toxic waste. In the United States, thousands of dumpsites clogged with toxic organic chemicals are dangerous enough to wipe out entire city populations.

4. The healthy, natural Sioux Indian lifestyle proved that illness is a teacher. When you regard illness as a teacher, it becomes a means of learning about yourself and the way you are moving through life.

5. We have perhaps no more than five years to make a choice in favour of a cleaner, safer world. Failure to make that choice could ensure that mankind is overtaken by a fate more horrific than nuclear war.

6. Why is it that we spend gigantic sums on the insignificant risk of disease sources in the environment, and completely ignore the obvious human problems of neglect, brutality, loneliness and ignorance?

7. A fundamental principle of any rational approach to health must be it makes more sense to prevent a disease than to put emphasis on treatment. This is especially important with cancer, since strategies of prevention show tremendous promise while treatment hasn't gained any ground on the disease.

8. The public demands information and will turn to the ill-founded, often dangerous diets of quacks and "health foodists" if reputable nutritionists do not provide dietary guidelines.

9. It is no coincidence that a kind of moralistic vegetarianism, often linked with a narcissistic interest in exercise as fitness, should come into vogue simultaneously with the "sexual revolution" and increased reliance on drugs for mental and physical effects.

Periodical Bibliography

The following articles have been selected to supplement the diverse views presented in this chapter.

Barrie R. Cassileth, Edward J. Lusk, et al.	"Psychosocial Correlates of Survival in Advanced Malignant Disease?" *The New England Journal of Medicine*, June 13, 1985.
Barry Commoner	"Acceptable Risks: Who Decides?" *Harper's Magazine*, May 1988.
Norman Cousins	"Let Wisdom of the Body Promote Natural Health," *Los Angeles Times*, February 1, 1988.
J. Gordon Edwards	"Let's Tell the Truth About Pesticides," *21st Century Science & Technology*, May/June 1988.
Howard H. Hiatt	"Prevention Is at Least as Worthy as a Cure," *The Wall Street Journal*, February 3, 1987.
G.M. Keller	"Industry and the Environment," *Vital Speeches of the Day*, December 15, 1987.
Edward Krupat	"A Delicate Imbalance," *Psychology Today*, November 1986.
Steven Locke and Douglas Colligan	"Is the Cure for Cancer in the Mind?" *New Age Journal*, January/February 1988.
Patricia Long	"Laugh and Be Well," *Psychology Today*, October 1987.
Peter H. Raven	"We're Killing Our World," *Vital Speeches of the Day*, May 15, 1987.
Carolyn Reuben	"Healing Your Life with Louise Hay," *East West*, June 1988.
Laura Kelsey Rhodes	"Toxics: A Blowin' in the Wind," *Public Citizen*, May/June 1988.
Martin L. Rossman	"The Healing Power of Imagery," *New Age Journal*, March/April 1988.
Kirkpatrick Sale	"Deep Ecology and Its Critics," *The Nation*, May 14, 1988.
Frank E. Samuel Jr.	"Let's Make the Self-Care Revolution Work," *Vital Speeches of the Day*, April 15, 1988.

Organizations To Contact

The editors have compiled the following list of organizations which are concerned with the issues debated in this book. All of them have publications or information available for interested readers. The descriptions are derived from materials provided by the organizations.

American Association of Retired Persons (AARP)
1909 K St. NW
Washington, DC 20049
(202) 728-4422

AARP, with 20 million members age 50 or over, is dedicated to improving life for older people. It sponsors a group health insurance program and community service programs on such topics as crime prevention and pre-retirement planning. Its publications include the monthly *News Bulletin* and bimonthly *Modern Maturity.*

American Cancer Society (ACS)
3340 Peachtree Road NE
Atlanta, GA 30026
(212) 736-3030

Over two million volunteers work in regional branches of ACS to do research and educate people about cancer prevention, detection, and treatment. It publishes *Cancer—A Journal of the American Cancer Society* monthly, *CA— A Cancer Journal for Physicians* bimonthly, and *World Smoking and Health* three times a year. These publications are available through the 3000 local ACS groups nationwide.

American College of Health Care Administrators
8120 Woodmont Ave., Suite 200
Bethesda, MD 20814
(301) 652-8384

The College believes special academic training and experience bring good administration of nursing homes. It advocates implementing a code of ethics in nursing homes and elevating administrative standards. It publishes the semimonthly *Long Term Care Administrator* and *Journal of Long-Term Care Administration* quarterly.

American Council on Science and Health (ACSH)
1995 Broadway, 18th Floor
New York, NY 10023
(212) 362-7044

ACSH provides consumers with scientific evaluations of food and the environment, pointing out both health hazards and benefits. It participates in a variety of government and media events, from congressional hearings to popular magazines. It produces a self-syndicated radio series of health updates, publishes five to six reports on health issues a year as well as *News and Views*, a bimonthly.

American Medical Association (AMA)
535 N. Dearborn St.
Chicago, IL 60610
(312) 645-5000

The AMA is a professional association for physicians. It publishes the *American Medical News* and *Journal of the American Medical Association*, both weeklies.

Committee for Freedom of Choice in Medicine (CFCM)
1780 Walnut Ave.
Chula Vista, CA 92073
In CA: 1-800-227-4458
Other Areas: 1-800-624-2140

CFCM advocates using alternative therapies for treating disease. It supports patients' freedom to choose treatments without government interference. It conducts seminars on metabolic/nutritional treatment and maintains a database of patients with degenerative diseases who have been treated with metabolic therapy. It publishes the quarterly *Choice Magazine* as well as several books, including *Freedom From Cancer, Now That You Have Cancer* and *Save Your Life.*

The Foundation for Advancement in Cancer Therapy
Box 1242, Old Chelsea Station
New York, NY 10113
(212) 741-2790

The Foundation supports the "total person approach" to cancer therapy which emphasizes nutrition and mental-physical unification to regenerate the body. It sees this approach as complementary to traditional therapies like chemotherapy which destroy the cancer without restoring the body to health. It publishes *Cancer Forum* bimonthly.

Group Health Association of America (GHAA)
1129 20th St. NW
Washington, DC 20036
(202) 778-3200

The GHAA works to promote the health maintenance organization movement by conducting research programs, sponsoring education seminars, and compiling statistics. Among its publications is the monthly *Group Health News.*

The Hastings Center
360 Broadway
Hastings-on-Hudson, NY 10706
(914) 478-0500

Since its founding in 1869, The Hastings Center has studied ethical issues raised by advances in medicine, the biological sciences, and the social and behavioral sciences. It publishes *The Hastings Center Report.*

Holistic Health Havens (HHH)
3419 Thom Blvd.
Las Vegas, NV 89106
(714) 645-1799

The HHH serves as a study and information center for the practice of holistic medicine. It publishes the journal *Holistic Health Quarterly.*

National Cancer Foundation
1180 Avenue of the Americas
New York, NY 10036
(212) 221-3300

Through social research and professional consultation, the Foundation seeks to determine the emotional, social, and economic needs of cancer patients and their families while developing social services to meet those needs. It provides to the public and government officials facts and guidelines on the care of the catastrophically ill. It publishes professional papers and *Lamp,* a semiannual periodical.

National Committee for Quality Health Care (NCQHC)
1730 Rhode Island Ave. NW, Suite 803
Washington, DC 20036
(202) 861-0882

NCQHC, whose members include hospitals, nursing homes, and investment bankers, believes the private sector, not government intervention, is the key to providing health care to all Americans. It develops health care proposals for government and the public to evaluate. It publishes *Capital Outlook* 12 times a year and numerous position papers.

National Environmental Health Association (NEHA)
720 S. Colorado Blvd.
Denver, CO 80222
(303) 756-9090

NEHA is a professional association for environmental health workers in government, industry, and universities. It publishes the bimonthly *Journal of Environmental Health* as well as *Environmental Health Trends Report*, a quarterly update of political issues.

National Foundation for Cancer Research (NFCR)
7315 Wisconsin Ave., Suite 332W
Bethesda, MD 20814
(301) 654-1250

The Foundation funds 68 laboratories to conduct scientific research into the effects of cancer on cellular structure and function. It publishes *Progress*, a quarterly newsletter, and numerous booklets.

National Foundation for Long Term Health Care
1200 15th St. NW
Washington, DC 20005

The Foundation funds the study of the elderly and long term care. It strives to improve the image of long term care through educational and media programs. It maintains a 10,000 volume long term care library and publishes *National Foundation News* six times a year.

National Geriatrics Society (NGS)
212 W. Wisconsin Ave., Third Floor
Milwaukee, WI 53203
(414) 272-4130

The Society consists of public and private nursing homes, sanitariums, and hospitals which care for the aged. It offers advice on maintaining operational and administrative standards in geriatrics programs. It publishes a monthly newsletter and the *Nursing Care Requirements In Nursing Homes In the States of the Union* three times a year.

National Health Information Center
PO Box 1133
Washington, DC 20013
(703) 522-2590

With a database of 1100 organizations, the Center assists consumers and health care workers in finding health information by referring them to appropriate sources. It publishes *Healthfinder*, a series of books including *Financing Personal Health Care, Medications, Vitamins,* and *Weight Control.*

National Wellness Institute, Inc.
South Hall
University of Wisconsin-Stevens Point
Stevens Point, WI 54481
(715) 346-2172

Members of the Institute include health care professionals from corporations, hospitals, and fitness clubs. It acts as a clearinghouse for information on fitness and health maintainance and offers referrals for additional information. It publishes *Wellness Management*, a quarterly newsletter.

Natural Food Associates (NFA)
PO Box 210
Atlanta, TX 75551
(214) 796-3612

NFA promotes the benefits of organic farming and natural foods while exposing the dangers of chemical contamination of land and food. It operates a natural living bookstore and publishes both a monthly magazine, *Natural Food and Farming*, and a monthly newspaper, *Natural Food News*.

Bibliography of Books

Henry J. Aaron and William B. Schwartz	*The Painful Prescription: Rationing Hospital Care.* Washington, DC: The Brookings Institution, 1984.
Herbert Bailey	*E: The Essential Vitamin.* New York: Bantam Books, 1983.
Arnold E. Bender	*Health or Hoax?* Buffalo, NY: Prometheus Books, 1986.
Edward Calabrese and Michael Dorsey	*Healthy Living in an Unhealthy World.* New York: Simon & Schuster, 1984.
Jon B. Christianson and Kenneth R. Smith	*Current Strategies for Containing Health Care Expenditures.* Jamaica, NY: Spectrum Publications, 1985.
Stephen Crystal	*America's Old Age Crisis.* New York: Basic Books, Inc., Publishers, 1982.
Tracy Deliman and John S. Smolowe	*Holistic Medicine.* Reston, VA: Reston Publishing Company, Inc., 1982.
Edith Efron	*The Apocalyptics: Cancer and the Big Lie.* New York: Simon & Schuster, 1984.
Catherine Feste	*The Physician Within.* Minneapolis: Diabetes Center, Inc., 1987.
John Fried	*Vitamin Politics.* Buffalo, NY: Prometheus Books, 1984.
Arthur C. Hastings, James Fadiman, and James S. Gordon, eds.	*Health for the Whole Person.* New York: Bantam Books, 1981.
Victor Herbert and Stephen Barrett	*Vitamins and "Health" Foods: The Great American Hustle.* Philadelphia: George F. Stickley Company, 1982.
Howard H. Hiatt	*America's Health in the Balance: Choice or Chance?* New York: Harper & Row, Publishers, 1987.
Pascal James Imperato and Greg Mitchell	*Acceptable Risks.* New York: Viking Penguin Inc., 1985.
Brian Inglis and Ruth West	*The Alternative Health Guide.* New York: Alfred A. Knopf, Inc., 1983.
Charles B. Inlander, Lowell S. Levin, and Ed Weiner	*Medicine on Trial.* Englewood Cliffs, NJ: Prentice-Hall, 1988.
Dennis T. Jaffe	*Healing from Within.* New York: Alfred A. Knopf, Inc., 1980.
Jonathan King	*Troubled Water.* Emmaus, PA: Rodale Press, 1985.
W. Harding leRiche	*A Chemical Feast.* Agincourt, Ontario: Methuen Publications, 1982.
Steven Locke and Douglas Colligan	*The Healer Within.* New York: E.P. Dutton, 1986.
William H. Masters, Virginia E. Johnson, and Robert C. Kolodny	*Crisis: Heterosexual Behavior in the Age of AIDS.* New York: Grove Press, 1988.

Thomas R. Mayer and Gloria Gilbert Mayer	*The Health Insurance Alternative.* New York: Perigree Books, 1984.
Earl Mindell	*Earl Mindell's New and Revised Vitamin Bible.* New York: Warner Books, 1985.
National Institute of Health	*Cancer Rates and Risks.* Washington, DC: NIH Publications, 1985.
Linus Pauling	*How To Live Longer and Feel Better.* New York: Avon Books, 1986.
Jesus J. Pena and Valerie A. Glesnes-Anderson	*Hospital Management.* Rockville, MD: An Aspen Publication, 1985.
David M. Prescott and Alvin S. Flexer	*Cancer: The Misguided Cell.* Sunderland, MA: Sinauer Associates Inc., Publishers, 1986.
Lewis Regenstein	*America the Poisoned.* Washington, DC: Acropolis Books Ltd., 1982.
Bennett M. Rich and Martha Baum	*The Aging: A Guide to Public Policy.* Pittsburgh: University of Pittsburgh Press, 1984.
Charles E. Rosenberg	*The Care of Strangers: The Rise of America's Hospital System.* New York: Basic Books, Inc., Publishers, 1987.
Louise B. Russell	*Is Prevention Better Than Cure?* Washington, DC: The Brookings Institution, 1986.
Ronald F. Schmid	*Traditional Foods Are Your Best Medicine.* Stratford, CT: Ocean View Publications, 1987.
Robert G. Schneider	*Cancer Prevention Made Easy.* Englewood Cliffs, NJ: Prentice-Hall, 1984.
Keith W. Sehnert	*Selfcare/Wellcare.* Minneapolis: Augsburg Publishing House, 1985.
Victor W. and Ruth Sidel	*Reforming Medicine: Lessons of the Last Quarter Century.* New York: Pantheon Books, 1984.
Harold M. Silverman, Joseph A. Romano, and Gary Elmer	*The Vitamin Book: A No-Nonsense Consumer Guide.* New York: Bantam Books, 1985.
Alvin and Virginia B. Silverstein	*Cancer: Can It Be Stopped?* New York: J.B. Lippincott, 1987.
Charles B. Simone	*Cancer & Nutrition.* New York: McGraw-Hill Book Company, 1983.
Douglas Stalker and Clark Glymour, eds.	*Examining Holistic Medicine.* Buffalo, NY: Prometheus Books, 1985.
Peter Ways	*Take Charge of Your Health.* Lexington, MA: The Stephen Green Press, 1985.
Elizabeth M. Whelan	*Toxic Terror.* Ottawa, IL: Jameson Books, 1985.
Elizabeth M. Whelan and Fredrick J. Stare	*The One-Hundred-Percent Natural, Purely Organic, Cholesterol-Free, Megavitamin, Low-Carbohydrate Nutrition Hoax.* New York: Atheneum Publishers, 1983.

Index

283